The Visionary Director

Margie Carter • Deb Curtis

The Visionary Director

A Handbook for
Dreaming,
Organizing,
& Improvising
in Your Center

 Redleaf Press
www.redleafpress.org
800-423-8309

Published by Redleaf Press
a division of Resources for Child Caring
10 Yorkton Court
St. Paul, MN 55117
Visit us online at www.redleafpress.org.

Book design by David Farr, Imagesmythe
Illustrations by Janice Porter
Printed in the United States of America

Redleaf Press books are available at a special discount when purchased in bulk for special premiums and sales promotions. For details, contact the sales manager at 800-423-8309.

Excerpt from *The Heart Aroused* by David Whyte. Copyright 1994 by David Whyte. Reprinted by permission of Doubleday, a division of Bantam Doubleday Dell Publishing Group, Inc.

Excerpt from "Catch the Fire" in *Wounded in the House of a Friend* by Sonia Sanchez. Copyright 1995 by Sonia Sanchez. Reprinted by permission of Beacon Press, Boston.

Library of Congress Cataloging-in-Publication Data
Curtis, Debbie.
    The visionary director : a handbook for dreaming, organizing, and
improvising in your center / by Deb Curtis and Margie Carter.
        p.   cm.
    Includes bibliographical references (p.   )
    ISBN 978-1-884834-55-4
    1. Day care centers—United States—Administration. 2. Early
childhood education—United States.   I. Carter, Margie.   II. Title.
HQ778.63.C87   1998
362.71'2'068—dc21   98-30881
                                                                    CIP

Printed on acid-free paper.

To MaryAnn Ready, who offered me my first experience of working in a program with a visionary leader who put the ideas throughout this book into practice.

—DC

To Denise Benitez, who has taught me to find my breath and stay with it and has served as an extraordinary role model for teaching.

—MC

We cannot neglect our interior fire without damaging ourselves in the process. A certain vitality smolders inside us irrespective of whether it has an outlet or not. When it remains unlit, the body fills with dense smoke. I think we all live with the hope that we can put off our creative imperatives until a later time and not be any the worse for it. But refusing to give room to the fire, our bodies fill with an acrid smoke, as if we had covered the flame and starved it of oxygen. The interior of the body becomes numbed and choked with particulate matter. The toxic components of the smoke are resentment, blame, complaint, self-justification, and martyrdom. The longer we neglect the fire, the more we are overcome by the smoke.

—DAVID WHYTE,
The Heart Aroused

I say

Where is your fire?

You got to find it and pass it on.
You got to find it and pass it on
From you to me from me to her from her
to him from the son to the father from the
brother to the sister, from the daughter to
the mother from the mother to the child.

I say

Where is your fire?

—SONIA SANCHEZ
"Catch the Fire"

Contents

Chapter 2

A Framework for Your Work 41

Chapter 3

Your Role in Building and Supporting Community 67

Chapter 4
Your Role of Mentoring and Coaching 115

Chapter 5

Your Role of Managing and Overseeing 161

Chapter 6
Moving From Surviving to Thriving— The Need for Nourishment and Activism 203

Finding Energy and Determination 204

Principle | **Know Yourself and Act on What You Know** 206

Strategies | Listen to your body 207
Be clear about your best time of day and healthy energy boosters 207
Be intentional when you doodle 208

Principle | **Know Your Resources and Access Them Regularly** 209

Strategies | Reflect on your experiences and values 209
Create a visual map of your resources 212

Principle | **Know Your Own Goals and Pursue Them with Vigor** 213

Strategies | Cultivate personal goals that will round out your development 214
Join a sports team, reading circle, or support group 215

Principle | **Be Aware of Your Friends and Your Foes** 215

Strategies | Spill out your worries instead of allowing them to pile up 216
Practice observation and stillness by doing nothing 217
Use focused meditation techniques to bring you back in touch with yourself 217

Principle | **Organize Yourself, Your Time, and Your Stuff** 218

Strategies | Create and maintain systems for nearly everything 218
Have a place for everything 218
Plan each week and day before it begins 218
Utilize the trash and recycling bins regularly 219

Principle | **Get Active Beyond Your Program** 220

Strategies | Learn from I Dream a World 222
Identify the components of real social change 222
Think in terms of zoysia plugs 223

Living Your Way into a Vision 224
Resources for Thriving 226

Afterword 229

Appendices

Foreword

Even after a short time in our field, it would be relatively easy for most people to list what's wrong with child care programs in the United States—poor salaries and benefits, too few materials, damaged equipment, unmanageable adult-child ratios, extraordinarily high staff turnover, a dwindling pool of reliable substitute teachers, gaps in language and culture between programs and the children and families they serve, and not enough training that meets our day-to-day and on-the-job needs. Every day, we witness the direct results of drastic neglect and underfunding of our child care system. We're pretty good at agreeing on the problems.

Over the last two years we have been working at the Center for the Child Care Workforce to conduct a series of trainings with center directors and teaching staff called "Taking on Turnover." Participants are quite forthcoming when we ask them to describe their problems at work. It's when we're asked to conjure up a vision of a good child care workplace— and to set priorities to bring the vision to life—that the trouble often begins. Perhaps tensions arise among directors, teachers, and aides about where the solutions lie, or what should be addressed first. The process of creating change in any kind of organization can be painful and slow. But I suspect that most of all we have trouble because as a field, we are so used to settling for what we can get, and "coping creatively" with too few resources, that we don't ask the fundamental questions about how child care *ought* to be. We don't raise enough challenges. We forget to dream.

Imagine the child care of our dreams, not just child care that's good enough. Imagine if people working with young children received adequate professional preparation, opportunities for ongoing professional growth, and earnings equal to their investment in their careers. Margie Carter and Deb Curtis invite us to imagine and dream, and they assist us in the process. They help us see how settling for the current situation dulls our enthusiasm and ultimately diminishes our efforts. Ultimately, they invite us to create an environment in our programs where the adults, not just the children, continue to learn, grow, and use their imaginations to guide their work, family, and community life. And they offer an array of strategies toward that end.

Why does using our imaginations matter so much? On the most basic level, this is a critical task. Our current work environments, more often than not, fail to attract and retain highly skilled teaching staff. The most recent follow-up to the National Child Care Staffing Study found that only one-third of the teaching staff in a sample of centers that were rated higher than average in quality had remained in their jobs for at least five years. Such high turnover signals inconsistent care for children and demoralization for staff and parents.

It is a steady combination of our using our imaginations, enhancing our skills, and mobilizing our collective will and political clout that will move us beyond the basics to create child care programs that really nourish and strengthen children, families, and staff. If we are to address the real issues in our programs and the early childhood field and, as Deb and Margie suggest, have our work influence the larger social change required, it is essential for us to reach a common understanding of goals. Otherwise, we will pull ourselves in opposite directions, leaving no one with a sense of accomplishment or satisfaction. We can start on a practical level. For example, if we can agree on how much paid planning and preparation time the caregiving and teaching staff really need, we can take steps—even if they are small at first—toward implementing a policy that's closer to our goals. But first and foremost, we have to have a vision. Without one, it is mighty hard to reach a destination and easy to get where we never intended to go.

I came to child care in the early 1970s, a time when envisioning alternatives was the name of the game. For myself and many of my peers, child care held the promise of the future. As I phrased it then, child care was the key to women's liberation and the path to a more just world. A good child care system, we reasoned, would enable women to help support their families and feel secure in knowing their children were well nurtured. Children would be helped to reach their full potential. Our society would recognize child care and other forms of traditional "women's work" as highly skilled professions. It was probably a good thing that I didn't know how formidable the barriers would be to realizing this vision, or I might have never begun! Although I have been exceedingly frustrated over the years at the slowness of progress in improving our child care services and jobs, I still find nourishment and direction in that early vision of child care as a service that supports parents, nourishes children, and rewards practitioners for the complexity of their work. Indeed, it is this shared vision that has helped me and others get through the hard times, put disagreements in perspective, and most important, keep reflecting on how best to do our work.

In the 1990s developing the Worthy Wage Campaign has served as another vision to guide our efforts to create quality, affordable programs for families and fair and decent employment for child care teachers and providers. The goals and growth of this campaign parallel the picture Margie and Deb paint on these pages—all that can happen when people germinate a vision together and roll up their sleeves to make it happen. The underlying idea of the Worthy Wage Campaign is to engage everyone involved or affected by child care in understanding that a skilled and stable workforce is the cornerstone of a good child care system. But stabilizing and adequately compensating the workforce only addresses the basics of what we really long for. Our dreams reach far beyond. The Worthy Wage Campaign aims to build a critical mass of people who begin to see issues about affordability and compensation in child care as political, not just personal issues. As people become engaged in seeking solutions, they will see the connections that ultimately suggest a vision and demand for larger social change. The vision of the Worthy Wage Campaign has not only sustained many of us "old-timers," but it has generated a new generation of advocates and activists willing to take on the challenge of improving child care jobs and services so that we can move a step closer to our dreams. For those of us working on child care issues over the last quarter century or more, the most heartening development is this group of new folks committed to refining and carrying forward the vision.

In this book, Margie Carter and Deb Curtis help take the "envisioning" process out of the realm of tasks that sound too overwhelming and impossible to begin, let alone complete, and in their inimitable way, they make it not only manageable but creative, inspiring, and playful. They are guided by a vision of child care that acknowledges the importance of both child *and* adult development, recognizing that adults, too, must be acknowledged as individuals, respected for their points of view, and challenged gently to see things in new ways. Their vision affirms the right and responsibility that we have as adults to make the world a better place, and they remind us that this vision underlies why many of us chose to work in child care in the first place. *The Visionary Director* offers us an essential tool for affirming and renewing our commitment to child care and to meeting the challenge of nurturing our society's future.

MARCY WHITEBOOK
Codirector, Center for the Child Care Workforce
May 1998

Acknowledgments

To the directors, caregivers, and teachers who have lent their stories to this book we extend sincere appreciation. They represent programs large and small; diverse and homogeneous; serving middle-class, upper-class, and poor families; private, parent cooperative, or sponsored by Head Start, government, corporations, school districts, and colleges; and located across the United States and on U.S. military bases in Europe.

Special thanks to Ruth Beagleholz, Julie Bisson, Cathy Burckett-St. Laurent, Wendy Cividanes, Jim Clay, Dana Connoly, Lisa Dittrich, Kathleen Gonzales, Mary Graham, Karen Haigh, Leslie Howle, Carmen Masso, Paul Moosman, Leslie Orlowski, Jan Reed, Caron Salazar, Teresa Senna, Margo Shayne, Linda Skibinski, Alicia Smith, Laura Walker, Ellen Wolpert, and Adina Young. While many of us have removed ourselves from the day-to-day work of leading programs, they remain on the front lines pursuing their vision with great tenacity. We see these folks as inventors, craftspeople, cultural workers, and artists.

Thanks to Jeanne Hunt and Lonnie and Casey Bloom, who put up with us once again as we abandoned them for another big writing project, and to Beth Wallace, who served as a fine editor and counselor during bouts of confusion.

Thanks also to Bonnie and Roger Neugebauer of *Child Care Information Exchange* for publishing the articles that were later incorporated into this book. They have spent the last twenty-some years bringing ideas and directors' voices together.

We are especially grateful to Marcy Whitebook and Rosemarie Vardell for their exceptional leadership and contributions to the Worthy Wage Movement, to our lives, and to this book. These women continue to do the nuts-and-bolts work that provides our profession with the research and the tools for creating a different vision of a child care system. Their ongoing efforts in the face of overwhelming barriers are a continued source of inspiration to us personally, professionally, and politically.

Introduction

Most directors of early childhood programs come to their positions with little experience or education to prepare them for the awesome task of trying to run a quality program with inadequate facilities, resources, and staff. They may have a handful of promising seeds, but before long, they are stretched too thin, frantically patching the holes that continue to pop up in their watering can. If directors are to be successful and satisfied with their work, they not only need skills and expertise, but a way to get a handle on their jobs, and a replenishing source of nourishment for themselves. Their professional development must not only include the skills of administration, business and finance, supervision, and human relations, but also the arts of dreaming, designing, organizing, and improvising.

As this book goes to press there are a number of exciting efforts aimed at enhancing the skills and leadership potential of early childhood program directors. We welcome these efforts. They address what we have intuitively understood and what research now confirms: the director's leadership is the primary nutrient for growing a quality program. We hope that this book will contribute to the ability of directors to summon the resources and skills to be visionary leaders for their programs; to "find the fire and pass it on."

How Can Directors Become Leaders?

It's easy for directors to feel helpless and victimized under the current conditions. There are so many factors that seem out of control. While this feeling of helplessness is understandable, we also know that directors seldom claim the leadership potential their position offers them. Instead, they let the limitations of the current conditions constrict their imaginations and creativity. Under the "be realistic" banner, directors tend to stay focused on how things are, rather than on a vision of how it could be. They hope that somehow more checklists and accountability systems will "fix" the problems of trying to provide quality in a service that is underfunded, undervalued, and operating with an inadequate workforce. All too often, however, paperwork and regulations serve to constrain directors from getting beyond the barriers to quality instead of helping directors surmount them. Imagining a different course and cultivating leadership to pursue a different vision is not a common practice among early childhood program directors. Our hope is that *The Visionary Director* will spur you into developing that leadership.

Whatever the external factors, we all have the power to shape the environment around us. If you do this thoughtfully in your role as a director, you'll find that your early childhood program can transform the sense of powerlessness and isolation that prevails in the lives of caregivers, teachers, children, and families. Your leadership toward that end has the further potential to influence larger social change, as Valora Washington (1997) of the Kellogg Foundation reminds us:

> Transformation of the social order often begins with acts of imagination that elevate a startling dream of change above the intimidating presence of things as they are. Yet if such dreams are passionate and clear, and if they can call a great many people into their service, they may ultimately give shape to the future.

This is the message you will find in the pages of *The Visionary Director,* along with numerous strategies to move your program in that direction. While we have been discouraged to hear many directors describe their vision for their programs in narrow terms, such as improving their playground or getting accredited, we have also been heartened to meet others who have bigger dreams for the role their programs can play in reshaping the communities where they reside. Some have made significant incremental changes in transforming the organizational culture, physical environment, activities, and interactions that shape quality in an early childhood program. Others have begun small steps toward creating a community of dreamers who are on the road to making changes.

Imagination and Activism Are Key

If you see yourself as the developer of an organizational culture, your leadership will extend beyond managing an early childhood program. As you create a culture of safety and respect, alive with a sense of possibilities, your program will attract staff and families longing to be involved in this kind of community. And, if your policies and actions go beyond lip service to diversity, you create the potential for using that diversity to transform the fear, alienation, and despair that are so pervasive in our wider community.

Cultivating imagination is as critical to a director's success as acquiring skills. So much in our world conspires to take away our dreams. With all the tasks a director needs to accomplish, it's easy to get consumed by the daily details, neglecting our hearts and minds. New energy comes when you step outside your "to do" lists, make time for activities that call forth your creativity, and do things that intellectually stimulate and nurture you. It's equally important to involve yourselves with people and efforts working on behalf of social change, within and without the early childhood profession. Some of the most promising efforts in our profession have come when directors begin linking up with others for support and action.

The Director on Fire

It's not uncommon to hear the words *program director* and *burnout* in the same breath. Our goal in writing this book is to help you avoid burnout by setting your heart on fire. We've come with kindling that has proven reliable. You can fan the flames with the beating of your own heart. On these pages you will find the spark of a guiding vision for directors of early childhood programs. We have seen the difference made when directors give attention to shaping an organizational culture of collaboration and excitement about growth and development. Rather than just running a program, this kind of director is creating a learning community and spurring others into activism on behalf of social change in the world. You will hear the voices of directors like this throughout these pages.

We once heard Carol Brunson Phillips speak of strengthening the power of children to develop through their culture. This not only influenced our thinking about the role of ethnic culture in shaping development, but also inspired us to imagine the kind of early childhood program culture that would support the power of the staff and families to develop. There are no quick fixes with this approach. It is steady, patient, improvisational work. You have to invent it as you go, shaping your program around the events and the lives that come through your door each day. *The Visionary Director* offers a framework for thinking about and organizing your work. In these pages we suggest principles and strategies to cultivate the kind of thinking and activities that would support a vision of early childhood programs as learning communities. We believe the dreams and inventions you draw from these ideas will surpass any specific formulas or directions we could offer.

Using This Book

The chapters of this book focus on a conceptual framework and self-directed activities to help you develop your own understandings and possibilities for working with the framework. Chapter 1 offers our vision of early childhood programs as the new neighborhoods of the twenty-first century, poised to transform the cultural ills of our society with genuine, mutually respectful, and empowering relationships. Included are lessons from African proverbs, organizational development theory, and our own childhood memories of life in a neighborhood or community. In chapter 2 we propose thinking of a director's work as a triangle, carefully balanced on all sides. Here you get a taste of "systems thinking" as it pertains to developing the culture of early childhood programs.

Chapters 3, 4, and 5 offer more details about working from each side of our triangle framework, with principles and strategies to consider. Chapter 6 stresses the need for self-care and activism, with strategies, stories, and quotes to keep you connected to a source of nourishment. At the end of this book, there is an afterword with snapshots of promising initiatives around the country, and an appendix that offers sample forms for some of the strategies we have described.

What you will not find on these pages is help with budgeting, fund-raising, and financial management. We know there are other valuable resources to assist you in these areas, and we have included some of these in this book's resource lists. *The Visionary Director* focuses on the strategies to light your fire and the vision to help you clear the smoke. For the ideas in this book to become part of your approach to directing, you will need practice in making them yours. Each chapter of this book concludes with a practice activity for further reflection on the ideas just discussed. It might be tempting to skip over this section, but we advise you to reconsider. We encourage you to use this book for more than inspiration or reference. Make it a workbook that you return to on a regular basis. Consider forming a support group with other directors to study this book and discuss ways to apply the principles and strategies to your work.

Chapter 1

Guiding Your Program with a Vision

What's Your Vision?

Before you begin reading our ideas about being a program director or supervisor, take a minute to consider yours. Which of the answers below is the closest to your thinking regarding the purpose of an early childhood program? Check the box that represents your highest priority.

☐ To provide a service for parents while they work

☐ To give kids a head start to be ready for school and academic success

☐ To enhance children's self-concept and social skills as they learn to get along in the world

☐ To ensure children have a childhood that is full of play, adventure, and investigation

☐ To create a community where the adults and children experience a sense of connection and new possibilities for making the world a better place

☐ _____

(add your own words here)

_____

We start this book where we hope you will start—describing what you see as the primary purpose of your work. There is no right or wrong answer in the choices above. Your view of your work may encompass some version of each of these ideas. Most likely you go through your days with a general sense of purpose. We recommend taking the time to be specific about your purpose and vision because, consciously or unconsciously, your image of an early childhood program shapes the way you guide your program. Your vision plays the same role in your program as your breath plays in your body—distributing the life force of oxygen throughout your system, exploring where things are tense and need some attention, and providing a rhythm for your muscles to do their collaborative work.

How often do you pay attention to your breath? Right now, for instance, have you noticed how you are breathing? As you read these words does your breath feel rushed, tight, or even hard to detect? Are you aware of where your breath is in your body? Take a minute to check this out. Likewise, consider how frequently you do your job as a director with a vision flowing through your mind. Developing a regular awareness of your breath in your body cultivates a mindfulness for all parts of your life. Similarly, when you move through your days with a vision of how things could be, you'll approach directing tasks and decisions in a thoughtful manner.

You've probably come to this book searching for answers, for solutions to the stresses and strains of directing an early childhood program. We suggest you start your search by finding your breath, not only because this is literally a good thing to do, but also because this action symbolically represents the essence of what this book has to offer. With all the pressures surrounding a director's job, no doubt you barely have time to *catch* your breath, let alone read a book. This means you probably spend most of your time reacting to how things are, rather than developing new ways of being. Consider the smoker who relies on cough drops to soothe a scratchy throat and neglects to find support for changing habits and healthier living. This is akin to directors who rely on management tips to survive instead of taking stock, reorienting their approach, and claiming their power to create something different.

Searching Your Heart for What's Important

When it comes down to it, looking for quick answers and formulas to run a child care program is like turning to diet pills and beauty products to improve your health. It's just not that simple. To be sure, it's important to acquire skills and learn the "how-to's" of developing a well-functioning management system, and there are a growing number of resources to help you with this. *The Visionary Director* suggests something less often discussed in books on supervision—finding the heart of what brought you to the early childhood field, remembering the vision you've had for how it could be, and drawing on this as you move through your days. As you take time to find your breath, literally and metaphorically, you will begin to discover a deeper longing that lives in your body—a desire for meaningful work that makes a difference in the world; time for joy and laughter; a place where you have genuine connections with others; and a community where you feel safe, have history, and enjoy a sense of belonging. When you embrace rather than ignore this longing, it can shape a vision that guides your work as fundamentally as your breathing guides your body.

Around the country, directors are attending conferences, seminars, and classes in search of ways to improve their work. We've discovered that though at the surface this appears to be a search for some quick ideas, a much deeper need often brings us together. Directors long for a place to unload the very heavy burden they carry. This work is probably very different than what they imagined it to be. People usually come to the work of directing early childhood programs with an eagerness to make a difference in the lives of children and families. Faced with the current conditions, many directors are aware of a lot of "if-only" feelings lingering below each breath—if only we had more money to pay the teachers, if only we could improve the facility, if only we could offer more scholarships, if only we could just get parents more involved, if only people understood the importance of this work.

Beyond the need for a steady paycheck, most of us seek jobs in early childhood care and education because it is work with real meaning and real people, and it offers the possibility of making a difference in the world. Yet all too quickly external pressures and the demands of this work make us lose sight of this original motivation. Budgets, regulations, reports, perturbed parents, and shrinking substitute lists soon overwhelm our hearts and minds. There is hardly time to get to the bathroom, let alone to that stack of reading to be done and the papers to be filed. Before long, you find yourself moving from crisis to crisis, too frazzled to remember all those time-management techniques, and exhausted down to your bones. The original dreams you brought to your job can easily fade or seem totally out of reach.

We want to rekindle a sense of new possibilities for you. Rather than helping you get better at working with how things are, *The Visionary Director* offers you a framework and beginning strategies for transforming the limitations of your current mind-set and conditions. At the heart of this book is our vision of early childhood programs as active learning communities for both children and adults. It's easy to talk about our problems and the things that bother us in our work, but too often directors neglect to describe how they would like their work to be; the specific elements of their visions. It's a challenge to let our minds spin out new possibilities when we are so used to adapting and accommodating ourselves to how things are. Breaking out of these confines can stir up old longings and remind us of how little we've settled for.

Imagining How It Could Be

The vision we have for early childhood programs replaces the institutional feel of items from an early childhood catalog with things from the natural world that keep us in touch with the life cycle of living, growing, and dying, and of the interdependence of living things. The walls are not adorned with commercially produced displays, but with images from the lives of the people who spend their days there together. There are a variety of interesting textures, colors, and things to discover and investigate. Inviting smells of food and flowers overtake the odors of stuffy rooms, urine, and disinfectants. Natural light and soft lamps create comfy places for people to enjoy each other's company. Staff members and children have a place for their things, their meetings, the tools they need for their work and play, and a soft, quiet place for when they need a break away from each other. People are building genuine relationships across age, economic, gender, and cultural differences. They are actively listening to and learning from each other, learning to show their passions, to feel safe in expressing disagreements, and to negotiate problems with remarkable creativity. Mutual admiration and appreciation flows between the staff, children, and families. Respect from others translates into respect for oneself and a desire to make a contribution in righting the wrongs of the world. The way people learn to listen and talk, play, think, negotiate, value, and care for themselves and each other in these early childhood programs spills out to other lives in the surrounding community. People have a taste of a different way of being and are no longer willing to settle for the inadequacies and injustices of how things are.

Our intention in writing *The Visionary Director* goes beyond trying to make your job easier, though we certainly hope it does that. We believe early childhood programs are in a pivotal position to foster relationships that can heal the rift we all feel between ourselves and others, and with the natural world. We can address issues of bias and inequality in our thinking, actions, and structural arrangements. Early childhood programs can give the children and adults involved an experience of empowerment, of democracy in action, so that they have the will and know-how to make this a priority in our country. On the whole, most early childhood programs haven't been developed with this as a vision. We've been focused on the more limited goals of keeping children out of harm's way or getting them ready for school. There is so much more we could be reaching for, seeing the connection between our work and larger social change. That vision could mobilize enormous energy and turn us into a force to be reckoned with.

If I hadn't maintained my vision of how this place could evolve, I could not have stayed in this job as long as I have. It's your vision that gets you through the very rough times.

—Paul

Fortifying Yourself with a Vision

In visiting directors around the country, we've found that those who actively work with a bold vision create programs that stand out from the grim statistics on mediocrity in child care. Think of your vision like the breath in your body. The more attention you give to it, the more it fortifies you. When programs are led by directors who breathe a larger vision into everyday tasks, people feel more alive in their bodies and their spirits lift with a new sense of hope. This is one of the greatest antidotes to burnout we have.

Por los horrores que veo ocurren actualmento pido por un milagro. El milagro que nunca más se le dé una paliza a un niño, que nunca más sean golpeados o abusados. Vivimos en una época en la que la violencia es normal. Debemos cuestionar las golpizas y humillaciones a los niños, el expresar la rabia y la frustración con violencia, de la misma manera que cuestionamos el tratamiento sexista y abusivo a las mujeres.

Cuando tuve la oportunidad de abrir un programa de cuidado infantil para madres adolescentes, sabía que la realidad actual de injusticias no se podría evitar en nuestro programa. Sabía que me agotaría muy rápidamente sino tenía una visión clara. Quería crear un lugar donde la gente pudiera participar en esta lucha por la no violencia y terminar con esta conspiración silenciosa, en torno a asuntos como darle una golpiza a un niño porque no quiere ponerse los zapatos. La clave para comprometerse en la no violencia es por medió de la comprensión del desarrollo del niño y el aprender a tener paciencia.

La visión que tengo cada día cuando vengo al trabajo es ofrecer a las madre un santuario de paz y de liberación del dolor de las calles. Un santuario donde se acepten sin juicios las historias de cada una de las adolescentes . Un lugar de sanación y cambio. Cuando las adolescentes vienen a nuestro programa, deben introducirse en esta noción que la violencia en contra de alguien está mal. Todas estas madres han vivido en violencia la mayor parte de sus vidas. Ellas deben querer hacer las cosas de una manera diferente, aun cuando todavía no sean capaces de hacerlo. Nosotras les decimos, "No las juzgaremos y ustedes no van a mentir o quedarse calladas acerca de lo que esté pasando. Pueden estar enojadas, pueden odiar lo que pasa, pero no habrá violencia." Ese es nuestro lema.

Es tan difícil y tenemos tantos contratiempos. A veces me canso y me pregunto a mí misma, "¿Cuántos años más de todo esto?" Y, sin embargo, este es el trabajo que me hace sentir que puedo influenciar y producir un cambio. Y lo hacemos. Cada año vemos a estas jóvenes madres hacerse más fuertes. Emergen la esperanza y la compasión. Se apoyan las unas a las otras y nosotras vemos cómo cambian su manera de ser. Creo firmemente que al final luchan por el cambio porque quieren tener esperanza para sus hijos.

—**Ruth**

With all the horrors one sees in our popular culture, I have a dream. If I could create one miracle before I die, it would be to stop children from being spanked, hit, or abused. We live in a culture where violence is normalized. We must question the cultural edicts that condone spanking and the humiliation of children, just as we must question the abusive and sexist treatment of women, and the expression of frustration or anger in the form of violence.

So when I had the chance to open a child care program for teen mothers I knew I couldn't divorce the politics of the wider injustices of the world from our program. Without a clear vision to focus on, I knew I would burn out very quickly. I wanted to create a place where people would take on this struggle for nonviolence and step out of this conspiracy of silence around such things as spanking toddlers for not wanting to put on their shoes. The key to making a commitment to nonviolence is through understanding child development and through learning patience.

The vision I form each day I come to work is to provide a sanctuary of peace and freedom from the pain of the streets for teen mothers. A sanctuary of acceptance without judgment where each teen's story is her own. A place of healing and change. When teens enroll their children in our program, they have to buy into this notion that violence toward someone without power is wrong. All of these mothers have been living with violence most of their lives. They have to want to do it differently, even if they aren't able to yet. We say to them, "We will not judge you and you will not lie or keep silent about what's going on. You can be mad, you can hate what is happening, but no violence." That's our mantra.

It's so hard and we have so many setbacks. Sometimes I get so tired and I ask myself, "How many more years can I do this?" Yet this work is what makes me feel like I can have some influence, create change. And we do. Every year we see these young mothers get stronger. Hope and compassion emerges. They support each other and we watch them change the tide. I firmly believe that ultimately people will fight for change because they want hope for their children.

—Ruth

Assessing Where We Are

In recent years we've begun to ask directors to describe the vision that is guiding their work. To our surprise, many have a limited response. Some talk of a new playground, more scholarship dollars, or an active substitute teacher list. We see these responses as goals or items on a wish list, possibly indicators of a dream not yet fully articulated. A surprising number of directors point to NAEYC Accreditation, Head Start Performance Standards, the Creative Curriculum, or their High/Scope program as their vision. To be sure, we have great respect for these guideposts and have used such things for many years in our own work. But as we begin to look around at the actual classrooms following these standards, and when we assess the focus of curriculum and interactions between the staff, children, and families, our hearts sink. Somehow the idea of a vision for a program has been reduced to a set of goals, standards, and regulations—lots of paperwork, checklists, and little boxes to be filled out. Our concern about vision begs other questions. Where is the heart and vitality in these programs? What gives them life? Who spends their days here and what are their hopes and dreams?

In the early years of developing programs for young children whose mothers worked all day, the vision was to create a home away from home. Teachers and directors took inspiration from the philosophies of early nursery school and kindergarten educators, as well as child psychologists—people such as Caroline Pratt, John Dewey, Maria Montessori, and Jean Piaget. The supervisor's focus was on providing meaningful play experiences for children, not managing complex programs with multiple demands. Time and history have brought us to a new place.

Over the last twenty-five years the early childhood profession has come of age. Early childhood caregivers and teachers have now become a full-fledged workforce with regulations, training systems, professional organizations, conferences, and a huge collection of resources. Visit an accredited early childhood program in any region of this country and you will likely see characteristics of what defines a profession—a body of shared language, definitions of core competencies, and standards. Early childhood care and education has an extensive body of literature, a code of ethics, certificates, and degree programs. On the one hand, we feel proud to be part of a cadre of people determined to see that young children in group settings are cared for in safe and healthy environments. We welcome the efforts of publishers and companies seeking to provide us with better equipment, multicultural materials, curriculum ideas, and child guidance strategies. However, when we visit exhibit halls at conferences, we fear our profession has lost sight of the need for a vision to guide our work. Many early childhood educators seem to have fallen prey to strong commercial interests and misguided pressures to get kids ready for school at a younger and younger age. How has this happened and what does it mean for our lives?

In large and small child care settings that are both for-profit and not-for-profit, from Florida to Alaska, and on U.S. military bases around the world, we see accredited child care and Head Start programs all starting to look the same. Most are furnished with items from the same early childhood vendor catalogs, have the same bulletin board displays, and curriculum plans posted on the wall. We've discovered that criteria and standards originally developed as guidelines for quality care and education have now become narrowly interpreted rules to enforce. Though there is lip service to the concept, the heart of a caregiving partnership with families is missing in most programs. We see teachers using happy face forms to give parents reports about whether their children ate, slept, or had a "good" day. Most of these end up stuffed in the bottom of a bag or on the floor of the car because they convey very little about what families really want to know about their children's time spent away from home.

Children spend more of their waking hours in these programs than with their families. What families really need are snapshots (both descriptions and photographs) of how their children are developing and making friends, what they are doing and thinking, liking and avoiding. A daily form with perfunctory information doesn't make up for what they are missing. Because parents often lack the experience to find meaning in their children's play, they pressure teachers to provide them with traditional signs of their children's academic progress. They like to see art products, dittos, and checklists indicating what they think of as school readiness. Teachers striving to be developmentally appropriate get frustrated with these requests. Caregivers and parents want assurances and appreciation from each other. Often neither feel very satisfied with what they get.

Meanwhile, from the children's perspective, life is getting more crowded, rushed, and regimented into scheduled, short time blocks. Children spend too little time outdoors, in the world of real work, or with meaningful relationships and a sense of community. They rarely get to be alone, to play for as long as they like, or to be with children not of their own age. Caregivers and teachers come and go, and no one takes a special interest in them for long, or gives them a sense of history or belonging. Most of the adults in their lives seem obsessed with whether they know their colors and their numbers, and talk of getting big enough to go to school sustains little hope for engaged interest or meaningful learning.

As we approach the twenty-first century, early care and education programs are a daily fact of life for children and families in the United States. On the way to work each morning, most parents leave their children in the care of someone outside their families, usually in settings that look far more structured and institutional than where they spent their own childhoods. Some children are fortunate enough to be in quality family child care homes, but before long, the provider goes out of business or parents move their children into a pre-school setting that they believe will help them be ready to succeed in school. Well-meaning parents focus on their young children's education in a narrow sense, not considering the larger picture of their childhoods and the real experiences needed for success in life.

Rethinking What We Need

It is estimated that young children today spend approximately 12,000 hours in group care and institutional settings before they even get to school. This means that children are spending the bulk of their childhoods in our programs. Childhood in the last decade or two looks very different than what most of us reading this book remember. Growing up in a neighborhood, roaming freely on the block, climbing trees, playing street games, making creations with logs, stones, or found junk, regular family gatherings, playing with children of all ages as the neighbors watched out for all of us—these are things of the past. The experience of participating in the daily life and meaningful work of the community is less and less available to young children. Instead, most children today are spending their days in programs with large groups of children their same age, isolated from their families and the real world, surrounded by institutional walls and chain-link fences, playing with single-purpose plastic toys, and spending time with underpaid, often unresponsive or disgruntled adults. As Jim Greenman (1992) asks, "Is this what we want for the one childhood our children will have?"

I want every room in our program to be one I would love to put my own child in. Each new baby I enroll in our program I personally take into my arms and say, "I will do my best to see that every day you are loved by someone here. In every way possible, we will find ways to let you know how special and important you are to us."

—Laura

Early childhood programs are microcosms of the larger world in which we live. Often they are devoid of spirit and meaningful connections, plagued with crumbling infrastructures, and distressed with lives on the brink. Staff, children, and families are filled with stress and assaults to their physical and mental health. To cope, we become desensitized and think of this way of living as "normal." Living with an unacknowledged but nagging discrepancy between how things are and how they could be easily leads to cynicism or depression. We lower our expectations to avoid our deep disappointment. Any vision we may have started with gets sacrificed in the name of saving our sanity.

Visit any early childhood center and you find everyone is needing more support. Scratch the surface and you find a profound need for a place to be nurtured and appreciated. People desire more than reminders to have a good day. We yearn for fuller connections with others and more meaningful daily exchanges. Why don't our needs assessments acknowledge this human longing for connection as our most vital need? This acknowledgment would give us a wake-up call we could respond to with commitment and know-how. The early childhood profession knows about nurturing human development. Within our control are buildings where people of different ages, and in many cases, different cultures come together each day with the potential of real interchanges of ideas, needs, skills, and resources. We come together with a clear focus on children. Everyone acknowledges that these children are our future. They represent our hopes, promises, and deepest longings. Are we using this daily opportunity to its fullest potential?

The often quoted African proverb "It takes a village to raise a child" is an important reminder for us. But perhaps in our consumer-oriented, technologically advanced, fast-paced culture, it will take a *child* to raise a *village*. When people genuinely come together around their hopes and dreams for children, a sense of possibility can be rekindled. This goes far beyond providing a service or a school readiness program. Early childhood centers can play a central role in recreating the new village, the new experience of neighborhood for our daily lives. They can become places that respond to the longings for community, meaningful relationships, and a sense of belonging. This is a vision we can have for our programs, and not just as words on paper. Our actions, our policies, and the experiences of our organizational culture can reflect and embody this dream.

Distinguishing a Mission from a Vision

The early childhood profession gives periodic lip service to the idea of having a vision, but it is uncommon to find much time or space devoted to this topic in our literature or professional development offerings. More typically we find discussions of appropriate practice, standards, regulations, and rating scales. Though these certainly may be part of one's vision, they are not usually discussed in this context. In all our profession's emphasis on the components of quality child care, specific mention of working within a larger vision is usually missing. Is this because we don't understand the concept or role of a vision in our work, or are there other explanations?

Many early childhood programs have something written on paper about their purpose. Often this is in the form of a mission statement outlining their intent to serve children in need of care, to treat them respectfully, and to meet their developmental needs. However, directors hired into programs are seldom asked how they would like to see the organization's purpose brought to life. Mission and philosophy statements are occasionally posted in programs and are usually found in handbooks or the organization's literature. Rarely do these statements make their way into the hearts and minds of the staff or in any way become a guiding vision for program environments, policies and procedures, or daily decision making.

A mission statement is usually about purpose, but it is seldom about a dream. Typically, a mission statement tries to address a problem with a statement of services. A vision, on the other hand, goes beyond how things are to describe how we would like them to be. In the words of Susan Gross (1987), a vision is "what the world or society or an environment or community would look like if that purpose were realized."

There are a number of possible reasons why the early childhood field has focused more on the delivery of services and neglected to project a larger vision for what we could be doing. As we have grown beyond the part-time nursery school model of providing enrichment experiences for children and battled the notion that full-time child care is just baby-sitting, the bulk of our attention has been on developing an agreed upon body of professional knowledge and ethics. The primary focus has been on the child's experience within our care and secondarily on parent support and education. While a growing emphasis has been placed on staff qualifications and training, little attention has been given to the working conditions and resources caregivers and teachers need to do their jobs well. If we projected a picture of what is really required, we'd have to admit how woefully inadequate our programs are.

Our profession is predominantly female, and in a world where resources are controlled by male priorities, we struggle to be taken seriously. To get the recognition and support we need, women tend to do what is expected of us, color within the lines, and play the game nicely. In early childhood care and education, our message is often, "We are doing such a good job with children, please give us more recognition and resources." If we spoke the bigger truth and acknowledged that most of our programs are mediocre at best, we'd feel like failures. Politically, we'd be shooting ourselves in the foot. Most early childhood professionals prefer to confine our sights to what seems possible, rather than face the pain of what Langston Hughes called "a dream deferred." Thus we strain under multiple stresses and minimal resources, and our workforce continues to turn over rapidly.

As children and their families come to us increasingly needy, with their family life and communities under assault from commercial interests, media culture, violence, poverty, and racism, we frantically put our fingers in the leaky holes. We have failed to mobilize a vision that would hold back the floodwaters, let alone dismantle the dike and build a new structure that would universally meet the needs of children and families.

Peter Block reminds us in *The Empowered Manager* (1987) that "a vision exists within each of us, even if we have not made it explicit or put it into words. Our reluctance to articulate our vision is a measure of our despair and a reluctance to take responsibility for our own lives, our own unit, and our own organization. A vision statement is an expression of hope, and if we have no hope, it is hard to create a vision."

Are there places in our profession where a larger vision is central to the discourse and is actively generating hope? It seems to us that most of our profession's romance with the Italian schools of Reggio Emilia stems from the hope they offer us. Reggio schools show us a vision of how programs could be if we genuinely dedicated ourselves to the lives of children. Early childhood educators are flocking to seminars and conferences about the Reggio approach, not just because it's a fad, but for the way it captures our imaginations. There are now books and videos inspired by the Reggio model, showing teachers ways to observe, document, and do in-depth curriculum projects with children. These resources imply a vision for our program. Often the authors quote Loris Malaguzzi, father of these Italian schools, who said "Start with your image of the child." In *The Hundred Languages of Children* we get a glimpse of what this approach means in terms of program structure, support, and policies, but most of the literature is focused on how the teachers carry out this approach with children.

The heart of the Reggio model includes not only an image of children, but a culture that is family-centered and attentive to sensual pleasure, reflection, intense discussion, and collaboration. These schools have grown from a vision of social justice in the politics of the Italian town for which they were named. The adults have created programs for children out of their real lives and values. If we are to draw inspiration from these Italian schools, we can't imitate their culture, but rather find our own way. We need to dive under the profit-driven popular culture of America and bring forth the things that we know nurture children and family life, such as having relationships with real people rather than television personalities, slowing

down to notice and celebrate how the light changes with different seasons, and taking time to create lasting traditions and memories. The challenge is to create a program culture that will support these things.

I work in an inner-city setting that is often stereotyped because it is riddled with all the problems of poverty. It's easy to have low expectations and become immobilized by the difficulties. But, if you want to find them, there are still many possibilities for the people who live in these communities.

From the beginning of my directing work here I knew my challenge was to go beyond just meeting the standards, which is what most people reach for as a goal for an inner-city program. I had a driving belief that children, families, and staff members all have the potential to continually learn and grow. With this in mind, I began to think in terms of instilling a sense of hope as a primary goal. Most inner-city child care and Head Start programs don't get access to progressive, visionary ideas. The focus is usually just about needs, deficits, and survival. My search for a way to change this led me to the schools of Reggio Emilia in Italy.

At Reggio I found an extraordinary set of infant, toddler, and preschool centers founded by a small group of determined people after their country had been ravaged by war. Over the years they got their municipal government to fund these programs. At first I was hesitant to try to use Reggio as a model for our programs. Reggio Emilia and the inner-city of Chicago are so completely different. I knew we would have to invent our own way, and I questioned whether we could.

I had to learn how to focus on opportunities and not obsess over the barriers and obstacles or allow ourselves to get stuck there. My dream is to create a different example of quality for others to see, especially in programs like Head Start and subsidized child care. Rather than seeing our children as just needing more social services, we have begun to recognize that despite the hardships in their lives, these children come to us with ideas, interests, and curiosities that we need to help flourish. Reaching our vision is an ongoing process, and we are figuring it out as we go. I don't think it will ever end. There are peaks and valleys, but we are continuing to move forward.

—**Karen**

Vision

your time as a director is spent nurturing hope and of possibility to those in your program? Are there ch you are cultivating a vision as part of your regular ions, parent orientation, and staff development efforts? ionary Director contains ideas on how to move in that direction. Throughout this book are snapshots of the many different ways directors are making this happen. As you hear their voices, let them strengthen your ability to guide your program with a vision and deepen your desire to be part of this spreading movement to turn our early childhood programs into genuine caring and learning communities.

Go back to why you're doing what you're doing. I don't mean going back to the regulations. Don't be outer defined. Do not allow the regs to define who you are. Do not allow any outside forces to define who you are. Allow for the possibility that the regs may actually catch up with your vision. There will be a flicker of fire that's very exciting.

—**Dana**

Going Beyond Managing to Leading

Guiding early childhood programs with a vision requires more than management skills. A manager is focused on the people, problems, and tasks at hand, using technical skills to address them. Beyond that, working with a vision requires developing oneself into a leader who inspires others to participate in and expand the vision. Of course, early childhood directors who are leaders attend to management concerns, but they also bring these concerns into a group focus through vision building. Linda Espinosa, who embodies these dimensions of leadership, says, "Leaders are those who provoke or nudge or elevate others into thinking, feeling, or behaving in ways they would not otherwise have demonstrated" (1997). Growing yourself as a leader goes hand in hand with growing a vision.

It's pretty easy to be a star if you are a hard-working director with aspirations. You can create some innovative things in a program and then move on to the next phase of your career. I strive to be a leader, not a star. A leader plans for what stays when they leave. The big difference between a leader and a star is in the size of a person's ego. I know that as I provide leadership, people won't always love me and be happy. But I'm trying to build an institutional structure that will outlast any focus on me.

—Laura

A vision can't be handed down like a mission statement or memo. The ground has to be prepared, seeds have to be planted, and tender shoots have to be protected from destructive pests and early frosts. This requires what Sharon Kagan and Michelle Neuman call "conceptual leadership," which they say is "more about how we think together about the field's identity and the role that early care and education must play in a democratic society" (1997). A conceptual leader continually steps back and sees the big picture. You need a working knowledge of systems thinking, human development, pedagogy, and group dynamics. Where can we find models to adapt for this kind of leadership in our field?

Looking for Models

Surprisingly, it is outside the field of early care and education that we find the most literature and training with an emphasis on leading organizations with a vision. For the last fifteen or twenty years, the vision of workplaces as learning organizations has been advancing in the corporate business sector, but this is only occasionally found in early childhood programs. Corporate consultants and CEOs have been influencing the direction of for-profit business using ideas that seem intrinsic to the early childhood field. Our work centers around ideas of human development, the processes of teaching and learning, and teamwork. Yet it is the business world that has taken off and prospered using these concepts. Since the 1990s there has been a proliferation of corporate business management books and trade journals discussing ideas that we think should be the foundation of our work in the early childhood care and education field—build from people's strengths, acknowledge contributions, develop shared visions, do systems thinking, see empowerment as the key to success, provide for and reward collaborations, and celebrate often. Shouldn't these concepts be filling our literature, conferences and professional development seminars? The corporate business world has created a vision and mobilized a workforce around a strong sense of purpose, ultimately to enhance their growing profit margin. What are equivalent actions we can use to become powerful in the world?

As one voice in the field, *Child Care Information Exchange* has consistently tried to bring the lessons of the corporate business world to our work in early childhood. As early as 1987 they featured an article by a business management consultant alerting us to the way organizations become powerful. Here's a taste of what Susan Gross has to say in her article "The Power of Purpose" (1987):

> What we mean by purpose is the end or result at which an entire organization is aimed. Purpose is the organization's driving force and reason for being. It is always translatable into vision—that is, an image shared by the organization of what the world or society or an environment or community would look like if that purpose were realized.

For early childhood programs, Gross is describing something different than uniting a center around the self-study for NAEYC Accreditation, as important and rewarding as that might be. She is suggesting using our imaginations, not our checklists, to define dreams that linger with us as we move through our days of stress, chores, meetings, and "to do" lists. Her point has to do with how we cultivate our hearts, make connections with other people, and create a desire to reach for something better. Gross goes on:

> The most potent ingredient in organizational effectiveness is a clear sense of purpose shared by every member of the organization. Organizational problems, including nasty interpersonal conflicts and wrenching internal schisms, can literally begin to dissolve when people in an organization rediscover the depth of their common vision.

Susan Gross and other people in the business world are reminding us that vision is central to organizational effectiveness. Peter Block, another business management consultant, reminds us that the very definition of leadership in an organization is tied to working with a vision: "Leadership is keeping others focused on the vision, and this means that we have to get comfortable talking about it" (1987).

To develop leadership, we suggest that you work with a clear set of principles. Each chapter of this book offers principles that we think are valuable for early childhood programs. Strategies you can use to bring them alive are also included. Here we introduce the first principle as a foundation for your work.

Principle

Begin by Developing Your Vision

A vision for an organization can't be just one person's idea. As a director, you may have the initial inspiration for your program's purpose, but for these ideas to grow, you must steadily invite the interest and involvement of others.

Because many early childhood program directors are inexperienced in working with a vision, they may be uncertain how to talk about it and bring their vision into focus for others. Here are some strategies that might prove useful for developing leadership skills.

Strategy

Regularly share memories of favorite childhood experiences

Whether our childhoods were generally positive or negative, most of us have some favorite childhood experiences to share with others. When adults take on teaching jobs in early child-hood programs, the primary memory bank we draw on is a school setting. But deep within us are other memories that fill us with warmth, giggles, and sensory details we want to describe. These can become frequent discussion starters to generate ideas about the activities and relationships that are valuable for children.

In the initial process of working with a staff to build a common vision for the program, it's useful to devote a large block of time to some specific storytelling about childhood memories. This gets people in touch with a vital set of experi-ences that have lasting meaning for them. Devoting precious staff development time to this sharing communicates the priorities of the program and the value that is placed on people's own lives as a rich source of learning. It also sets the tone for creating a "storytelling culture" in the program.

This idea might be introduced during a meeting by asking the staff to break into pairs and each share a favorite memory from their childhood. Acknowledge that some may have had difficult childhoods, but nearly everyone has something special they remember. Tell the group you will give each pair about ten minutes for sharing. After the first five minutes, alert them to the time for the second person to share. Reconvene the whole group and ask for reflections on what they heard. Rather than repeating these stories, ask them to name the themes they heard. This process of analyzing and drawing out the meaning of these stories is where "ah-ha's" happen. Many people have memories of endless hours playing outside without any adult supervision. Others remember playing with kids of all ages in the neighborhood, eating peanut butter sandwiches out on the steps, turning found objects into toys or inventions. As you list these kinds of themes—endless hours outdoors, no adults around, making mischief, make-believe—consider which are currently available to children in your program. Obviously, we can't do some of these things, but can we find ways to create similar feelings for children today?

Discussions like this are the tender shoots of a growing vision. As the months go on you can further develop this aspect of your organizational culture by devoting ten to fifteen minutes of each staff meeting for continued storytelling. What you want to cultivate is a climate where stories are everywhere in your program, reflecting a genuine enthusiasm and engagement with what is happening. This initial story sharing practice will lay the groundwork for giving attention to the details of children's conversations and their play. It will further the respect and appreciation staff and families will have for how stories offer a window into who they are and how they think.

The way you launch an activity of sharing childhood memories among your staff depends on your assessment of who they are. Getting to know your staff well will help you determine how to set the stage and introduce the activity. If you have a large staff, you may need to allow more time, or you may want people to share their stories in pairs or small groups. If people are hesitant to talk in a group, bringing some objects and pictures can help spark people's memories. When people have good listening skills and feel at ease to talk in group settings, this activity usually runs smoothly. If one or two people tend to dominate the discussion, you will need to monitor the time and the structure of the activity so everyone has a turn. When you have a group that seems hesitant to talk about themselves, you might do better to keep the talking in pairs or have them make some written lists.

We've also found caregivers and teachers respond well when asked to use open-ended materials such as toilet paper rolls, wire, and blocks to represent their favorite memory or a favorite place they remember from their childhood. This often generates creative thinking and playful interactions, reminding people of the spirit of childhood. Sometimes it helps to suggest a specific focus for a childhood memory, such as remembering a time when you took a risk as a young child. You can experiment with free form sharing, letting anyone who is ready have a turn to speak, or you can just go around the room, giving everyone a turn. Use these questions with any childhood memory activity to generate the components of a child- and family-centered program:

- *What were the themes in the stories you heard?*
- *If you were going to give this story a three or four word name, what would it be?*
- *Which of these themes would you like to be part of the children's and families' lives in our program?*
- *How can we simulate some of these experiences within the confines of our safety regulations?*

One director we know wanted to build a playground that would provide children with opportunities for risk taking and adventure. She used childhood memory activities to raise funds for and design a playground built for risk and adventure in her program. In meetings with her staff, child care licensers, local business people, and parents, she asked them to recall their fondest memories of being outdoors. Their memories included lots of sensory elements, such as water, dirt, and even pricker bushes. With fondness, most of them recalled favorite hiding places, taking risks, and doing things their parents might not have allowed had they been around. After brainstorming lists like this, the director suggested they compare their experiences with the lives of children in full-time child care today. The contrast was striking enough that this director was able to mobilize the support and resources to build a playground that simulates many elements of these childhood memories. It is designed around nature and adventure, with more money put into landscaping than plastic, immovable climbers. For a fuller account of this inspirational story, see our book *Reflecting Children's Lives: A Handbook for Planning Child-Centered Curriculum.*

Finally, if you happen to have a group that is slow to participate in sharing memories and stories, you might want to launch this activity by reading a children's book that captures some aspects of your vision. Books that work well in launching childhood memory activities are listed in the strategy that follows.

Strategy

Use children's books in staff meetings

There are a number of reasons to regularly read children's books in staff meetings and workshops. Overall, we need to improve the way we typically use picture books with children. Books are usually given to children as a holding pattern, a way to keep them occupied during transition times, with little support for any real interest in the books. Often a requirement is to put them away as the teacher is ready for the next activity. Story reading in many early childhood programs usually happens in large groups at circle time, with repeated reminders to sit quietly and not interrupt. This habit is counter to much of what we know about helping children become life-long readers and lovers of books.

To explore a child's perspective on books, ask the staff to share their favorite childhood memories with books. They most likely will share stories about curling up with a book and a flashlight under the sheets or in the closet, or sitting outside on the steps or under the trees. Or they may remember being snuggled in the lap of a family member or at bedtime, with few distractions and ample time to talk about the pictures and share wonder and related experiences. Sharing these memories and regularly using picture books in our staff meetings alerts us to possible changes we might want to make in using them with children.

If you model book reading or invite teachers who are expressive to do this, reading books in staff meetings helps cultivate good story reading voices and listening habits. They are also a terrific way to jar our memories of what things are like from a child's perspective. Stories told with a child's eye are not only useful in considerations of issues like child guidance, but often provide an opportunity for us to dream a little, and to remember the kind of environment and experiences that create close relationships, a strong sense of identity, and the wonder and magic of learning in the company of people who love you. Choosing picture books with childhood themes nudges us to explore their implications for our programs. They are great vision-building tools.

A good story to start with is *On the Day I Was Born* by Debi Chocolate. The text of this book is simple, but uses engaging language to accompany the rich texture of the illustrations. The child in this story talks about being wrapped in a soft cloth, being adored by his family members, and making his father stand tall and proud. Read the book with expression as you would with children. You can read the book all the way through or stop after a few pages. Use the following questions for discussion of the themes in this beautiful book:

- *How is our program like the feelings of the child in this book?*
- *What is our softness curriculum? Can you describe specific things we do that make children feel they are wrapped in a soft cloth?*
- *Do we convey to the children and their families that they make us feel proud? If so, how?*

Another text that helps teachers explore the specific components of childhood that we should be providing in our programs is *Roxaboxen*, a true story by Barbara Cooney. It is filled with images of children engaged in meaningful, self-directed play that involves all the goals we have for our block and dress-up areas, for our nature and science activities, and for physical, social, emotional, and moral development. Ask staff members to reflect on questions like the following, together as a group or in pairs:

- *When the children in our program grow up and think back on their time with us, will it be with the same fondness and meaning that Roxaboxen offered? If not, how can we make it so?*

- *What are the elements of childhood portrayed in Roxaboxen and how can we recreate or simulate them in our program?*
- *What are the jewels that children find in our program? Are there enough to go around?*
- *Where in our program do children experience the sensation of riding fast like the wind on a pretend horse?*

Miss Tizzy, by Libba Moore Gray, offers another wonderful picture of how children and adults could be spending their time together. Many aspects of our vision for early childhood programs becoming genuine caring and learning communities are in this book. Miss Tizzy is part of a neighborhood and engages children in predictable routines and unexpected treats. She shares herself fully with the children and involves them in meaningful work and joyous play. In her care, the children learn to make a contribution to the neighborhood and ulti-mately to Miss Tizzy herself. To guide the discussion of this book, ask staff to reflect on the specific things Miss Tizzy does with the children that make her so wonderful. Consider ques-tions like the following:

- *How do we connect children in our program to nature in the spirit of Miss Tizzy with her garden and cat and songs to the moon?*
- *What special things of ours do we bring to work to share with the children?*
- *What risks do we take in sharing ourselves with children, like Miss Tizzy having a house and garden that looks different from everyone else's, or being willing to sing even when she is slightly off key?*
- *How do children in our program experience a similar sense of neighborhood when they are in our care?*
- *How do children in our program learn to make a contribu-tion to those around them?*

Each of these books generates wonderful discussions and provides twinkles and tears for our eyes. They help us remember how it could be and inspire us to move in that direc-tion. If you spend much time in the children's section of a library or bookstore, you will likely find other books to use in your vision building. Consider children's books for meetings not only with staff, but also for gatherings with families, at board meetings, or even hearings with licensers or legislators.

Having tried this strategy of reading children's books, many directors have told us of exciting results. In one program, some of the staff were so inspired by *Roxaboxen* that they put all their plastic, commercial toys in storage and replaced them with open-ended materials from nature, such as driftwood, rocks, shells, and old wooden boxes and baskets. The quality of play among children that·followed was unlike anything they had seen before. When shelving units and furniture needed replacing, they began shopping at garden stores and the IKEA store that had opened in their area, instead of using the traditional early childhood catalogs. The atmosphere became more relaxed and parents started lingering more at drop off and pick up times. Soon they began to find parents snuggled with children on a wicker love seat looking over children's artwork or favorite books, while others helped to add finishing touches to a fort made of bedsheets and driftwood pieces.

Since we read *Roxaboxen* to a group of licensers, several of them have remarked that they now regularly read children's books in their office meetings. A family provider called and told us her licenser had a sudden change of heart after rereading *Roxaboxen*. She decided the huge pile of dirt in the backyard didn't really constitute a health and safety hazard. In fact, she thought it might be an exciting playground if the children were given some natural props and simple tools like sifters, pails, shovels, and rakes.

Strategy

Get to know the dreams of families

Each family enrolling a child in an early childhood program has hopes and dreams for their children. This is easily overlooked as schedules and fees are negotiated. To coax it out of families, put something in your application form that asks about their hopes for their child as they form relationships with caregivers and teachers. During home visits, interviews, or orientation sessions, respectfully raise questions that get to the values and longings they have for their children.

Make the families' values and their dreams for their children visible to the staff and others in concrete ways, such as bulletin board displays that feature different families every month. Put interviews and photographs that tell a story of a family in your newsletter or in a homemade book for others to read. To make this welcoming for everyone, be sensitive to issues that families may feel awkward disclosing, such as the configuration of their home life, their economic circumstances, or health. These strategies and your sensitivity go a long way to create an inclusive environment that acknowledges that all families have strengths, just as all families struggle.

Nuestra labor comenzo por que habían pocas opciones para las familias que necesitaban programas bilingües. Mi esposo y yo teniamos una visión (sueño). Determinamos mantener el español como el primer idioma de nuestros hijos. Queríamos un ambiente que le diera valor a su cultura Puerto Riqueña. Otros padres de diferentes culturas y razas también querían tener estas oportunidades para sus hijos, nuestra dedicación a estos valores creó un compromiso y un sentido de comunidad.

Hemos descubierto que nuestra visión no es estáticas, ha sido moldeada, modificada y puesta a prueba por los niños, maestros y agencias regulativas con los que nos relacionamos a travez de los años. El interés mutuo de los participantes por el bienestar y supervivencia del programa ha sido la fuerza que ha ayudado a realizar lo que hemos forjado. Hemos hecho grandes cambios en el ambiente físico, en nuestro curriculum, en nuestras políticas, en superar los problemas económicos y todavía nos mantenemos como una agencia independiente y privada. Esto nunca hubiera sido posible sin el sentido de comunidad que se ha forjado en nuestro Centro.

—**Carmen**

Our journey began because there were very few options for families looking for bilingual programs. My husband and I had a vision. We were really determined to maintain Spanish as the primary language for our children. We also wanted our children to be in an environment that validated their Puerto Rican heritage. This vision was shared by many other parents across racial lines. They too wanted a program that would provide these opportunities for their children. Our commitment to these issues created a bond and sense of community.

We have discovered that visions are not static. Our vision has been molded and put to the test by the many children, parents, staff, and regulatory agencies that have been involved over the years. The vested interest of all the participants in the survival and well-being of the program has been a very powerful force in accomplishing what we have. We have made major changes in our physical environment, curriculum, and policies. We have overcome financial hardships and have managed to remain an independent and private agency. This never would have happened without the sense of community that has emerged at our center.

—**Carmen**

Strategy

Reinvent the idea of quilting bees

Bring people together for meaningful tasks that aren't always about cleaning, painting, and repairing. Entice them with an enjoyable and useful activity, such as organizing their family memories into scrapbooks and photo albums. With busy lives, this is something most people don't make time for. They are usually grateful for the opportunity to rekindle memories at this type of bookmaking party.

Suggest that families and staff members bring photographs, special mementos, or just their memories to create visual stories about their lives. Offer a variety of colorful background papers, magazine pictures, stickers, and old greeting cards. Get a frame shop to donate a supply of recycled mat board or foam core. Provide glue, markers, scissors, and other tools for making bulletin boards or homemade books.

Offer initial ideas to get people started. They could create a book or display board around family history, favorite memories, holiday celebrations, or special accomplishments. Not only do you end up with visual stories of people in your program, but as they work on these projects together, staff and families are learning about and from each other and building a caring community.

Strategy

Develop a vision statement together

At some point it's useful to create a public declaration of the vision you are trying to build. When the ground has been adequately tilled and fertilized with activities such as the strategies above, invite people to collaborate on writing a vision statement. Using the accumulation of notes from your childhood memory sessions and input from the staff and parents about their values and what's important to them, invite people to collaborate on writing a vision statement. Use the lists from previous activities as well as the bulletin boards and homemade books to remind people of images they have already painted.

Ask people to look over these lists and visual representations and then brainstorm some words that describe the ideas or themes they reflect. Put these words into concept groupings and encourage people to brainstorm specific images to add more detail. As they begin this process, suggest they think of the special things they already experience in the program and then add more ideas about what else they would like see. Ask for volunteers to record what is being said. Use the words and phrases to develop a statement. It might take a couple of sessions to come up with a statement that sounds pleasing to everyone, but keep at it. The process itself continues to feed the vision.

Here's an example of a vision statement created by one program in Seattle:

> ### Hilltop Children's Center
> *A Learning Community for Children and Adults*
>
> *Where children are valued for their ability to do mean-*
> *ingful work, their wonder and curiosity, their perspec-*
> *tives, and ability to play—*
> *Where families are valued for their bonds and traditions,*
> *their ability to play, their commitment to work, home,*
> *and community, and their dreams for their children—*
> *Where staff are valued for their vision, their delight in*
> *children, their skill, heart, and knowledge, a commit-*
> *ment to families, and an ability to play—*
> *We cherish what we learn from each other.*

Strategy

Represent pieces of your vision with blocks

People need to see examples of what your vision looks like on a daily basis. After some initial time spent identifying and working toward your vision, get your staff focused on acknowledging how they see it in action. Bring a pile of blocks and sticky notes to a staff meeting. Ask people to again look over the components of your vision and then think of an example they've seen lately. Have them write a brief story description of this on a sticky note, put it on a block and then place the block so as to begin to build a foundation that represents your vision. As the foundation gets built, have each story read aloud so that the examples are visible to everyone. You might even find a way to display this block foundation on a table with a sign for parents and staff members to continue to add more story blocks as they see your vision coming alive.

Strategy

Expand your vision

We have offered you a vision of early childhood programs as learning communities that can serve as the cornerstone for larger social change. Take some time now to gather your own thoughts and reactions to this idea. If your program was to move closer to this vision, how might this look in your particular setting? Remember the words of Sylvia Ashton-Warner: "Dreams are a living picture in the mind generating energy."

Try to imagine the feel, the look, sound, and even the smell of such a place. What words would you use to describe this picture? Jot down some phrases that describe how the environment would influence the interactions and activities for children, staff, and families.

Now look over your list. Do any of your words match your image of a school? Are they similar to any elements in your current program? Go through the list again. Can you identify three things you could do, with negligible impact on your budget, that would reflect some of the elements you pictured? Perhaps your list would look something like this director's list:

- soft music and seating in our entry way

- chocolate chip cookies baking

- small groups of parents talking about weekend plans together
- monthly toy and clothing exchange for families
- community garden in a section of our play yard
- hosting ESL and citizenship classes for the community

1. Set up tape player and wicker love seat by sign-in table.

2. Have potpourri or scented candle for interim.

3. Call Refugee Alliance to discuss and offer space.

Practice Assessing Your Vision

Management consultant Carl Sussman once suggested that the typical early childhood environment does not cultivate the kind of risk-taking behavior that is needed to conceive and carry out an expansive vision. Inherently the work of taking care of children involves patience, consistency of routines, the utmost vigilance to safety and health, and gentle, accepting, nurturing behavior. Perhaps because of this, many of us in the early childhood profession have a temperament less inclined toward risk. In fact, most directors associate the idea of risk with liability and strive to keep everything safe, literally and figuratively. But if you are to be a leader and move your program toward a larger vision, you will need to cultivate yourself as a risk taker.

I didn't always know this. The learning took years. But once I learned how to make Army regulations work for us rather than letting them work against, I felt powerful and helped the people who worked with me feel empowered.

Yes, we do have to be 100% in compliance with Army regulation 608-10 in order to maintain our Department of Defense certification (the Army equivalent to state licensing). But what I've discovered is that somehow rules get "made up" that are not and never were in the regulation. Why this phenomenon of making up rules occurs in early childhood programs might make another whole

story. Maybe we make them up because we're inve
profession as we go. Maybe we do it because we're s
inspections. Maybe it's because we have such different i
understanding about best practices for early childhood pro
It could be a combination of all of these.

For example, when I was a preschool teacher there was a "rule"
among the child development centers and family child care homes
in our community that said the children must wear their shoes at
all times, even during nap time, because there might be a fire drill.
Does that make sense to you? Did you ever try to sleep comfortably wearing your shoes? Did you grow up never being allowed to
go barefoot? It made no sense to me, but we did as we were told
by our directors and kept the children in shoes.

So how did we work through this in my program? We began to
question the rules—the ones that didn't make sense to us. We
began to expect inspectors to "show us where it says that in the
regulation." We learned that the Army regulation actually stated
the intent for each rule. When we found that out, we began to
work with rule makers to develop plans and solve problems. Our
goal was to meet the *intent* of the regulation rather than continue
to comply with arbitrary rules. We began to feel that we were in
control of the rules, not that the rules were in control of us. We
began to feel powerful. We began to think for ourselves. We
became thinking people caring for our nation's children. We
began to be creators rather than followers of regulations that
didn't make sense.

—**Kathleen**

Take a minute to assess yourself. Do you see yourself as a
risk taker? A visionary? Are you satisfied with how things are
in your program, in our profession, and in society at large?
How close to your dream are you? Which of the following
statements feels most like you?

- I avoid taking risks and tend to put my head in the
  sand when it comes to big changes that are required.
- When I feel something really needs changing, I'm
  willing to stick my neck out.
- I'm always ready to challenge the status quo, to speak
  up or advocate for something that obviously needs
  changing.

- My program is pretty close to how I want it to be.
- I have a list of changes that need to be made if our program is going to meet our profession's definitions of quality.
- My vision for our program goes far beyond what is typically discussed in our professional literature. I have big dreams and am willing to work to achieve them.

Getting the most out of this book will require you to take some risks. Lay aside any skepticism or list of "yes, buts." Approach the coming chapters as a dreamer, making notes of what appeals to you, what you'd like to try. Let your mind stretch to spin out possibilities, your spirit fill with courage and determination, and your heart draw strength from your breathing. It's possible to change how things are when you remember and recommit yourself to how it could be.

Resources for Growing Your Vision

This selection of titles offers ideas from corporate business world consultants and community organizers, as well as three selections from the early childhood field, all pointing us toward a new vision of how it could be.

Block, Peter. *The Empowered Manager: Positive Political Skills at Work.* San Francisco: Jossey-Bass, 1987.

Carter, Margie, and Deb Curtis. *Spreading the News: Sharing the Stories of Early Childhood Programs.* St. Paul: Redleaf, 1996.

Chang, Hedy, Amy Mukelroy, and Dora Pulido-Tobiassen. *Looking In, Looking Out: Redefining Child Care and Early Education in a Diverse Society.* San Francisco: California Tomorrow, 1996.

Espinosa, Linda. "Personal Dimensions of Leadership." in *Leadership in Early Care and Education.* Ragan, S., and B. Bowman, eds. Washington, DC: NAEYC, 1997.

Greenman, Jim. "Places for Childhood." *Child Care Information Exchange* No. 86 (1992).

Gross, Susan. "The Power of Purpose." *Child Care Information Exchange,* No. 56 (1987).

Kagan, Sharon, and Michelle Neuman. "Conceptual Leadership." in *Leadership in Early Care and Education*. Ragan, S., and B. Bowman, eds. Washington DC: NAEYC, 1997.

Senge, Peter, et al. *The Fifth Discipline Fieldbook: Strategies and Tools for Building a Learning Organization*. New York: Doubleday, 1994.

Shields, Katrina. *In the Tiger's Mouth: An Empowerment Guide for Social Action*. Gabriola Island, British Columbia, Canada: New Society, 1994.

Sussman, Carl. "Out of the Basement: Discovering the Value of Child Care Facilities." *Young Children* No. 1 (1998), 15.

Washington, Valora. "Commentary," in *Leadership in Early Care and Education*. Ragan, S., and B. Bowman, eds. Washington DC: NAEYC, 1997.

Chapter 2

A Framework
for Your Work

The job of directing

an early childhood program has many faces. Whatever your intentions on any given day, the ebb and flow of events at your program places consistent demands on your time. Consider how your time has been spent over the last few weeks and place a check in the box below that most closely represents how it has felt.

Currently, most of my time at work is spent as:

☐ an air traffic controller
☐ a welcome wagon hostess with the mostest
☐ a midwife
☐ Mary Poppins
☐ _____
   (place your images here)
_____

When you begin the work of directing an early childhood program you may have a strong sense of purpose and be clear about your vision. Perhaps the first chapter of this book has sparked some new awareness for you and your mind is full of ideas. But consider this scene, which is no doubt a familiar one for you:

On the way to work this morning you've been thinking about the growing vision you have of your program becoming a caring and learning community for all involved. There are signs that many of your teachers are understanding the significance of their work in the larger context of changing the culture of consumerism and violence that surrounds us. Parents, too, are beginning to recognize the contrast between how vibrant it feels at your center and the environments where they live and work. They see how much people at the center seem to enjoy each other's company and help each other out. You feel inspired and resolve to work on behalf of this vision, knowing that it will make a difference in the lives of the children and adults.

Walking in the door you learn that one of your teachers has called in sick and no substitute has been found. A parent approaches, impatient to speak with you before she heads off to work. In the back of your mind you notice the payroll accounting begging for attention so checks can be cut by the end of the day. On your desk you find a long "to do" list that must be accomplished before your board meeting this evening. The glow of your morning thoughts fades as you face the pressing issues of the day.

In scenes like this, how do you keep hold of your dreams as you move through your day? Do you have strategies that keep your head above water, your mind focused, your eyes clear and bright? The work life of directors and supervisors is so encompassing, so filled with squeaky wheels and daily crises, that it's easy to lose sight of where you want to be going. Building and sustaining your vision takes more than your imagination or a head full of dreams. You need a structure and systems to help you organize the tasks that lead to your vision, one that keeps you intentional in your planning and responses. Directing with a vision requires a conceptual framework and a practical grasp of effective tools to meet the multiple demands of this complex work.

Looking for Tips and Techniques

When you seek out resources to help you in your work, what is usually on your mind? Are you looking to acquire particular skills such as budget development, time management, or delegation of tasks? This know-how is obviously important for program managers and there are a number of other competencies you need to be an effective supervisor. For example, recruiting, orienting, supervising, and evaluating staff; marketing and advocating for your program with parents, potential funders, and policy makers; writing handbooks, correspondence, and newsletters; maintaining contracts, policies, and documentation; solving problems, managing conflict, and accessing resources. The good news is that there are now some management books and resources designed to assist you with the day-to-day activities of your job. You can find these within and outside of the early childhood field, and we have listed related ones at the end of each chapter of this book.

As well as management tips, however, directors are seeking ideas to cultivate their leadership skills. As we discussed in the first chapter, learning to lead as well as manage is what makes it possible to bring a vision to life. If you are a leader, you work with a larger framework for thinking and responding. At any given time you intentionally choose which of your management roles is most likely to bring you closer to your vision. Directors need an approach, a presence of mind, that keeps their attention on the process of nourishing the vision they're after. This obviously involves more than checklists, good software, and management techniques. While you work to uphold standards, you translate them into meaningful concepts to guide the everyday activities in your program. Human development and making connections are as central to your thinking about quality as are those rating scales and component checklists. With each situation they encounter, leaders find a way to frame their thoughts, tasks, and decision-making process in the service of their visions. When you organize your work with attention to a vision, you find yourself moving forward, not spinning your wheels. Your spirit is awakened rather than drained.

What framework makes sense to guide the work of early childhood program directors as they seek to lead with a vision? Without funds for an ever-expanding administrative staff, how can you fulfill your multifaceted responsibilities? The ideas and inspiration a leader needs are often found outside of the typical early childhood publishing house. You might try visiting a magic shop, becoming an understudy to the Sorcerer's Apprentices, or perhaps contacting a laboratory specializing in clones. Keeping a sense of humor is essential to maintaining your sanity. Equally important is finding a way to think of the many aspects of your job. You need a framework that gives you a picture of your leadership tasks, one that keeps your work in a balanced perspective as you take on the discrepancies between how things are and how you envision they could be.

In recent years our Head Start has grown exponentially. Like every other Head Start program, we had a hierarchical structure. This worked fine when the problems were simpler and only required limited intervention, like speech services. What started to change was the growing needs of children and families. The numbers of families needing intervention grew and their problems became more involved and complex. I remember very clearly a defining moment during a staffing where we assigned eight to ten program people to intervene and address the problems in one family's life. I remember thinking, "This is stupid. This is the most fractured family, and this approach will disrupt their lives enormously." As a director, you have to stop blaming and listening to excuses and start assessing what change is needed. You must learn to discern the difference between idiosyncratic blips and problematic structural patterns.

At that point we had to redefine how we wanted to deliver services. The performance standards were segmented into many components and we had to find a more holistic way. We had to back out of the existing model and reorganize ourselves from the family's problem, rather than from the institution's structure. This change process included the entire staff. We were committed to this vision and we had to create an organizational structure to support it.

The beginning of the process was very hard. There was old baggage among staff members, and they were unable to let go of past injustices. But we stayed with it, and the outcome has been very positive. People were able to create a new structure that has worked very well for us. They believed in it, they owned it, they developed better working relationships. They had experienced a crisis, worked through it, and saw they could come through with good results.

As a result of this experience, I tried to build into our system more opportunities for collaborative planning, reflection, and problem solving. This involved restructuring our staff scheduling to create more paid time away from children. We ran up against a number of barriers, and we are still working to bring them down. There are no easy solutions to limited funds, time, and know-how, but we are determined to create a way out of no way.

—Dana

One of the definitions Webster offers for the word *framework* is "the larger branches of a tree that determines its shape." There are any number of management frameworks designed to help you make the current shape of your organization work better. What we are suggesting is that a new shape be considered for early childhood programs, one that nurtures the growth of individuals and a community in a way that transforms business as usual in the wider world. A framework like this infuses everyday tasks with opportunities for collaboration, reflection, and the discovery of other perspectives on children and families. Developing this kind of framework will most likely require you to shift some old habits and ways of thinking. To get off the typical treadmill of directing from crisis to crisis, it is helpful to step outside the early childhood field for some fresh ideas. We recommend turning to sources that may not have occurred to you, ones that offer you a new way to conceive of what you need to do. For instance, consider this concept of balance which is so critical to your thinking and functioning.

Learning about Balance

Learning to effectively juggle all the aspects of your work requires some understanding about the notion of balance. What will keep things from spinning out of control or, conversely, prevent your spirit or your program from shriveling up and dying from inertia? How do you balance sanity in your life with expediting quality in your program?

Balance is more than an abstract idea of how to lead one's life. When the dictionary defines balance as the relationship between debit and credit, we know this refers to both money *and* energy. Webster says balance involves comparing, prioritizing, decision making—a daily way of life for early childhood program directors. The demands and details are so plentiful that you find it hard not to be in a continual reactive state. Taking time to compare and prioritize may seem like a luxury, given all those fires to be put out. On the other hand, balance is certainly a key factor in staying healthy and effective as a director. We need models who have mastered the practice of balance, who have strategies we can adapt for our work. Where can we find those with examples for us? Take heart! There are people whose lives depend on a precise under-standing of balance and they have lessons to share.

Expand your mind's eye and consider the work of jugglers, figure skaters, whirling dervishes, and gymnasts. Perhaps this suggestion makes you chuckle but here's what jugglers tell us about their art. The trick to keeping all those balls in the air is to find one spot to focus on as all the balls are tossed in a path. If your eyes shift, trying to follow the individual balls, all that dispersing movement will cause you to lose concentration. You'll drop the ball. (Ever had this experience during your days of directing?) Figure skaters offer us a similar message. They say they are able to keep their balance while doing those amazing twirls and spins by focusing on one spot. They train their eyes to immediately find this spot as they make each whirl and turn.

Are you familiar with the religious order of Sufism, whose members are called whirling dervishes? As they dance into a trancelike state, they too follow this approach. When you watch dervishes dancing, you see them simultaneously whirling in individual circles while moving as a group around a big circle. They do this for up to an hour without ever losing their balance. Dervishes explain this practice as one of complete abandonment to their spiritual focus.

During one of the Olympic games we heard a gold medal gymnast describe her success as more than a matter of skills and techniques. She said the most important thing to do is to get an image in your mind of what you want to achieve. She asks herself, "What does it look and feel like, going up in the air, over the bar, and landing on your feet?" Similarly, directors can create specific images in their minds of what their center might look, feel, smell, and sound like when their vision is accomplished. The images will guide you as you master the techniques to get there.

Try asking yogi masters how they manage to keep a sense of balance while stretching their bodies into seemingly unimaginable positions. Their response will start to sound familiar. Yogis say one strategy for maintaining balance is to find a spot on the ground to focus on as you begin to position your body. They stress that this approach to physical balance helps to empty our minds of clutter so that we can find an internal place of balance. As we store a physical sense of balance in our brain's memory, it helps nourish this balance in our mental, emotional, and spiritual lives.

The lessons from all these folks have a common thread. There is a relationship between our ability to use our imaginations, find a focus, and keep ourselves in balance. A program director using these notions of balance is attentive to what nourishes people, not just whether they are meeting the requirements. More than learning the skills of long-distance running or doing triple toe loops, one has to develop an internal sense of strength and ability to stay focused and clear about where you want to be. Furthermore, our bodies can teach our minds about balance. Translating this to the work of an early childhood program director suggests two things: it is essential to find a focus and return to it again and again, and we need to give attention to our bodies as well as our minds.

Mary Catherine Bateson, author of *Composing a Life* (1990), suggests that we explore the concept of balance by looking at a tightrope walker. Many of us use the term "walking a thin line" to refer to some aspect of our work, but have we ever watched closely to study how those on a high wire do this? The tightrope walker usually carries a thin rod and continually moves this rod while walking along the high wire, changing the angle to maintain balance. This rod is equivalent to the framework we use to keep ourselves balanced in our work. A conceptual framework is something we can continually hold on to as we move through our daily tasks. It helps us know what shifts and adjustments we need to make to stay on track.

Finally, Bateson also suggests we consider music composition and visual arts for insights into composing a life of balance. Musicians and artists are skilled at finding a way to fit things together—different movements, forms, and colors—into a composition that is balanced, pleasing, and nourishing to the listener or viewer. Learning how they think and approach their compositions might be useful for directors who face parallel challenges of combining disparate elements into an engaging work of art. Directing really is a creative process, a pulling together of different elements to create a tapestry. You can approach your work not as a dot-to-dot ditto of meeting requirements, but rather as an ever changing, growing canvas on which you make bold strokes all the while paying attention to details and the creative process.

We recommend that you continue to explore insights in the worlds of the physical, spiritual, and visual arts. You are likely to always find metaphorical, if not practical, ideas that will help you shape an approach to your work. Metaphors are actually very useful in learning to shift your thinking and discover new insights. They help you access a different part of your brain. With metaphors you can find personal meaning and connections with something outside your normal frame of reference. For instance, if you begin to think of the work of a director as similar to that of a gymnast, inventor, or landscape architect, your mind begins to reorganize understandings and possibilities. Metaphors are useful in creating new emotional as well as cognitive associations. They help us redefine the familiar and make sense out of the unfamiliar. You can find new ideas for your work by exploring new words to describe what you do.

Searching for ideas in unusual places isn't just a wild idea from Deb and Margie. You find recommendations like this in established icons like *Fortune* magazine. For instance, in the December 29, 1997, issue there was an interview with business consultant guru Tom Peters who said, "The point is that in any business it's a matter of breaking completely out of familiar ways of thinking, of not limiting yourself to what is comfortable or comprehensible to you." He goes on to suggest that it's critical to find places where you experience a different kind of learning, like going dogsledding at the North Pole, rather than attending a management seminar. For early childhood folks, this suggestion might actually sound more appealing than exploring the business strategies of transnational corporations. We like to play, express our creativity, and take new field trips!

Taking Bright Ideas from the Business World

Because their overall world is so different from ours, perhaps it hasn't occurred to you to seek out ideas from the big business corporate sector of our society. Certainly they have resources far beyond ours, and goals that are often antithetical to our values and priorities. How surprising, then, to discover the familiar concepts and language of human development in their literature and seminars.

As the early childhood profession has been growing and changing over the past twenty-five to thirty years, so has the approach to corporate business management. So-called innovators in the business world continually speak of whole systems thinking, and what was once called the personnel department is now referred to as human resources. The literature for corporate managers is filled with charts illustrating various conceptual frameworks for all roles, functions, human dimensions, and processes that must be considered in effectively leading an organization. Managers are encouraged to focus on team building and diversity training, to be risk takers and visionaries. There is an emphasis on eliminating hierarchies and bureaucracy, strengthening the imaginations and autonomy of employees, and creating permanent flexibility. Much of their talk is what we would expect to find in early childhood management literature because these are the values that seem inherent in our work with children. For some reason this hasn't been translated in our professional literature about teacher education. Few of our professional resources offer a comparable set of guidelines with a conceptual framework, and strategies for building a vision and organizational culture that reflects those values. Sadly, we've found that most corporate management books and seminars offer far more inspiration and motivation for moving beyond the status quo than their counterparts in the early childhood field.

If you browse the business management shelves of your local library or bookstore you are likely to find books by Peter Block, Steven Covey, Tom Peters, and Peter Senge, all highly regarded business management consultants. Consider what they have to offer us. For instance, in his book *The Empowered Manager*, Peter Block stresses that all management structures and systems reflect a framework for the distribution of power. This is the foundation for an organization's culture. Block describes how managers can use their power to advance an organization to one where employees are pleased to be spending the best days of their lives. He presents the fundamental choices managers must make as those between maintenance and greatness, caution and courage, dependency and autonomy. Block's discussion of the kinds of mentalities that hold managers back from greatness, that have leaders slip into bureaucratic and narrow thinking systems, matches much of what we see in large early childhood programs. We see directors more focused on maintenance than greatness, cautious about stepping out and trying to reach for something currently beyond their reach, and often waiting for someone else to address the larger economic and political constraints that

...d us. With the overwhelming forces marshaled to ...scourage and drain us, early childhood directors would do well to heed Block's reminder that creating a vision of greatness is the first step toward empowerment. He hits the nail on the head when he says, "The struggle to create a vision is the struggle with hope."

In most early childhood programs our paperwork has grown faster than our vision or our capacity to design systems that respond to the real lives of children, families, and our employees. Taking some cues from innovators in the large world of business, we need a conceptual framework for organizing our thoughts, roles, and tasks so that we can steadily build and sustain a vision for our programs. Keeping in mind the ideas about balance discussed earlier, it is useful to conceptualize the work of early childhood directors in terms of a triangle.

The programs I see that are in trouble are ones where directors are not willing to be unpopular and make hard choices. Someone has to make hard choices. It's not fair to leave that to be resolved by the group. When you are a leader you have to learn to live with discomfort. It's easy to lead when things are going well. What's not so easy is to make hard decisions to push forward change.

Change involves a dynamic process that people have to go through. Unless things become uncomfortable, nothing changes. If directors insulate themselves, they can become too complacent. When you are complacent you aren't moved to see any discomfort there might be in your program, let alone get beyond it. Discomfort is fertile ground for change. Allowing yourself to be uncomfortable is where vision comes from.

—Dana

Considering a Triangle Framework

A number of years ago while consulting with a Migrant Head Start program, we worked with our colleague, Gloria Trinidad, to draw on the image of a triangle as a simple framework for conceptualizing the work of program supervisors and directors. Our experiences as a child care director, bookkeeper, and Head Start education coordinator, along with our understandings about cultural diversity, group dynamics, and pedagogy for adults, led us to the idea of an equilateral triangle, with three

sides equally balanced and focused on our vision of early childhood programs as learning communities for children, families,
and staff. Each side of the triangle (managing and overseeing,
coaching and mentoring, and building and supporting
community) is integral to the whole, and incorporates our
values of inclusion and anti-bias practices.

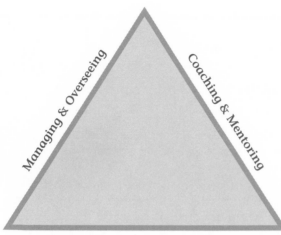

Building & Supporting Community

The image of a triangle to represent this framework works
well because we believe that each side of our management
work is of equal importance. Keep in mind the notion of
balance. If attention isn't given equally to the roles on each
side of the triangle, it becomes lopsided. At that point, both
director and program are in danger of collapsing. What follows
is an overview of this triangle framework as it pertains to your
human resources work. We conclude this chapter with an
opportunity to practice applying this framework to your
current work as a director or supervisor. The next three chapters will explore each side of the triangle in depth, offering
strategies to build and sustain the vision of early childhood
programs as caring, learning communities.

The Roles of Managing and Overseeing

All you have to do is look around your office for concrete representations of this side of the triangle. Perhaps you'll find the
Developmentally Appropriate Practice (DAP) book, accreditation
criteria from the National Association for the Education of
Young Children, Head Start performance standards, or your
state's child care licensing requirements. Your particular

program probably has a handbook of policies and procedures, and no doubt there are personnel files in your cabinets and computer. Maybe you've been working on your current staffing patterns, drafting a caregiver's performance evaluation, or processing a teacher's request for supplies from an early childhood catalog. The managing and overseeing side of the triangle involves many of these kinds of tasks. For staff supervision it especially includes things like the following:

- clarifying professional standards and expectations,
- developing a salary scale,
- arranging staffing patterns and schedules,
- establishing effective communication systems,
- organizing training options and meetings, and
- conducting performance reviews and evaluations.

The numerous activities related to managing and overseeing are critical to the functioning and well being of your organization. If you do not have clear standards and effective systems to guide your program, it is on very shaky ground. Any dreams you have of creating a learning community will be undermined if you aren't well organized and guiding your program with a strategic planning system and policies that reflect this vision.

As a director or supervisor, you are probably most familiar with the work on this side of the triangle. Because they are so very demanding and tangibly lend themselves to a check off list, these tasks define the primary way most administrators approach their jobs. If you are mainly operating from this side of the triangle, you find yourself constantly dealing with paperwork, as well as assessing, reminding, evaluating, and reporting. These are important management tasks, but in and of themselves they don't lead to a program where the children and staff are learning and thriving. Your managing and overseeing role has limitations when it comes to applying what we know about adult learning theory and effective staff development work. Just because they've read your manual or attended some early childhood classes, caregivers and teachers don't necessarily understand how to genuinely meet children's needs. Effective staff development requires a different mind-set and a different set of behaviors than managing and doing performance reviews. We think the tasks of helping teachers learn and grow belong on another side of the triangle.

The Roles of Coaching and Mentoring

Directors and supervisors often bring to us complaints like this one: "I've developed a really good staff handbook and I regularly send out memos and have conversations with my staff. Still, no matter how many times I tell them, they just don't seem to get it." Comments like these come from the mistaken notion that if supervisors can just get their staff to remember all of the regulations and guidelines, they will have a quality program. This reflects a managing approach to teachers' learning. Not only is this approach ineffective for staff development, it reinforces ideas about teaching and learning that we would never want teachers to use with children. Most of us would be aghast to hear this sentence coming from a teacher: "If I can just get the children to recite their ABC's at circle time, then they'll learn how to read."

Adult learning theory suggests that we must be mindful of the family and cultural background and the life experience that early childhood staff bring to our programs. These are as influential to their learning process as is any guidebook we might offer. Adults also learn more enthusiastically and effectively if they are taught in a way that is meaningful for their needs and interests. When you work from the coaching and mentoring side of the triangle, these ideas about pedagogy, family, and culture of origin systems are central. You use multifaceted strategies to meet the needs of early childhood program staff. These include:

- creating coaching methods for diverse learning styles,
- offering opportunities for self-assessment and goal setting,
- allowing time to practice new skills, and apply new understandings,
- nurturing dispositions favorable to effective teaching,
- giving feedback and support for growth and change, and
- fostering mentoring relationships.

When you cultivate your ability to work from the coaching and mentoring side of the triangle, you have more success with staff development. The roles you play here strengthen people's own power to develop, a central theme in strong, caring, learning communities.

The Roles of Building and Supporting Community

Because building and supporting community is at the core of our vision and our beliefs about what is important in early childhood programs, we put these roles at the base of our triangle framework. When staff and families identify them-selves as a strong community working together on behalf of children, there is a solid foundation for a program. This side of the triangle is critical for all our human resources, bringing connections and liveliness to our time together with mean-ingful activities and interactions.

Most early childhood directors operate from this side of the triangle in an intuitive way. Do you see your work of building relationships and offering support and recognition to the chil-dren, families, and staff of your program as part of your "real" work of managing human resources? You probably do nice things like periodically putting treats in the staff room, orga-nizing secret pals for staff birthdays, and hosting occasional potlucks or special events for the families or staff. These should not be seen as extra tasks outside of your regular role as a pro-gram director. Rather, we encourage you to see your community-building work as central to your role, regularly devoting time to be intentional about the efforts needed in this area.

The building and supporting community side of the triangle includes activities such as the following:

- designing an environment that promotes a sense of belonging,
- developing a shared vision with empowering roles for staff and families,
- acknowledging and respecting each individual and the contributions they bring to the group,
- learning the family contexts and cultural frameworks that shape the individual lives in your program,
- helping people make connections and establish bonds with one another,
- creating opportunities for shared experiences that establish traditions and a sense of collective history, and
- linking the people in your program to the wider community around them.

Building and supporting community requires more than good intentions or an annual celebration. Deliberate processes must be developed and negotiation skills harnessed. This side of the triangle requires a commitment to collaboration and a persistence in working with conflict and across different cultural perspectives. Sometimes the efforts are hard and the work goes slowly, but the fruits of your labor have a definite payback and will sustain you through other difficult times.

Consider How Different Directors Respond

Early childhood professionals are such seasoned problem solvers, that we have a tendency to want to jump in and "fix" things immediately. A quick fix may offer a temporary solution to a problem, but it usually doesn't build the deeper foundation necessary for a caring and learning community. If you don't have a framework for moving towards your vision, you often use knee-jerk responses to situations. This results in a hit or miss approach and doesn't create a sustaining organizational culture.

To explore how this might look in action, consider the different approaches to a common early childhood scenario described below. Which director's approach is similar to your instinctive response?

The Scenario

Teresa is a hard-working assistant teacher in your program. She's a cooperative team player on your staff and is extremely gentle and nurturing with the children. When it comes to her family life Teresa is a very private person, but you know that her husband works the graveyard shift and she has three kids to get off to school each morning. She is often late to work, showing up anywhere from ten to thirty minutes late. Teresa's tardiness is a problem for the other teachers and for you in maintaining appropriate adult-child ratios. You've spoken with her about this on several occasions, and she always promises she won't be late again.

Rhonda's Approach

Director Rhonda has just about had it with Teresa. When she again arrives late to work, Rhonda stops her in the hall and tells her, "You've been hired for the morning shift. It is your responsibility to be on time! I could understand if this happened only once, but it's a regular habit with you. I know you have a lot to do at home in the morning, but you have assured me you can be here on time. Our policies are very clear about this. Your lateness jeopardizes the safety of the children and puts other staff members in a very difficult position. I'm putting you on probation. If you are late one more time, you'll be fired."

Teresa meekly continues down the hall to her room. Overhearing this confrontation, two of her co-workers comfort her: "We don't want her to fire you! You're a member of our team and the children would be so sad. We have to get Rhonda to back off. Let's talk during naptime and figure this out."

Donovan's Approach

When director Donovan approaches Teresa about being late again he asks, "Teresa, how can I help you overcome this habit of being late? You're a valuable member of our staff and I don't want to lose you." Teresa, who doesn't usually share much about her personal life, bursts out, "I just wish I had more time in the morning with my children. We always have to rush and I get so stressed out. Today we ended up yelling at each other, which woke up my husband, and then I had to calm him down. We just never have an easy morning and it makes me cranky and late. I just don't know what to." Donovan 's face shows he has empathy for Teresa. "I really want to help. There are some good articles on time management and balancing work and family life in my office. I'm sure you'll find some good tips in them." Later that day he brings the articles to Teresa's room. Teresa smiles politely and accepts the articles, but thinks to herself, "I don't know how reading is going to help me find more time."

Maria's Approach

Director Maria loves Teresa. She values her ways with children and sees the quiet, calm strength Teresa brings to the dynamics of the staff. But Teresa's tardiness has been contributing to large group sizes and unacceptable adult-to-child ratios in the mornings. To address the problem, Maria has been arriving early so she can cover for Teresa if she's late. This makes Maria's day really long, but she knows Teresa has her hands full in the morning and doesn't want to put more pressure on her. She wishes Teresa would figure something out soon because the staff is starting to grumble about it and she's getting a bit resentful herself.

Analyzing the Three Approaches

Rhonda's response to this situation shows her emphasis on the managing and overseeing side of the triangle. She sees her job as creating systems to make sure the standards and regulations are followed, without regard to the impact this approach has on the climate in her workplace. Rhonda certainly has legitimate concerns about Teresa's tardiness. Required adult-to-child ratios have been developed in our profession to keep children safe and to enhance opportunities for individual attention.

Donovan, on the other hand, started on the right track by indicating to Teresa that he would like to help. He is working from the coaching and mentoring side of the triangle. But in the end, he didn't prove to be a very effective listener. From Teresa's perspective the issue is not about time management, but about the stress in her family life and having someone to talk to who really understands. Donovan thinks that he can "fix" Teresa's problem by giving her something to read.

Finally, Maria's efforts to "fix" this problem rely on her own good will and a "finger in the dike" model. She is primarily working from the building and supporting community side of the triangle. She has genuine empathy for the stress in Teresa's family life, but her neglect of the other two sides of the triangle keep her from finding a balance that works for her whole program. Ultimately, Maria's approach backfires, creating a disgruntled climate among the staff and the conditions for her own burnout. Rather than supporting Teresa to take action on behalf of her needs, Maria is trying to mop up behind her.

Each of these approaches to solving the problem of Teresa's tardiness is constrained by the limits of the director's vision. The example demonstrates that any one side of the triangle is inadequate to handle the complexities of the human problems that face directors. Only by thinking through the problem from all three perspectives could a workable solution be reached that furthers the vision of the program as a caring, learning community for all the children and adults involved. Each director has a piece of the puzzle, but is missing the overall framework.

For example, Rhonda has a good handle on management, and is clear about the limits to acceptable behavior in her program. She knows what the standards are and is not afraid to name them. However, because Rhonda limits her focus to "fixing" Teresa's problem, she misses an opportunity to enhance her program. Rhonda might find it useful to think about the problem from the other sides of the triangle. If she was actively growing a vision of a caring, learning community, she could work from the building and supporting community side of the triangle to try to discover a way to support a change in Teresa's behavior. Keeping the coaching and mentoring side in mind, she might find a way to work with Teresa that is less stressful and isolating for both of them. This, in turn, might lead her back to her managing and overseeing roles with the goal of designing more flexible systems for the real lives of her staff members. With such a vision Rhonda would be modeling respect and active listening. If she turned to the staff for their ideas, she would also be creating a climate for collaboration and problem solving.

Donovan's response reveals some understanding of the coaching and mentoring side of the triangle. He knows Teresa needs some help and is trying to think in terms of resources. He would be more effective if he worked with Teresa to identify what kind of help would be meaningful. Together they might consider strategies to meet Teresa's family needs and enable her to be responsible on the job. An effective coach knows that people learn best when they build from their strengths. If Donovan acknowledges the importance of Teresa's family life and explores ways to reduce her stress there, he will be a more useful mentor. A vision of workplaces as caring, learning communities must recognize the needs of a whole person, even as you coach them to let go of behaviors that undermine their work. Donovan could also work from the building community side of the triangle to involve other staff members and perhaps parents in finding a solution to heavy enrollment at the beginning of the day. Like Rhonda, he might also find himself moving to the managing and overseeing side of the triangle to rethink staffing and enrollment systems.

Maria is right in valuing Teresa's contribution to her team. However, she takes an intuitive approach to the building and supporting community side of the triangle, and seeks to avoid conflict by taking the sole responsibility to mediate the consequences of Teresa's tardiness. If Maria were approaching this side of the triangle in an intentional way, she would use this as an opportunity to work with the staff to support Teresa through this stressful situation. Maria's approach, too, would be strengthened by attention to both the other sides of the triangle. Working from the managing and overseeing side would help her to set clear limits for staff members, including Teresa and herself. Taking up the slack for Teresa without a plan to improve the situation is not a sound management technique, because of the stress it places on Maria and the other staff members. Her coaching and mentoring skills could also help her work with Teresa to build from the strengths Maria sees so clearly and address the stress in her family life.

Using the Triangle Framework

With the myriad tasks and decisions early childhood directors face each day, it is useful to have a framework for choosing your responses and the role to play in each situation. The triangle framework offers you a balanced approach to analyze and respond to the daily demands of your work. The intent of this framework is not to lead you to the "right way" or a "right answer." Rarely are the choices simple or clear-cut. Any number of responses may help "fix" a problem, but using the triangle as a framework can help you clarify your priorities and spot how a response might undermine or help grow your vision.

In formulating an approach to something like Teresa's tardiness, it is helpful to analyze the issues from each side of the triangle. Here are some questions and considerations you might pose for yourself, using the particulars of your program and the staff and families involved as the context for your thinking. Once you've clarified the issues as they relate to each set of roles you have, you can determine the responses that will best serve your vision.

Building and Supporting Community

- What impact does Teresa's tardiness have on the staff, children and families, and all of the working relationships?
- Are there contributions that Teresa brings to the community that offset the problem with her tardiness?

If Teresa's tardiness creates problems with ratios and tasks to be accomplished, her co-workers are likely to become disgruntled and children will show signs of stress. The issue then goes beyond an employee's tardiness and job performance. Are there any signs that families are beginning to question Teresa's reliability and viability as a caregiver? If not, working on this issue in the context of staff problem solving seems a more suitable approach.

If Teresa is a valued and well-liked caregiver, the parents and her co-workers would be upset if she were dismissed rather than given some alternative options. Because Teresa is an employee who brings many positive, tangible qualities to her work, her director might prefer to work with her rather than find a punctual employee who offers less to the children and her program. These issues must be weighed against a hard and fast rule about dismissing anyone who is tardy to work.

Coaching and Mentoring

- What are Teresa's views and values about balancing work and family time?
- Does she understand the impact her tardiness has on the program?
- Have we helped her understand this issue as it relates to her own needs, values, and learning style?
- What skills, knowledge, and resources might be helpful to Teresa in balancing her work and family life?

Many times early childhood program regulations are unconsciously designed around one cultural framework. If Teresa's lifestyle, values, and cultural framework are different from that of the overall program culture, it is important to examine cultural assumptions and consider other possibilities for regulations that allow for real differences and more inclusiveness.

Asking Teresa to share her perspectives, what she values and thinks is important, is a good starting point for problem solving on this issue. Exploring the goals she has for herself, and how she goes about learning new things will help her identify what needs to be addressed, what can be compromised, and what can't. This approach gives the priority to Teresa's learning rather than immediate compliance. On some occasions a director can make this choice.

- Do the regulations and standards for quality on this issue support our program's vision?
- Does Teresa's tardiness negatively impact the quality and safety of the program for children?
- Are the expectations, policies, and job descriptions related to tardiness clearly formulated for the program as a whole and with Teresa in particular?
- Is there any flexibility built into our system of staff scheduling to respond to people's real lives?
- What resources are available to help address this problem?

If a vision of a learning community guides your thinking, your management systems and responses from this side of the triangle will keep the whole picture, not just a particular rule in mind. If you choose to take disciplinary action toward Teresa or move quickly to fire her, the impact on both Teresa and the overall program climate could be quite negative.

There are some personnel issues that require immediate corrective action in order to keep children safe and parents confident in your program. This should be a thoughtful and timely decision as opposed to a knee-jerk reaction. In Teresa's case, you can examine the ratios, staff scheduling, overall morale, and communications to determine your priorities for action. Reexamine your orientation procedures for new staff members, as well as your written and oral communication systems to make sure expectations have been clear, rather than left to general assumptions.

If you consider Teresa's contributions, her stage of development, and cultural framework you may conclude she is a bigger asset than liability to your program. There may be possibilities for reassigning your human resources, schedules, or training dollars. All of these are considerations of the managing and overseeing side of the triangle.

Looking at issues from each side of the triangle may initially seem daunting for day-to-day situations. You will find that as you practice using the triangle framework, analyzing the issues from each side becomes second nature to your decision making. This kind of intentionality will strengthen your competency as a director and make it easier to grow your vision.

Practice Using the Triangle Framework

Before going on to a more in-depth consideration of each side of triangle, practice analyzing the issues in each of the following scenarios, using the chart provided. Try formulating questions and answering questions related to each side as demonstrated in the previous example. This will help you overcome the urge to respond with a "quick fix" for the situation. Once you've identified the possible issues related to each side of the triangle, then consider responses and strategies. Pay attention to how each of your strategies may undermine or enhance the vision of a caring and learning community.

Scenario 1: New Director Dilemma

Mary Beth and Katrina have worked together in the two year olds' room for the past eight years and they run a tight ship. Everything looks neat and tidy in the room and the children are always kept busy with activities. Still, you can see some need for improvement. Charts, pictures, and toys in the room look like they have been there forever. The curriculum is organized around art projects and seasonal themes, and though the children will do these activities, they seem meaningless and not very engaging.

Recently hired as the new director, you have gotten a cool reception from Mary Beth and Katrina. They tend to ignore you and go about their business when you enter the room. You have tried making a few friendly suggestions, but can't tell how they are being received. Another teacher, Doreen, has let you know that Mary Beth and Katrina have been complaining about you and are trying to get other teachers to do as they are and not respond much to your suggestions. Doreen herself has only worked in the program for three months. She is enthusiastic when you are in her room, and she seems eager for your suggestions on how she can improve.

Use the chart at the top of the next page to answer these questions:

1. What issues are raised from each side of the triangle by this situation?
2. What strategies from each side might you use to address the issues?

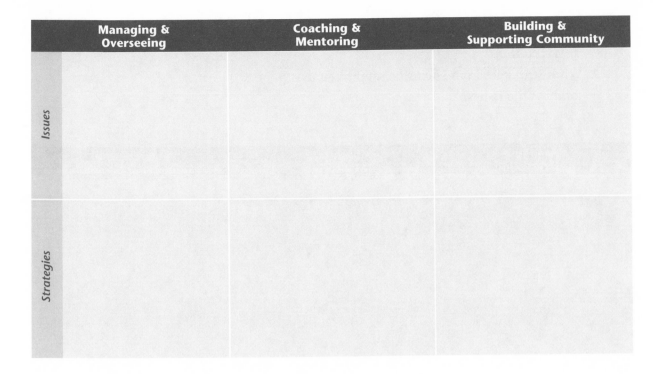

	Managing & Overseeing	Coaching & Mentoring	Building & Supporting Community
Issues			
Strategies			

Scenario 2: Messing with Michael

Michael works as the lead teacher in the four- and five-year-old classroom. He has a strong philosophy guiding his teaching style and approaches. One of the beliefs he often mentions is the importance of giving children meaningful responsibilities and decision-making in their day-to-day lives. Each of the children have their own large cubby located in the school entryway. This is the main walkway used by parents dropping off and picking up their children. Michael leaves the care and ownership of these cubbies and what is put in them entirely up to the children.

You often notice that the cubbies are in a complete shambles, with papers, toys, clothes, and various other items overflowing into the hallway. Michael's classroom is often in disarray as well. You've discussed this issue with Michael once before, suggesting that he spend more energy keeping these areas clean. You dropped the subject when he very strongly objected, stating this was an important learning experience for the children. Michael has resisted other suggestions from you, citing his teaching philosophy as the reason. Today the cubby area is a real mess. You notice the smell of rotten food and have to step over items as you go through the walkway.

Use the chart on the next page to answer these questions:

1. What issues are raised from each side of the triangle by this situation?
2. What strategies from each side might you use to address the issues?

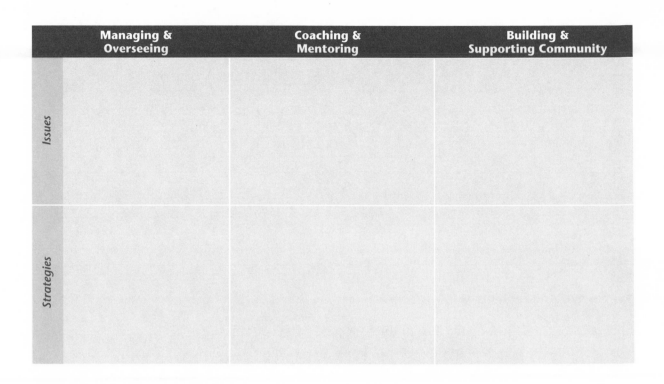

	Managing & Overseeing	Coaching & Mentoring	Building & Supporting Community
Issues			
Strategies			

Practice Assessing Yourself

Reflect on the analysis you did in the above situations. What side of the triangle felt more familiar to you or was easier to generate responses for? Which side seems more difficult for you to work with?

After this exercise, consider any goals you want to set for yourself to cultivate a more balanced approach to directing from each side of triangle. The following chapters are designed to help you explore how to better use each of the three components of our triangle framework. The ideas and strategies offered may help you move closer to your goals.

Resources for Learning to Work with a Framework

These titles combine several perspectives on working with a framework. In its own way, each enhances concepts of leadership that are useful for early childhood program directors.

Bateson, Mary Catherine. *Composing a Life*. New York: Penguin, 1990.

Berry, T. H. *Managing the Total Quality Transformation*. New York: McGraw-Hill, 1991.

Bolman, L., and T. Deal. *Reframing Organizations*. San Francisco: Jossey-Bass, 1991.

Center for the Child Care Workforce. *Creating Better Child Care Jobs: Model Work Standards for Teaching Staff in Center-Based Child Care*. Washington, DC: Center for the Child Care Workforce, 1998.

Peters, Tom. *Circle of Innovation: You Can't Shrink Your Way to Greatness*. New York: Knopf, 1997.

Chapter 3

Your Role in Building and Supporting Community

Imagine these scenes:

Kianna and her dad, Jackson, have planned to arrive early at the center today so they can have breakfast together. As they walk in the front door, an inviting smell of apple muffins greets them. "Ummm," Jackson hums softly to Kianna as he carries her to the booster seat at the table where a few other families and staff have already gathered. "It sure smells like we're having something good for breakfast today."

It's mid-afternoon and director Sandria has some errands to run for the center. On her way to the bank and post office, she stops by to pick up the two preschool children whose turn it is to go with her today. Abby and Rochelle are eagerly waiting at the door. On the way to the car they chatter excitedly. "Do we get to help put stamps on the letters? Can we put them in the mailbox?"

After a tense day at work, Maia is delighted to find that the children and staff have lemonade and snacks waiting for families at pickup time. As she enters the gate, Maia's school-age daughter, Audrie, proudly greets her. "Hi, Mom. Come on and sit under the umbrella and I'll bring you some snacks we made." Maia sits on the lawn chair right next to where her baby, Ronnie, is sleeping in a baby seat. Maia relaxes and smiles as she joins the other parents enjoying this special treatment.

On a sunny Saturday morning Alexis, a staff member, and Darcy, a center parent, are weeding together in the child care's pea patch garden. As they work, they can easily watch their children playing *nearby. Developed by staff and families who don't have their own space or who wanted to work with others, this is an impressive garden of vegetables and flowers. A small section is designated as the children's garden, while the rest is tended by adults who are center staff and families.*

As you read over these scenes, what's your first response? Are there elements described that sound similar to things in your program? Did you think to yourself, "That sounds so wonderful, I want to try that!" Perhaps you found yourself immediately reviewing all the reasons why this couldn't be done in your program.

It's true, few early childhood programs have typical scenes like these. Most attempts to define professional standards and practices have all but eliminated the home or neighborhood feel to our programs. Instead, the atmosphere in early childhood programs feels more institutionalized, either cluttered and dreary, or brightly colored rooms where play is orderly and controlled, and lessons are taught. Your reaction to the scenes described above probably reveals the vision or mind-set you bring to your work. When you think of a desirable early childhood program, is it an institutional model like school or does it include elements of childhood, family gatherings, and life in a neighborhood?

The scenarios above are glimpses of real programs whose directors and supervisors are breaking away from the institutional model that has become the norm in the early childhood profession. These snapshots reflect programs that are not only designed for children, but are also places for families and provide an experience of community. The emphasis in these programs is on strengthening the bonds between children and their families and creating positive connections with other children and adults. The directors at the helm here realize that when adults and children are removed from each other's daily life and work, neither develop or live as fully as they could. The approach these directors take reflects their understanding that children today are spending the majority of their childhoods away from their homes and neighborhoods. They are trying to respond to the lack of support families with young children receive in the larger popular culture of our country. These directors have a vision that goes beyond how things are. They want children in their programs to experience growing up in families with an extended kinship network, a revived sense of neighborhood and community.

Bringing a vision like this to life requires a shift in how you think about your program, the role you play as a director, and the way you spend the bulk of your time. This vision suggests that you consider all who cross paths in your program as a part of your community. When you are planning and carrying out various aspects of your job, all of these players are included in your thinking. You are consciously helping each individual feel included and recognized. Your program culture intentionally shapes shared experiences that cultivate a sense of belonging and evolving history together.

If you use the triangle as a framework for thinking about your directing job, the tasks of building and supporting community form the base of your work. This requires more than an incidental or "get to it when I can" approach. You need strategies specifically designed to nurture the experience of community in your program. And you need methods to cultivate the skills required for collaboration, working with conflict, and across differences such as culture, family structure, and communication styles.

You can think about doing this community-building work in ways that parallel how we think about planning for children. We give attention to organizing and maintaining the physical space (indoor and outdoor learning environment); we plan for engaging activities and skill development (curriculum); and continually foster connections and the building of relationships (social, emotional, and identity development). What follows is a discussion of each of these areas with examples of strategies to help you carry out your role of building and supporting community.

Creating an Environment that Nurtures Community

We live in a highly mobile culture where most people live far from their place of birth and extended family. We conduct our daily lives in cars, at jobs, or schools away from home or a neighborhood. The environments of our schools and workplaces often contribute to a sense of isolation, if not alienation. They seldom offer any meaningful context for us to be fully human, to learn from, or contribute to each other's lives. We usually feel more stressed than nurtured when we leave.

Early childhood programs can either contribute to or counter the effects of living in a culture that gives only lip service to family life and community. As you walk in the door, the organization and aesthetics of the environment communicate a program's culture. Is this a place where there are rules posted on the walls, along with commercial alphabet charts, calendars, and curriculum materials? Or are there things children have created on the walls and around the room, along with other materials inviting curiosity and investigation? Are there bulletin boards and cubbies crammed with papers you want to avoid, or do you see pictures and words that pique your interest? Do you find yourself ignored and uncomfortable, or welcomed with a comfy place to sit and people eager to greet you? If you spent your childhood or adult days in this place, would it leave you cranky or satisfied, dreading or eager to come back?

The typical early childhood program is situated in a less than ideal space with more limitations than we know what to do with. In an inspiring article entitled "Out of the Basement: Discovering the Value of Child Care Facilities," Carl Sussman describes our situation this way: "Years of budget balancing and widespread acceptance of inadequate facilities has desensitized providers to their environment and created chronically low expectations" (1998). This problem is compounded as programs become furnished with little attention to aesthetics or imagination. Across the country most early childhood programs have begun to look alike. Usually there are child-sized tables and chairs, primary colors, an abundance of plastic materials, commercial toys, and bulletin board displays. You have to search to find soft or natural elements, places where adults, as well as children, can feel cozy, alone or with a friend. The smell of disinfectant often floats in the air. Have we forgotten how a cluttered or tattered environment quickly seeps into our psyche? Do we know how a sterile and antiseptic climate shapes our soul?

Caregivers, teachers, and children are spending the bulk of their waking hours, living their lives together in our programs. The way you organize the space, create traffic and communication patterns, furnish and decorate, all affect the experience people have in your building. To guide your thinking about a physical environment that connects and nurtures people, consider the elements of a comfortable home and a vibrant neighborhood.

Principle

Make the Center Feel Like a Home

In the early years of professionalizing child care services, a homelike atmosphere was often the emphasis. As we've grown to incorporate concepts of giving children a head start or school readiness, even family day care homes have been encouraged to look more like preschools. It is our belief that reversing this trend will provide a stronger foundation for children. Getting children ready for school is best done in the context of their full lives and developmental needs. The elements of a good home and community environment create the best conditions for their learning and thriving.

Strategy

Incorporate elements from home design magazines

You can create an inviting atmosphere in your program by thinking about what you are most drawn to in magazines that feature pictures of home designs. You could adapt ideas like the following:

- *Make spaces for the children and adults that include colors more interesting than just the standard primary ones.*
- *Add a variety of textures and natural elements throughout the environment—plants, rocks, shells, baskets, fabric, sculptures, and other art objects to look at and touch.*
- *Create cozy lighting by using dimmer switches, floor and table lamps, mirrors, and other materials that catch, reflect, and disperse light, and create interesting shadows to explore.*
- *Frame and display children's art attractively on walls, along with work from well-known artists.*
- *Find inviting ways to include photographs of families, children, and staff on tables, shelves, and walls. Change these in a timely manner.*
- *Engage everyone's senses with inviting aromas at the beginning and end of the day—dough baking, cinnamon- and clove-spiced cider simmering, peppermint leaves in the sensory table, extracts in the playdough.*

Strategy

Explore professional architecture and design resources

There are professional resources you can turn to as well. Adding to the earlier European influence of Maria Montessori and Rudolf Steiner, in the 1970s Elizabeth Jones and Elizabeth Prescott began writing for early childhood educators in this country about "environments as regulators of our experience." By the 1980s and 1990s, Jim Greenman, Gary Moore, Anita Rui Olds, and the educators of Reggio Emilia were adding to this body of literature, bringing us further insights from artists, poets, architects, researchers, and landscapers. If you're not familiar with this work, full citations can be found at the end of this chapter. It is resources like these, rather than commercial catalogs, that should be shaping our thinking about the design of physical space, and materials we purchase. They remind us of the elements that support human interactions, invite curiosity, and sustain attention for problem solving and learning.

Jim Greenman's voice has been one of the consistent calls for creating spaces in child care centers that work as well for the adults as they do for the children. In our minds, no director should be without his book *Caring Spaces, Learning Places* as a resource to return to again and again. With an understanding of the link between quality experiences for staff and quality care for children, Greenman offers practical strategies as well as inspiration to draw on. Keeping this concept as a focus, take a minute now to review your program's environment, in your mind, or on your feet, with pen and paper in hand.

- *Is there adult-sized, comfortable furniture tucked in spaces here and there where a staff or family member can spend a cozy moment with a child, or a child can curl up alone and be reminded of those cozy moments with an adult?*
- *Are there floor seats with back support so that adults can spend extended time at the children's eye level?*
- *Do you have a room away from the children with a couch and adult-sized tables and chairs for relaxing, working, eating, and meeting?*
- *Are families and staff members encouraged to add artifacts, photos, and things they treasure to the classroom, the staff lounge, and other gathering spaces so that the*

*children, parents, and co-workers see them as people with
real lives, skills, and interests to share?*

Principle

Give the Program the Feel of a
Real Neighborhood

Most early childhood programs in the Unitied States are organized into isolated classrooms where the same group of children, usually of the same age, spends the entire day playing,
eating, and sleeping together. The doors stay closed to keep
children in, and others out. Often there are no windows to look
out and time outdoors is limited. Most other spaces in the
center, like the kitchen or office, are off-limits to children. They
rarely spend time with others of different ages, including their
siblings, older or younger children, or adults in the program.
Parents usually leave children at the classroom door, and there
is limited time or encouragement to stay a while to play with
children or talk with other adults. Is this your view of a real
neighborhood? If you have managed to free your program
from some of these dehumanizing constraints, take heart. You
are already on the road to change. You have recognized that
the isolation and disconnection that has come with urbaniza-
tion, fast food, commuting, and technology shouldn't be repli-
cated in our programs. Instead we should be organizing time
and space to build and enhance our connections with each
other. We have included some models to consider. Perhaps
there are elements you can adapt further, even if your space is
rather limited.

Strategy

*Use homebase rooms and make time for
children to roam*

Jim Greenman promotes the idea of "homebases" rather than
classrooms for child care programs. Children have a homebase
and primary caregiver or teacher, but doors are often open and
hallways are designed like blocks in a neighborhood to be
roamed and explored from time to time. Some of the centers
Greenman has been involved in designing have the equivalent
of indoor parks with play equipment, benches, large potted

trees, and space for children and adults from around the center to come together to talk and play. Children often visit the kitchen, which is designed to accommodate their observations and conversations with the cook.

Strategy

Set up larger programs as villages

Architect Gary Moore has written in *Child Care Information Exchange* about designing early childhood programs with a neighborhood concept (1997). He proposes interconnected "houses" or "dwelling areas" designed for smaller groups of children all surrounding a common core of shared facilities. This design offers opportunities for interactions with other people and spaces in the building throughout the day. Moore reports that large child care programs built as villages or campuses offset the difficulties of maintaining a homelike sense of scale. When a center is conceived as a series of inter-connected homes, staff are able to individualize their systems and schedules in smaller groups rather than following one large institutional model.

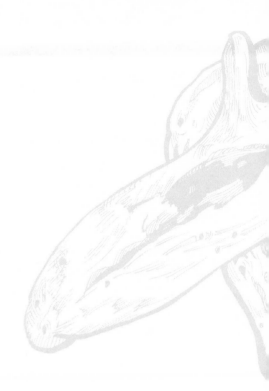

Strategy

Design space to resemble a neighborhood

In the January 1998 issue of *Young Children*, Carl Sussman describes a Head Start program's transformation of an old school building. They worked with an architect to create corridors that look like play streets, with classroom doors and windows designed like those of houses opening out onto them. The corridor widens in front of the kitchen with storefront fixtures, dubbed the Head Start Cafe, where children can visit the cooks. The center has a parents' room and staff room, each with their own special ambiance and supply of resources.

Our U.S. Military Child Development Center was fortunate to have an outstanding German kindergarten nearby. I invited their director to do a presentation at our center. She described how they had changed over the years to address some of the very child behavior problems we were experiencing. This motivated our teachers to visit the German kindergarten, and one of our staff became particularly excited to adopt their philosophy. I worked to support her idea of using an outer hallway as a block and book area and allowing children to expand their play outside of the regular classroom space. This experiment was very successful, and her self-esteem and maturity grew by leaps and bounds. She no longer thought in terms of time out and strict control of the children's behavior. She began to trust children and value their choices. Before the end of the year she announced she had decided to go to college to get a degree in early childhood development.

—Cathy

Strategy

Use natural shapes and soft lighting

Anita Rui Olds, a developmental and environmental psychologist, has also pioneered the innovative design of environmental facilities for children. In her workshops and consulting with both architectural and child care businesses, Olds stresses the importance of creating spaces where people can heal, work, play, and grow. Her innovations include softening rooms by creating more organic shapes and lighting to be responsive to our sensory needs, and moving human bodies to fulfill our need to gather, be comforted, rest, and explore. Olds reminds us that innovations do not have to be expensive or splashy. By using elements of the natural world, adding things such as mirrors, ramps, and lofts to create different levels and perspectives on space, a building can be transformed in both its ambiance and function.

Strategy

Use the beginning and end of the day

The self-initiated efforts of smaller programs with fewer resources can inspire us as well. The opening scenes described in this chapter highlight a few. Remember Kianna and her dad eating breakfast together? Her center has created a family-style kitchen and dining area with a designated morning time for families and staff to eat together. They also offer parents the opportunity to come for lunch or have a snack with their children. Wonderful aromas are an added benefit to this idea. Those who come to eat pay an extra fee to cover costs, but for busy working parents it's worth it. This is an opportunity to slow down and spend some quality time with their children and center "neighbors." When you revisit our opening stories you'll find that Audrie's school-age program created a similar feeling with their end-of-the-day lemonade picnic.

The seeds for a sense of community are often found in the early and latter part of a day when children are combined into one group as numbers dwindle. We know of a program that shifted this idea to include "open door time" for the first and last two hours the center is open. During these hours the reduced staffing pattern is spread between several classrooms and the hallway so that children can move throughout the small building. This "roam the neighborhood" model allows children, families, and staff interact across age groups and become more familiar with what is happening in other rooms.

Principle

Involve Parents and Staff in Considering the Space

As you consider the physical space available in your program, try thinking in terms of creating community, not just maintaining ratios. Perhaps you don't have the luxury of removing all the barriers to creating your ideal building, but you can knock down the walls in your mind and begin to think differently about how time and space are used in your program. Here are some strategies to try in staff or parent meetings.

Strategy

Assess how a space makes you feel

To broaden your ideas about early childhood environments and begin thinking about a model other than school, gather a group of magazine or calendar pictures that include a range of environments such as bank lobbies and high-tech office buildings, seascapes, forests, mountain ranges, health spas, cozy fireplace gatherings, temples, churches, sacred rock structures, Disneyland sites, and toy stores, early childhood classrooms, playgrounds, and school catalog scenes. As these pictures get

passed around, post the following questions for discussion in small groups:

- *How do each of these environments make you feel?*
- *What elements in this environment are influencing your feelings?*
- *How might you behave in this place?*
- *If you spent lots of time in this environment, how might it impact you?*

Come together after this initial discussion and make a list of the elements that were identified. Place them in two columns, one labeled with a plus for positive elements, the other with a minus for negative elements. Most groups who do this end up with a list of positive elements that bear little resemblance to a school. Here are some examples of positive elements other groups have identified, using this process:

- *Organization—a sense of order that makes it easy to get work done.*
- *Aesthetics—beauty, an invitation for curiosity and discovery.*
- *Softness—cozy places for the eyes and body to rest.*
- *Lighting and color—natural light and soft lamps in a range of shades, tones, and intriguing shadows.*
- *Things from the natural world—different textures, water, sand, rocks, plants.*
- *Flexibility—allowing for intimacy or expansiveness.*
- *Belonging—reflecting the lives of people there.*

Whatever elements you list, the next step is to use them as an assessment tool. Invite the participants to move around your building with them in mind. When you regroup consider the following questions. What examples of these elements did you find? Did you come across anything from our negative list? What changes should we think about making?

This strategy provides a concrete way for staff and parents to see ways you can begin to transform your program. As you begin to create an environment that is less school-like and more cozy and beautiful, the children, staff, and families feel immediate benefits. They want to linger, investigate, and enjoy each other's company and the work at hand.

Most programs wait until they have money before they work on clarifying their vision. I've learned how important it is to write down our vision and continually refine our goals and action plans. I don't want to settle for small results. We are going for more than what seems possible at any given moment. For instance, we have developed extensive environmental plans for each site. We have done this partly by having bi-weekly planning meetings with our site directors, coordinators, and an architect. When our state announced that it was accepting proposals for quality enhancement dollars we didn't have to scramble to write a proposal that probably wouldn't reflect our real needs. We already had a thoughtful, well-researched plan to submit.

—Karen

Strategy

Explore the environment as a child might

During a staff, parent, or board meeting use this activity to explore your environment with a focus on childhood, neighborhood, and community. It will alert you to what your environment now offers, as well as provide a way for the adults who participate to play together as a community. Have people work in pairs or small groups. Give them the assignment to go on a scavenger hunt and bring back an example, representation, or story of each item on the following lists:

Find contrasting elements:
- *something heavy/light,*
- *something smooth/rough,*
- *something dark/bright,*
- *something natural/manufactured,*
- *something huge/tiny,*
- *something scary/comforting.*

Find four kinds of:
- *holes,*
- *sounds,*
- *things that move,*
- *smells,*

- *places that challenge your body,*
- *symbols or writing,*
- *dangers.*

Find places for pretending:
- *you are powerful,*
- *you are small as an insect,*
- *you are at home,*
- *you are on TV,*
- *you are a detective,*
- *you are an artist,*
- *you are a scientist.*

Find in the natural world:
- *a new texture to explore,*
- *an intriguing shadow,*
- *something the wind does,*
- *animal tracks,*
- *something alive,*
- *something dead.*

Strategy

Create "A place where I belong"

You can also do a scavenger hunt to consider how your environment currently fosters or defeats a sense of belonging. Send small groups around the building to find something that represents each of the following:

- *something that reflects what you like or are interested in,*
- *something that tells who spends time in this place and what they do here,*
- *something that sparks a favorite childhood memory,*
- *something you don't understand,*
- *something that makes you feel respected,*
- *something that insults your intelligence,*
- *something you would take to a deserted island, and*
- *something that has at least three uses other than the obvious.*

The ideas, representations, and objects that get brought to the group discussion from both of these scavenger hunts will help you get to know each other better and provide a new look at your work and learning environments. End each activity by brainstorming a list of changes you'd like to bring about in your work environment.

At one point we were starting to see a discrepancy in the quality of the environments in our classrooms. Rather than just pass this off to differences, we developed Saturday work parties where each room took turns getting ideas and help from the rest of the staff. The teachers in a room would explain what was working well and where they needed help. Other staff members would then choose different tasks to pitch in and help. Some cleaned, painted, sewed, or built things, while others shopped for needed items or brought lunch for everyone. This plan not only improved the look of our rooms but also our morale and sense of teamwork.

—Wendy

Strategy

Create the skeleton of a grant proposal or the inspiration for a work party

Use a brainstorming process to ignite dreams that you can use as the basis for creating change in your environment through a work party or a grant proposal. Have handy some catalogs from garden and plant nurseries, architecture and home design firms, and art and display suppliers to serve as resources in envisioning equipment that might be used in a home or neighborhood. Building on the elements described in the previous strategies or other discussions, ask key questions like the following to get creative juices flowing:

- *If we were to knock out two walls, which should they be?*
- *If someone were to donate six large plants and three love seats or park benches, where would we put them?*
- *Where could we add some special lighting effects with dimmer switches, lamps, ceiling spots, or wall sconces, in order to create some new feeling in our building?*
- *What are five things from the natural world that would enhance our program?*
- *Where would you put three new windows and four new mirrors?*

- *If we were to build a loft, a cave, and a corner cafe, where would we put them?*
- *What's something from your home or community you'd like to see included in our program?*

If people are stuck in "yes, but" thinking, you may need to coax them along in generating a wish list. These questions are intended to help people think the unthinkable, to break out of the confines of the way they think about what's possible. It's important that all ideas in an initial brainstorm be considered of value so that the people involved don't censor their ideas before even raising them. You can create this feeling by including each one on your list. Then, conclude by doing some prioritizing and sequencing of the ideas on the list, as a group. Finally, take this list, get some cost estimates, and develop a grant proposal or plan for a work party to begin making some of these dreams come true.

People easily let their thinking get confined by the limitations of the space they are in. With each of the programs I have directed I started by reconfiguring the physical space to create a sense of possibility that we could be something different. It's a way of raising the issue of working with a vision. I look for how to create a more open feeling, how to create special feelings with lighting and interesting visual elements. There are all these walls around how people think in this work. My motto is, "If it's not load bearing, tear it down." When the physical walls come down, it opens up the imagination, as well as communications.

—Jan

Planning Your Community-Building Curriculum

As an administrator, take a minute to consider the various activities you plan and oversee in your program. You'll probably list things like staff meetings where you review schedules, discuss policies, curriculum, and current problems. No doubt you plan parent meetings that you coax families to attend. If you lead a nonprofit program there are board meeting agendas to prepare and probably fund-raising events. With the exception of the latter, directors typically plan activities that reinforce a traditional school model, focusing on the tasks to be accomplished, rather than the relationships to be built. There are occasional events for socializing, but these are usually seen as something outside the "real" work of managing a program.

Principle

Use Time Together to Strengthen Relationships

When you view your program as merely caring for children while their parents work, social events are seen as "extra-curricular activities." However, if a primary emphasis of your work is building community, your focus will be on strengthening the relationships among staff members and between children, their families, and the staff. Consider the policies you develop and activities you plan as a form of curriculum that strengthens the social/emotional development of the adults as well as the children. Sometimes this requires special events, but mostly it's a matter of rethinking the ordinary events of the day. Here are some examples to adapt as strategies for your own program.

We are fortunate to have staff meetings every week in our program, short as they are. For a while we didn't realize how our time in these meetings could be better used for staff and community development. After we surveyed the teachers we came up with a much more meaningful use of our time. Now only the first week of the month is devoted to center business. The second and third meetings are staff choices where people do a variety of things, from requesting workshops to working on improving some aspect of our mission within their team. The last week of the month our staff comes together to work on creating documentation displays. We help each other with the writing and visual layout and simultaneously feel more connected to what's happening in our different rooms.

—Wendy

Strategy

View staff meetings as circle time

Typical staff meetings in early childhood programs involve the director coming with a list of tasks, policies, and important dates to remember that she goes over with the staff. Rather than using the precious time you carve out for meetings on managing and overseeing tasks that can be handled in a memo, you can use this time for the important work of building community.

It may help if you think about your staff meetings the way a good teacher thinks about circle time with children. We know that a good circle time with children builds a sense of belonging and a shared early childhood culture. Why not see our staff meetings as having the same goal? Good teachers also plan activities throughout the day that create a sense of respect and community. They invite individual children to talk about themselves and make choices, and encourage groups of children to share their ideas and work together on projects. Rather than filling staff meeting time with announcements, scheduling details, and the authoritative voice of the director, can't we use them for genuine sharing, reflection, and collaboration? This might involve changing the idea of who's in charge, finding other means to take care of business, or creating an atmosphere that is physically comfortable, emotionally safe, and full of active listening.

Circle time is most effective when there is a welcoming leader, some thoughtful planning, and an opportunity for everyone to be acknowledged. Music and playful moments counterbalance serious stories. If our staff meetings have a different cultural feel to them than this, we might need to orient the group to a new set of routines and guidelines, just as we do with a new classroom grouping each year.

Strategy

Learn about listening

To build a community and work with the differences that will exist in any group, good listening habits need to be developed. Introduce the following framework and activities to promote listening between staff, parents, and the children. Begin by introducing the concept of three different kinds of listening:

- *Autobiographical Listening—You hear things that relate only to your own experience or perspective.*
- *Merry-Go-Round Listening—You are waiting or biding your time until it's your turn to speak.*

- *Deep Listening—You are genuinely trying to understand and learn something new.*

Whether in a one-to-one exchange or during staff meetings, the practice of deep listening goes a long way toward enhancing the self-esteem of both the speaker and the listener. Develop this skill by devoting a few minutes of each meeting time to any of the following:

- *Role-play the different kinds of listening and discuss how each feels.*
- *Share a story in pairs, and examine kinds of listening that occur.*
- *Point out the kinds of listening at work during a group discussion.*

Strategy

Set ground rules, share feelings, and develop facilitation skills

As a group, develop some agreed upon ground rules for behaviors, communications, and decision making. Take time to draw in all the ideas and voices about this. Post these agreements and review them regularly in the early months of this effort.

Devote some training to group facilitation skills so that responsibility for staff meetings can be rotated, allowing for individual style differences in facilitation. Post future meeting agendas with space to add ideas for discussions and who will plan for them. Include some specific activities for getting to know each other and for building a group culture at every meeting.

In our team meetings I have three goals for staff development. I want to create a climate where people become confident and excited about learning. I want to help them become more reflective in their work, to set goals, and be able to explain why. Finally, I want them to share their thinking and hear other perspectives. In addition to our own viewpoints, we have begun to make sure we think in terms of three perspectives at each of our meetings: the child's, the teacher's, and the parent's. Sometimes the administrative perspective is needed as well.

—Karen

Strategy

Use a fuss box

It's also important to take time to acknowledge our disappointments, things that upset us or make us sad. Periodically try using what Jean Illsley Clarke calls a "fuss box."

Put a cardboard box, large enough to step into, in front of the group. Establish a few ground rules and then invite anyone to step into the box for a bit of fussing. Ground rules should include points such as a willingness to physically dramatize one's feelings as "fussing," using "I" messages rather than blaming language, and a commitment to confidentiality and creative problem solving once the fussing is over.

Strategy

Make tear-water tea

Owl at Home, a children's book by Arnold Lobel, includes a short story entitled "Tear-Water Tea" that provides another strategy for dealing with disappointments. Owl periodically takes a kettle out of the cupboard and sits with it, thinking of things that are making him sad. As he calls them out, for instance, "Books that cannot be read because some of the pages have been torn out" and "Spoons that have fallen behind the stove and are never seen again," large tears begin dropping into the tea kettle until it is full. He boils it for tea and happily begins drinking saying, "It tastes a little bit salty, but tear-water tea is always very good." You can read or tell the story, then pass around a tea kettle, asking people to acknowledge with an equally dramatic flare things that are upsetting them. Use the ritual of symbolically boiling our disappointments to turn them into something good.

Strategy

Become storytellers

To build a group culture and sense of community, we need to know who we are and why we are here, and to begin to discover who we can be together. Devoting at least fifteen minutes of every staff meeting to self-discovery will lay the foundation for this building process. Share childhood memories on various topics. Ask staff members to "tell a funny story

about your family," "tell the story of how you got your name," or "talk about a time you were naughty." You also might use questions like these: Did you have a favorite toy, book, or song? How did your family treat a common cold? What celebrations were important to you?

A great resource for specific strategies on drawing out people's stories and using them for community building is *Telling Your Stories* by Donald Davis. Personal stories help us get a fuller picture of each other. Bringing in actual photos or objects form our childhoods makes it all the more vivid. As we hear more about each other's lives, we discover how we are alike and different. We weave threads that ties us together in collective memories.

These stories may not always be pleasant and that should be acknowledged as well. Suggest to staff that they choose a memory that will enhance their learning and not stir up emotional blocks. Remind them to keep their ears and hearts open to their colleagues, while being sensitive to confidentiality when it is needed. Shared stories and pictures are a vital part of any culture or community.

Strategy

Create visual stories of your life together

In our book, *Spreading the News: Sharing the Stories of Early Childhood Programs,* we offer detailed instructions with examples of how to observe children and create a visual story display that reveals your understandings. This process is a powerful tool for staff development and learning to communicate effectively with parents.

You can also put these stories into book form. Photographs of curriculum projects along with annotated descriptions from teachers can become handmade books which, when added to the reading corner, provide hours of continued revisiting and storytelling. Likewise, you can capture stories of the evolving development and thinking of individual children with handmade picture storybooks, and provide families with the impetus to create these at home for a wonderful back-and-forth storytelling exchange.

Amidst intense feelings about how we were going to handle holidays in our program, I introduced an idea I came across at an

NAEYC anti-bias session. Each family and staff member at the center was given a piece of mat board to create a small display about how they celebrated the winter holidays. As we began to hang these in our vestibule, this became a new gathering place where parents lingered and learned more about each other and our staff. It was definitely a community-building experience that became an annual practice.

—Julie

Strategy

Refocus parent newsletters

Many programs produce monthly newsletters for parents. Typically these require teachers to write a column with news of their curriculum and classroom events. For a teacher this can be about as meaningful as doing a ditto, and parents respond with about as much enthusiasm as to a coloring book page. We are all inundated with far too much to read. Unless it's real and meaningful for our lives, why go through the motions? Let's not waste this opportunity to have the teachers put forward their identities—who they really are and what matters to them.

Try having the staff write about such things as the following:

- *a favorite childhood memory that relates to their current work with children,*
- *a person they look to for inspiration or leadership,*
- *a book or author who has influenced how they see and work with children, or*
- *something metaphoric like a fable, poem, or song to describe how they experience their time with the children or respond to a particular event.*

Principle

Grow Community-Building Curriculum from the Lives Around You

If you work with a vision of creating a caring, learning community for your program, you see your role as director in some different ways. Just as the staff plans curriculum for the children, a good part of your work is planning "a curriculum"—systems, interactions, and activities that build relationships among all involved in your center. This takes time and specific strategies to ensure it occurs. You can draw upon the principles of good curriculum for kids:

- View curriculum as everything that happens.
- Arrange the environment and systems to bring people together around shared interests, curiosities, and reflections.
- Plan activities and responses from observing and listening.
- Facilitate interactions, mediate conflicts, and scaffold learning.

Here are some strategies, including examples of directors using these ideas to build community in their programs:

Strategy

Rethink daily routines

Mull over a scene like this and imagine it happening in your program.

Kali got to bed late last night and her dad, Doug, wants her to sleep in as late as possible this morning. He packs her clothes for the day, and right before it's time to leave home, he gently wakes Kali, wraps her in a blanket and puts her in her car seat. On the way to the center, he sings softly to her in the car. When they arrive, Kali's dad walks with Kali as she toddles through the hallway still in her PJ's. He smiles at Kali's caregivers, grateful that later during the dressing time they will help her and the other children who arrived in PJ's get dressed for the day.

The transitions and routines of our daily lives with children are often the most stressful times for us. Helping children separate and reconnect with their families is a critical aspect of our work. Too often programs view "separation anxiety" as a problem that children and parents must resolve on their own. Instead of viewing these times as something to endure, why not thoughtfully plan for them? Rituals and activities around pick-up and drop-off times should be a part of curriculum planning. Trying some of the following activities might encourage everyone at the center to slow down and use transition times as opportunities for connections and community.

- *Include families in shared snacks or meals.*
- *Create consistent rituals for the beginning and ending of the day that families can participate in, such as singing, dancing, or playing music to signal these times.*
- *Design a cozy corner for families to read or cuddle together to ease the transition.*
- *Provide a dressing area for parents to help children who come early to change from their pajamas and get clothes on or hair brushed.*

This approach implies that the adults see themselves as partners in caring and educating children. It supports parents in talking with staff about their children and encourages staff to be respectful of family values and routines. As these relationships grow it will be easier for both family members and staff to discuss any issues of concern with each other. From this kind of weekly communication a more meaningful curriculum can be developed for the children as well.

Strategy

Grow curriculum from family life

Could you imagine any of these scenes happening in your program?

Emily's mom is pregnant with a new brother or sister. It's a big event for Emily and her family. The children and staff are interested too as each day Emily talks about how big her mom's belly is growing. At circle time she reports on changes happening at her house to get ready for the new baby. Peter, the director of Emily's child care program, asks her mom to help create a display with photos of pregnant mothers, including one of her carrying Emily. The display soon grows with other center moms adding their pregnancy pictures. Emily's mom agrees to let the children trace an outline of her body on a large piece of paper. Each month they use string to measure around her belly to see how much it is growing. They label and hang the string next to the silhouette of Emily's mom. Soon families are found around the displays at the end of the day, sharing stories about births and how they handled the arrival of a new sibling. Excitement continues to grow as does this real life curriculum.

Luis's mom started school this fall learning new computer skills to improve her job skills. Luis talks a lot about how he and his mom both go to school now. Caramel, the center director, arranges with Luis's mom to have, and a small group of children from the center visit her at her school's computer lab. They take pictures during the visit and Luis's teacher puts the photos in a book for the classroom. There is now a lot of talk about computers, and Caramel invites small groups into the office to see her computer. Several children now regularly run to greet Luis's mom when she picks him up.

As a program director, consider it part of your job to help teachers plan curriculum out of the children's family life. When real events and experiences in the lives of your families are the source of your activities, you never run out of curriculum ideas. You not only build meaningful curriculum, but a sense of community grows in the process.

Families, of course, do not always have happy events in their lives. It is just as important to acknowledge difficult ones. Sharing hard experiences is often not easy, but it can be the source of deeper connections and more meaningful relationships.

I really discovered how our center has become a community through a tragic event. A father at the center died suddenly and what happened next still affects me. The morning we received the information, I was in the car and got the call on my cell phone. One of the staff asked another to call me because she was afraid she would be unable to tell me he had died. The first words out of my mouth when I heard were "Tell me you're lying!" She said "No, I'm not. We just got the call and we're concerned about how to give the information to the teachers and to others."

When I hung up the phone I knew I had to deal with my own emotions quickly so I could be strong for the others. An hour after I arrived at the center the mother called and said the two children had asked to come to school and what should she do. I assured her the teachers had the information and wanted to support the children. They would certainly welcome them that day. I also told her to let me know if there was anything she needed. After she dropped the children off, the mother came and told me the entire story. Through hugs and tears I comforted her as best I could. To take care of myself throughout the day I would close the doors of my office and allow myself to cry.

That weekend I went to the funeral home with some of the staff. Much to our surprise there were many families from our center, both alumni and current children, parents, and staff. One parent came up to me and said, "I didn't realize until today that we really are one big family at the center." She then told me that her son said that the children who lost their father didn't have to worry because everybody at day care would take care of them. A food tree was set up for three months for the family and the oldest son's class cooked dinner once a week. Other parents offered to take the children home with them so their mother could have time for herself. This support still continues for this family, even though it's been a year.

—Wendy

Strategy

Grow curriculum from teacher passions

Teacher Gail is an avid recycler. She proudly boasts to everyone that she has recycling down to such an art that she only puts out half a can of garbage every week on her curb. Director Pam encourages Gail to bring her passion and knowledge about recycling to the child care program. Gail immediately begins planning a number of projects she can do with children. First on her list is building a worm bin so the children can see composting in action. She tells Pam her big dream is to set up a recycling center for families in the program.

Jamilla is a talented craftsperson and artist. Recently she has been designing whimsical felt hats and selling them at street fairs. Director Rhonda encourages Jamilla to show the children how she makes hats. Jamilla brings in supplies for her own work and scraps and pieces for the children to try their hand at hat making too. Within a few weeks the children are planning a hat sale as a fundraiser for the new climber they want on the playground.

When we think about favorite adults from our own childhoods, they are often people who shared a passion or skill with us. Children thrive when they are with adults who respect them enough to share things that are important in their lives.

Having the opportunity to apprentice themselves to a mentor is a great way for children to acquire skills and a love of learning. As a director, are you interested in the skills and interests your teachers have outside of their work with you? Do you encourage them to find appropriate ways to share these with the children and their families?

Strategy

Find curriculum in your wider community

Each year during the town Tulip Festival many of the families and staff feel they don't have much time to get involved in the events. The director, Colleen, helps arrange for the children and staff to participate in the parade that goes down Main Street and to ride through the fields in farmer Bob's hay wagon. She writes a newsletter sharing stories of the activities at the center and invites the parents to share this at their workplace. This enables many of them to get time off to participate in the festival with their children and center staff.

A new hospital is being built down the street from the center. Most of the children and families pass this construction site on their way to the center and talk about it with great interest. Leon, the center director, contacts the construction company requesting to have the children visit the site. He also invites a representative from the company to visit the center with some of their tools to talk with the children. In the meantime, Leon helps the teachers gather construction materials for their classrooms and designates an area on the outside playground for building.

As a director who seeks to build community and cultivate a program for childhood, your surrounding community is a possible source of rich experiences for curriculum. Your program and the larger community mutually benefit when children are visibly involved with their curiosity and contributions.

Strategy

Connect people to one another

A strong feeling of community comes from the meaningful connections people have to each other. These don't just happen automatically, especially with the fast-paced lives we all lead in today's world. Consider all the ways you as a director can help people in your program get more connected to each other.

Connecting children to one another

- *Create opportunities for children to be in mixed-age groupings and to see each other throughout the day.*
- *Schedule regular opportunities for older children to help younger children—zipping, tying shoes, washing hands, serving food, rubbing backs, reading books, writing letters, making gifts.*
- *Develop a program phone book, listing children's and families' phone numbers and addresses so that they can visit with each other away from the center.*
- *Display photos of children and their families on walls around the center and in homemade books or photo albums.*
- *Share verbal and visual stories of the children's friendships and activities with each other.*

I really wanted to do something different in our program, to create the feel of a family. To me this meant a wider age range in our rooms. There was resistance at first on the part of the staff and the parents. I had to hold fast to my vision and steadily grow the idea.

People were afraid that the toddlers and preschoolers might hurt the babies. Parents were worried that their older children might not learn as much if they were with babies. We had many staff discussions about the potential problems and benefits, and finally they agreed to try it. It wasn't long before we found that even young toddlers wanted to adopt the babies as special friends, someone they needed to watch out for. They would regularly put their arms around them and kiss them. I think it was my patience that ultimately paid off. A friend kept reminding me, "When you feed someone an elephant, give him one piece at a time."

—Leslie

Connecting families with one another

- *Develop a "Skill and Resource Exchange Bank" where staff and families can trade skills, tools, baby-sitting, and other helpful resources.*

- *Organize family gatherings not related to the operation of the program, such as dances, book fairs, barbecues, and family field trips to museums, zoo, and swimming places.*
- *Arrange your insurance and janitorial services so that you can make the center available to families for other activities, such as gardening, aerobics classes, and birthday parties.*

One of the children in our program lived with her grandmother. Her method of discipline was to swat the child, which we witnessed a number of times when they were at the center together. We wanted her know that this was something we didn't want her to do while she was in our program and to suggest other options for discipline. We met with her and let her know that, of course, she could follow her own methods of discipline at home, but in our program swatting isn't appropriate. We shared other options for guiding children and the reasons we do things this way. This meeting was very difficult for us to think about and plan for. We wanted to be respectful, but also firm in our philosophy. Our concern and commitment must have come through because the meeting turned out really well for all of us. The grandmother shared her frustration and difficulty in controlling her anger with her granddaughter and asked for our help. She asked us to watch and help her recognize what was happening with her granddaughter and to tell her what else she could do. We also helped her contact and get involved in a program for grandparents raising their grandchildren.

—**Paul**

Connecting staff with one another

- *Organize periodic outings and gatherings for staff and their families.*
- *Create visual displays around your building reflecting the lives and interests of staff members.*
- *Use part of each staff meeting for activities to learn about each other—life experiences, values, skills, and passions.*
- *Provide comfortable space and time for staff to have breaks, snacks, or perhaps exercise together.*
- *Give staff the equivalent of cubby space for personal belongings, treasures, photos, and books.*
- *Plan celebrations to mark special events and shared history.*

Sin embargo, lo que más necesitamos es hablar y escuchar nuestras propias historias, y sentir el apoyo y amor entre nosotras. En el día de entrenamiento del personal, después de que tuvimos talleres sobre varios tópicos, terminamos con una ceremonia para sanar a la sanadora, en la que encendimos una vela y nos lavamos mutuamente los pies. Nosotras hicimos esto por todos los pasos que nos esperan, por todo lo que debemos enfrentar para cumplir con nuestra filosofía. Esto tuvo un fuerte impacto en nosotras y nos llevó de sentirnos cansadas y desalentadas a sentir que éramos siete mujeres con la fuerza necesaria para cambiar las cosas.

—Caron

Mostly what we need is to tell and hear our own stories and feel our love and support for each other. During our staff training day, after we had workshops on topics, we ended with a healing-the-healer ceremony where we lit a candle and washed each other's feet. We did this because of all the steps we have to take and how much standing up we have to do for our philosophy. It made a big impact and we went from feeling tired and discouraged to feeling that we are seven women strong and able to change how things are.

—Caron

Connecting with the larger community

- *Schedule regular visits for children to go on errands with you or other staff members, for instance to the bank, post office, library, or grocery store.*
- *Invite members of the community to make regular visits or attend events the center offers.*
- *Arrange a monthly exchange with another early childhood program, a retirement home, or youth center.*
- *Expand staff development opportunities to include such things as attending a concert, museum, or local art exhibit.*
- *Arrange your insurance and janitorial services so that you can offer use of the center for community events such as classes or meetings.*
- *Offer your center's building for community events such as yard sales, book and art fairs.*

Tratamos de crear una comunidad tanto en nuestro programa como entre nuestro programa y la comunidad en general. Nuestra meta es ofrecer a cada madre adolescente un tutor académico de una organización de mujeres de la comunidad y una mentora de la comunidad. Los "Día de llevar a nuestras hijas al trabajo", mujeres de la comunidad llevan a una mamá adolescente al trabajo. Ponemos un énfasis especial en trabajos no tradicionales y otros a los cuales no estarían expuestas de otra manera. A menudo las mujeres pueden ganar más dinero en oficios como plomería, en electricidad o conduciendo autobuses, que en trabajos femeninos más tradicionales como en oficinas o en el sector de servicios.

—Caron

We try to build community both within our program and between our program and the wider community. Our goal is to provide each teen parent with an academic tutor from a community women's organization and a woman in the community as a mentor. On "Take Our Daughters to Work Day," women in the community take a teen mom to work. We put a particular emphasis on non-traditional jobs or ones they might not otherwise be exposed to. Often women can make more money in trades like plumbing and electrical work, or careers like bus driving than they can in more traditional women's jobs like office or service industry work.

—Caron

Working with Differences and Conflict

As you read the strategies above you no doubt found yourself with some "yes, buts." Perhaps you wanted to say, "What about staff, parents, or children who are difficult to be with?" "What can I do when my staff members don't get along?" "How can I do this with a parent who does nothing but complain?" We know these are concerns common to most early childhood centers. They will periodically appear whatever your vision or effectiveness of community-building efforts. When you focus on the real lives and issues of people in your program there will almost certainly be conflict and difficulties. Group dynamics are seldom easy, even among people who genuinely like each other and share the same vision.

A community cannot be built overnight and certainly won't be built by directors who spend all their time managing and overseeing, to the neglect of mentoring, coaching, and building community. The tasks of this side of the triangle are probably not in your formal job description. They take time, intention, and hard work. You need to cultivate shared leadership and involve others in developing procedures, processes, and decision-making guidelines. From the beginning, set the stage with some specific strategies, anticipate where coaching and facilitation will be needed, and give attention to improving communication channels. When you take this approach and develop the skills for this kind of leadership, the payoff is enormous. You can feel it in the air, sense it in your heart, and see it in the living, breathing relationships among those in your program.

Our program is richly diverse with a large percentage of families having English as their second language. We have many Asian languages spoken and some Spanish, as well as English. At parent orientations and subsequent meetings I demonstrate our commitment to inclusion by offering simultaneous translation services. Initially the English-speaking parents were uncomfortable. They complained that the meetings take twice as long this way and suggested we have separate meetings. I helped them see the value and richness of the diversity in our program by sharing what is happening with the children. The children are very able to work through language differences, and in fact they are delighted in the many ways they can be with each other while learning new words to say. The adults have slowly come around to see that if the children can figure this out, so can they. We are committed to never separating our meetings.

—Mary

Principle

Acknowledge and Respect Differences

Whenever a group of people come together, especially with the conscious intent of influencing the next generation, the personal and professional growth available to them is enormous. This is a disposition to continually cultivate, especially as you enter the troubled waters that are sure to come. Having some initial practice in consciously naming and working with different viewpoints establishes a foundation before the going gets rough. Over the years we've seen strategies create a climate and develop skills that help programs work through the inevitable conflicts that are part of any gathering where people are building genuine relationships.

Cuando se trata de eleguir el personal de nuestro programa hago la selección basándome en el corazon y no en la educación. Me es más fácil entrenar profesoras que desentrenarlos. No encuentro a las profesoras a través de anuncios, sino pasando la voz. Cada profesora trae sus propios talentos y en eso es que nos concentramos. Cuando alguien se va, no siempre encontramos una persona con las mismas caracteristicas, sino a menudo, a alguien con talentos diferentes. Los éxitos que hemos logrado en nuestro programa provienen tanto de aquellos que han estado antes en el programa como de los que están actualmente con nosotras.

—Ruth

When it comes to staffing our program I ultimately recruit staff based on heart, not education. I have found it easier to train teachers than to untrain them. I find teachers not by advertising, but by word of mouth. Every teacher brings their strength and that's what we focus on. When people leave we don't always get a new person with the same strength, but often someone with a different one. The tapestry of success that we have created in this program comes from who those who have come and gone as well as those who are currently here.

—Ruth

Strategy

Create a representation of a community

Sometimes the best way to learn about difference among us is to work as a group to create something. An hour to an hour and a half spent in the following activity and debriefing can illustrate the dynamics that are often present in working cross-culturally, or with those who have different life experiences and values than our own.

Give the group an ample supply of scrounge materials (paper towel rolls, small boxes from food packaging, bottle caps, straws, newspaper, masking tape, wire, yarn) and tell them they have thirty to forty minutes to work together to create a representation of a community they all want to live or work in. After they are nearly finished, add the following tasks to their group work:

- *Elect a mayor.*
- *Create laws, and a story about the history of the community.*
- *Give the community a name.*
- *Decide how to present it to others.*

At the end of the hour, have a debriefing that includes not only the presentations of the community but a discussion on how the group worked together. Were they actively involved with each other or engaged in parallel play? Did they build a common vision together? Was anyone left out, marginalized, or made invisible? How were differences accommodated? What did the person do to get elected mayor? What does this tell us about leadership among the staff? With an immediate experience to reflect on, new insights often emerge that are more difficult to get from abstract discussions. Helping teachers identify their own points of view and see why others might differ can lay the basis for respectful teamwork and conflict management. This activity also creates a sense of excitement and possibility for the vision of our programs as a community.

Strategy

Explore different values

In many early childhood programs, there are policies and practices that are taken for granted with little discussion or questioning. Someone in the past may have set these up according to a personal preference, or the policies may have been adopted from professional definitions of best practices. In any case, it is useful to periodically explore the assumptions underlying certain practices so that everyone is clear about why the program has certain policies. A chance to discuss these issues also provides an opportunity to identify and manage any conflict of values among staff, and possibly between a teacher and parent.

Teachers and caregivers benefit from the opportunity to examine and name the influences on their own values and preferred practices. A simple way to do this in a staff meeting is to write on separate pieces of paper possible opposing viewpoints on policies and then post them around the room. Ask everyone to find one viewpoint they wish to discuss, go to that paper, and talk with others there. They don't have to agree with the viewpoint, but they should at least have strong sentiments that they would like to discuss. Things we typically write on these separate papers include:

- *Children should be seen and not heard.*
- *Children should primarily be allowed to make choices and negotiate with adults.*
- *Children should primarily be offered limited choices and non-negotiable guidelines from adults.*
- *Children should call adults by their first names.*
- *Children should address adults by Mr. or Ms. or Teacher with her or his name.*
- *Children should usually be separated from the group or put on time out when they don't follow the rules.*
- *Children should usually be redirected and involved in other activities when they don't follow the rules.*

In the debriefing discussion following this activity, ask whether people found similarities or differences with others in their group. Were they there because they agreed or disagreed with the viewpoint? When teachers are asked to carry out practices different from their own belief systems, or when there is a difference between a family's practice and that of the early childhood program (for instance, in allowing a child to negotiate with an adult), this typically undermines the teacher's effectiveness with the child. In some cases, it may serve to discredit the parent or family values. Neither of these options is desired. Exploring the values and belief systems underlying practices with children can result in a willingness to accommodate a different viewpoint in order to create a better fit for a child, family, and the program.

We started discussing our anti-bias work as part of our accreditation self-study. At one point I said, "We are going to have to deal with the gay issue if we are going to be truly anti-biased." Several staff members were objecting to our need to take up this topic because we didn't currently have any children with gay or lesbian parents in our center. This could have gotten me off the hook, but I pressed forward and asked them how they knew that. I asked, "Do we feel confident that our center is a welcoming and safe place for a parent to tell us she is a lesbian or he is gay?" We took a walk through our center looking at the images and written materials around. We looked at our enrollment forms, handbooks, and newsletters to see if they gave any messages of inclusion or exclusion of families with gay or lesbian parents. It was a real eye-opener.

Several committees were formed to address our findings. Over the course of a year we struggled to develop several written statements. The first was our "we believe" statement, which was followed by a piece for our parent handbook that said our commitment to embracing diversity welcomed all kinds of staff and families to our program and would expose children to all kinds of families in our discussions and materials.

In developing the "we believe" statement we started with the idea that our program should be a safe haven for every child and family. As we got to the gay issue I had to repeatedly clarify that we are not talking about sex education here, but rather an appreciation of diversity in the world. I had to help several teachers who had vocal religious objections to homosexuality see that they already knew how to keep their personal religious beliefs out of the program without compromising themselves. I told them I knew they had strong ideas about God, the Holy Trinity, being "saved," Bible reading and prayer, but that they didn't impose this on the children, their families, or co-workers. I said, "You know how to keep these things separate, maintain your self-respect, and still respect those with different beliefs. You can do that on this issue too." It took some work, but we learned how to bring the concept of "agree to disagree" to life with what felt like genuine respect.

—Alicia

Strategy

Name your assumptions

Even programs that pride themselves on having a great team spirit have periodic tensions. This may be a result of patterns of relating to each other that stem from dysfunctional family dynamics imprinted on us at an early age. At other times, tensions represent the dynamics of power and privilege in our wider society. It is especially useful to identify our assumptions about working with diversity so that we have a frame of reference when conflict arises. The assumptions we work with go something like this:

- *Adults come to child care programs with a complex web of influences from backgrounds that must be untangled as they learn and unlearn across diversity.*
- *As adults come to deeper understandings about themselves and working with diversity, these understandings will influence their work with children, helping them to go beyond tokenism to counter biases and to be culturally sensitive.*
- *Everybody has a culture; culture is learned and includes, but goes beyond, ethnicity.*
- *Bias comes in many forms; invisibility and lack of cultural relevancy are as detrimental as stereotyping.*
- *Anti-bias practices require that we recognize European American cultural dominance and learn how its assumptions become a bias when applied universally. We must learn new attitudes, information, and behaviors as we unlearn acquired biases.*
- *To be inclusive and genuinely multicultural requires that we make a place for those historically left out, misrepresented, or disenfranchised. Given the stakes, this will likely stir up emotions and conflict that we must learn to work with.*

When I interviewed for the director position at our center, I was clear about my commitment to anti-bias practices and that I would want to immediately begin bringing more diversity to this white, middle-class program. At the same time, I had to be open if the staff had a different vision. To begin, I talked about how much my own life had been enriched when I diversified my circle of friends to include more people of color.

We began to discuss what would need to happen if our center were to become a place where families of color would feel comfortable. As we explored more what appeared to be the small diversity among us as a staff, some personal stories began to deepen understandings. We had great conversations about grandmothers, meaningful traditions, and religious issues. A Jewish teacher shared what it was like to be on the outside of the main-stream culture, as did one of our few teachers of color. Over time these stories chipped away at the mountainous task of rearranging understandings and attitudes.

It's a tricky thing to get a mostly white and privileged program to struggle around these issues. It takes way longer than you want. I had to keep tailoring my vision to a realistic time frame without ever giving up or diluting my vision. The success of small steps rewarded me and encouraged me to stay longer than I might have otherwise.

—Julie

Strategy

Create persona doll stories

Often teachers need help in finding a child, parent, or coworker's perspective, and you can develop what Kay Tans in *Anti-Bias Curriculum* calls persona doll stories to help them learn to do this. It's important to not oversimplify or create black-or-white attitudes with persona doll stories. In fact, their value lies in providing opportunities to explore the complexities of a topic or given situation.

Persona stories are most effective when they are developed out of real life stories or composites of ones you are familiar with. Develop stories by first making a list of the concepts you want to explore. Then search your memory for specific images that reflect these concepts and gather your images into a single tale that outlines the setting, an incident or two, and the thoughts of the persona you have developed.

When you tell the story, hold or pass the doll around. Then have the staff generate a list of what stands out for them in the story and discuss these as examples of the concepts you have in mind. When the personal story has a number of important details and is to be the centerpiece of a discussion, you might provide a written copy to pass around. If the goal is to do some problem solving around an issue, ask pairs or small groups to create possible endings for the story. This often stimulates thinking that moves below the surface and wrestles with the complexities involved.

Strategy

Examine the elements of culture

Other peoples' stories are useful in getting us to think concretely about culture, how to be inclusive, and how to avoid bias in our programs. Useful resources for discussing cultural differences are the Lakeshore poster pack entitled "Children of the U.S." or the photo books *Of Many Colors: Portraits of Multiracial Families* and *Love Makes a Family*. Pass around these photos during a staff meeting asking each person to read the related story and then introduce that family to the rest of the staff. As a group, discuss ways your program could make this child and family feel included and acknowledged. Generate a list of the elements of culture to be aware of, including those that are visible and obvious, as well as elements that are less so, like communication practices and patterns of handling emotions, values, beliefs, and attitudes.

Develop a working definition of "stereotyping" and contrast this with a definition of "culturally sensitive practices" that you will use. This sets the stage for drawing lessons from the experiences of working together as diverse staff and families. Conclude by asking teachers to consider any experiences they have had at your center where a cultural difference might account for a conflict. Once we take the time to explore the roots of our differences, we can usually find a respectful way to work with them.

After a number of years of steadily working to implement an anti-bias program at our co-op, we hit a major crisis that put us to the test as to whether we were really the community of parents we professed to be. As the new school year began we had taken a number of preparatory steps to communicate to parents that we planned to include families with gay and lesbian parents in our anti-bias curriculum this year, but we had no indication of the controversy that we were stirring up. When the day came to begin reading *Daddy's Roommate*, a number of parents kept their children home and our typically small evening board meeting swelled to include half of the school. Normally restrained parents were overtaken by emotions. Tempers flared and accusations were made. This led us into a long and remarkable process where we learned how democracy really works and how people with different views can still live in harmony in the same community.

Over the course of several months we held meetings, conducted surveys, and designed a ballot, all of which involved carefully defining the problems at hand, identifying guiding principles, and developing possible solutions. A committee invented processes to take us through this time of conflict and to everybody's credit, we stuck with it and came out with agreed upon goals and a good compromise. We replaced *Daddy's Roommate* with teacher-created persona stories, but we retained the rest of our curriculum, including the use of photos and discussions of families with same-gender parents and using the words "two moms," "two dads," or "partners" rather than the terms "gay" or "lesbian." In the years following this controversy we have continued to develop a conflict resolution model and training in its use each year for parents. We are stronger than ever since this undertaking and I'm pleased to say that this year's parents voted to begin including the terms "gay" and "lesbian" in our curriculum.

—Linda

Principle

Explore and Mediate Conflicts

Contrary to our instinctive feelings, conflict is not all bad. It has the potential to balance our relationships and expand our resources. When we just stay on the surface and avoid or smooth over areas of disagreement, we rarely get to the depth of what we truly care about. Our programs become richer when we can work through sources of friction caused by different perspectives, skills, and interests. Moving through bumpy times together forms deeper connections and more authentic relationships. The investment you make in really learning to work with other perspectives has a significant payoff. Here are some strategies to strengthen your ability to do this.

Strategy

Explore different communication styles

Sometimes people make judgments about each other based on differences in communication styles. This could be a personal or a cultural issue, but whichever, it's useful to understand what's happening. Here's a playful way to explore how we send and receive information and feelings.

Ask your staff to consider possible labels for acceptable communication styles and then choose four or five to work with. The term "acceptable" is a subjective one. Our intent here is to avoid negative labels such as caustic, attacking, manipulative, or defensive, and identify a variety of other styles that have a useful place in communicating. For instance, friendly, humorous, creative, decisive, analytical, direct, or indirect could be selected as styles for exploration. Spend a minute defining what is meant by each of these styles. Then, divide the large group into as many small groups as there are styles, and assign one style to each small group. Ask each group to generate a list of common phrases that you might hear someone from that style use. For instance, the lists might look something like this:

Friendly style
● *You have great ideas.*
● *I like what you said.*
● *They might not like that.*

Creative style
● *Anything is possible.*
● *Let's keep brainstorming.*
● *What if we flipped that around?*

Decisive style
● *Let's not waste time.*
● *We have to decide one way or another.*
● *I want to know what we're going to do.*

Analytical style
● *I think we should do a survey.*
● *The facts speak for themselves.*
● *We need more evidence.*

Once you've given each group the time to come up with a list of three or four phrases, ask for a volunteer from each group, and conduct a communications role-play. Choose a topic that isn't emotionally loaded for the volunteers to discuss. An example might be what color the center should paint it's walls, what kind of plants to get for the lounge, or what software should be purchased for your computers. As you facilitate the brief discussion, ask each volunteer to try to use as many of the phrases on their list as possible in the discussion.

Along with being able to laugh and get a new perspective on how style might look in a group setting, you can debrief this activity to explore the strengths and weaknesses of each style, and the barriers that can occur when we judge a person's contribution by their communication style. Staff members might enjoy identifying their own style and exploring how it can potentially conflict with another.

Building a community takes time. For me it took about eighteen months for the staff to know that when I say something, I mean it, and when I make a mistake, I'll admit it. I had to build trust before they would join me to form a community with a shared vision and purpose.

A lot of the staff had been there a number of years when I first arrived, and they had accumulated a lot of baggage. I wanted to start out with my vision of open and assertive communication to overcome the negative history. When I observed difficult interactions between staff members, I wouldn't walk away pretending I didn't see it. I would walk up and describe what I saw without judgment. I'd offer support and model conflict resolution. It took lots of work, and with each bumpy spot we had to come to new understandings and forge new agreements.

The staff came to understand that this was important to me. They slowly stopped complaining that their issues wouldn't get addressed. The whining mentality dwindled as everyone realized that they could articulate concerns and they would be heard and responded to in a safe and productive manner.

It's been a long haul, but we're ready now to do amazing things together. We're a team with a safe, supportive system in place. There's no limit to what we can do, because we won't be stopping ourselves anymore.

—Alicia

Design a conflict resolution process

With the demands and stresses of child care work, sometimes staff tensions can mount to an intense level before you know what happened. As part of the list of working agreements you develop, it's important to include a process for how conflicts will be handled. Ideally, the expectations and approaches to conflict resolution you develop should parallel what you set out for the children in your program. For instance, you might have a general statement that would read as follows:

> *"At our center we all share in caring for each other and for the environment. When someone forgets or breaks this agreement, we remind them of how it hurts the group, explore why this happened, and work together to help the person get back on track. We work out disagreements by taking turns listening carefully to each other, explaining what we understand, and exploring what changes are possible and acceptable to those involved."*

You then need a clear process for how this takes place and staff meeting time to practice on some minor issues. At the top of the following page is an example of an agreement and process developed in a program Margie directed.

There are common elements any conflict resolution process should have. These include:

- *using active or deep listening, with the use of paraphrasing to check understandings;*
- *providing opportunities for each person to state needs and wants in the situation;*
- *generating an active, creative brainstorm of possible solutions, and reserving judgments;*
- *evaluating possible solutions and choosing what to try;*
- *developing an action plan with specific details; and*
- *evaluating the plan at designated intervals.*

Examples of documents several programs have developed for their conflict resolution process are found in the appendix.

Agreement:

When necessary, we will use a criticism/self-criticism discussion process to identify attitudes and behaviors that are negatively affecting our agreements.

Questions to ask oneself before giving a criticism:
- Is my criticism based on investigation or on assumption?
- What is the most important element of the criticism?
- What is secondary?
- What is my side of the problem, my responsibility, or my contribution to it?
- Are there any things I hide to avoid being criticized?
- Is my criticism intended to hurt, attack, or improve understandings and communication?
- How are our staff agreements hurt or helped by my criticism?
- How can I play a concrete, positive role in helping the other person change?
- What changes do I need to make in myself?

Stating a criticism:
- When you do _____, I feel _____.
- It hurts our agreements because _____.
- Therefore I want you to _____.
- In the future I will behave differently by....

Discussion to investigate the criticism:
- Why do you feel that way? What happened?
- What other things were going on?
  (Include events taking place around you at the same time, as well as feelings and impressions happening within you.)
- What is the main thing that needed to happen here?

One of our infant caregivers had a style with the babies that many of our staff found offensive. She used inappropriate language, sometimes swearing in front of the children. Her sense of humor was often annoying rather than funny to most of the staff. We met as a team to discuss the concerns. This was a difficult discussion as many of the staff wanted her to change immediately. Her response was "This is me, I can't change who I am." I tried to guide the discussion toward the tangibles of words to not use with babies. I reinforced that we didn't want to change who she was, but her language was inappropriate in this setting. This proved helpful as she felt less personally attacked and more able to hear the specific criticism. The rest of the staff was also able to let go of the emotions around these issues and see her as a person beyond her language. She's made changes in her language with the babies and staff relationships have improved tremendously. I believe this is the result of working through a conflict in a direct, yet inclusive manner.

—Paul

Cultivating New Roles, Dispositions, and Skills

Your daily actions to build and support community in your program are some of the most powerful aspects of your job. It is easy to get overwhelmed and feel victimized in our work, and in our culture as a whole. When you create an experience of connection between people, you are creating a set of possibilities. When you view tension as a sign that people really care about what's happening, you can move past discomfort and fear to a place of discovery and integrity. If you dare to take up a vision and not settle for the status quo, you are on the road to nurturing it into reality. In the words of Peter Block, "The challenge is to pursue our vision with as much courage and intensity as we can generate" (1987). This is the heart of claiming your power and acting on it.

Think of yourself, not with the limited mind-set of a manager, but with the eyes and ears of a storyteller. Linda Espinosa reminds us that, "Storytelling is a means of communicating the substance of who we are and what we stand for. The vision we hold for children, for early childhood programs, and for families can be vividly captured in the stories we choose to remember and repeat." Howard Gardner specifically relates this to the role of a director: "A leader is someone who has a compelling story to tell; he is able to forge a group identity and sense of community through his effective storytelling." When you see yourself as a storyteller, your tales will spread the news of what's happening in your program and shape its growing culture.

Practice Assessing Yourself

Spend some time considering other metaphors that help you assess how you are doing in your community-building roles. If you thought of yourself as an architect, what skills would you need to design plans for improving the physical and emotional space of your program? If you were a weaver, how could you cultivate your eyes and hands so that each day you could pull together threads for this tapestry you are weaving?

If you thought of yourself as a sculptor, a mediator, or horticulturist, what skills would you need to learn? Use each of these professions as a heading, and make a list of skills and qualities that each might require or nurture in you. How do those skills apply to your work as a director? Consider what you already know about this work, and what's not yet clear to you.

Set some goals for yourself and step outside the early childhood field for some of the resources you might need. The act of moving across professional boundaries can be a community-building process in and of itself, making the world of early childhood care and education visible to others, and bringing their knowledge and resources within our reach.

Resources for Building and Supporting Community

This list includes several titles that may not be familiar to most early childhood professionals. There are several important books by architectural designers alerting the reader to how space can be designed to nurture or oppress the gathering of people in them. Other titles are from professional storytellers who describe their work as part of a community-building process and offer tips on how to use storytelling in everyday life and teaching toward that end. Finally, you may recognize some titles more familiar to the early childhood field, helping us think about the organization of space and working across cultures and bias.

Alexander, C., S. Ishikawa, and M. Silverstein. *A Pattern Language.* New York: Oxford University Press, 1977.

Bisson, Julie. *Celebrate! An Anti-Bias Guide to Enjoying Holidays in Early Childhood Programs.* St. Paul: Redleaf, 1997.

Bruchac, J. *Tell Me a Tale.* San Diego: Harcourt, 1997.

Davis, Donald. *Telling Your Stories.* Little Rock, AR: August House, 1993.

Day, C. *Places of the Soul: Architecture and Environmental Design as a Healing Art.* San Francisco: Aquarian, 1990.

Gillard, M. *Story Teller, Story Teacher: Discovering the Power of Storytelling for Teaching and Living.* York, ME: Stenhouse, 1996.

Gozdz, K., ed. *Community Building: Renewing Spirit and Learning in Business.* San Francisco: New Leaders Press, 1995.

Greenman, Jim, and Anne Stonehouse. *Prime Times: A Handbook for Excellence in Infant and Toddler Programs.* St. Paul: Redleaf, 1996.

Kivil, P. *Uprooting Racism.* Gabriola Island, British Columbia, Canada: New Society, 1996.

Moore, Gary. "The Common Core of a Child Care Center." *Child Care Information Exchange.* No. 114 (1997).

———. "Houses and Their Resource-Rich Activity Pockets." *Child Care Information Exchange.* No. 113 (1997).

Olds, Anita Rui. *The Child Care Design Guide: Day Care Centers that Honor the Spirit of Place.* New York: McGraw-Hill. Forthcoming, 1999.

———. "From Cartwheels to Caterpillars: Children's Need to Move Indoors and Out." *Child Care Information Exchange.* May 1994.

Sussman, Carl. "Out of the Basement: Discovering the Value of Child Care Facilities." *Young Children.* Vol. 53 No. 1 (1998).

Williams, Leslie R., and Yvonne DeGaetano. *ALERTA: A Multi-cultural, Bilingual Approach to Teaching Young Children.* Reading, MA: Addison-Wesley, 1985.

Chapter 4

Your Role of Mentoring and Coaching

Consider these scenes.

Director LeAnn has a staff-training plan this year that includes the required health and safety review, and how to identify child abuse and neglect. Because she has a number of new teachers she has also planned an in-service on developing lesson plans and child assessments. Even though they've covered this before, she thinks her long-term staff will still benefit from this training. Today, as she goes through her list of announcements at the staff meeting, LeAnn is discouraged as several teachers groan when they hear the training plans. She thinks to herself, "They don't know how lucky they are that we have money for staff training. I wish I could find some more enthusiastic teachers. They hardly pay attention at staff meetings, and no matter how much training I offer, teachers rarely change their behaviors."

Director Ramona is reviewing the required monthly lesson plans that her staff has turned in. Most of her staff complete these forms as mandated except for Lucy, a teacher in the preschool room. Her lesson plans are always sketchy, and Ramona notices when she visits the room that Lucy never follows what she's written down. Lucy's children are always very busy and happy and Lucy relates well with them and their families. Ramona doesn't know what to do. She's talked with Lucy several times, showing her the plans that Brandi in the next room writes and follows so well. The truth is, Brandi's room, like most of the rooms in the program, doesn't have much creativity or child-initiated activity. Apart from issues of required paperwork, Ramona secretly wishes that Brandi and the other teachers were more like Lucy in their work with the children.

A director's approach to staff supervision and development has a significant impact on the culture of your organization and the quality of a program. We highlight this point, not only because we know that everyone does their best work when they feel supported and respected by their peers and supervisors, but also because of what we know about how adults grow and learn. When meetings and staff training are centered around checklists, rules, and regulations, you are operating from the managing and overseeing side of our triangle framework. Furthermore, by example, you are demonstrating a way of teaching that you would most likely be critical of in teachers' work with children—teaching by lecturing, pointing out the rules, and requiring quiet, passive learners.

The model we see above in Directors LeAnn and Ramona will likely translate into a program culture where people are focused on schedules, lesson plans, and compliance issues, rather than thoughtful interactions, because these are the things the director is focused on. If time spent together isn't viewed as precious, if conditions aren't conducive to self-reflection and collaboration, staff tends to view training opportunities in terms of requirements, rather than thinking of them as opportunities. Like the director who is modeling this for them, the focus is on the tasks and paperwork to be done and the requirements to be met. Rather than enthusiasm for new discoveries, or the warmth of genuine community, the tone is one of boredom, detachment, and going through the motions. You may create a program that technically meets the standards for quality, but where is the heart and spirit? How is the quality of life for the people in the program? Is there a sense of community with caring and learning for all its members?

Yes, it's important for staff to follow policies and procedures and to participate in ongoing training opportunities. However, unless caregivers and teachers are exceptionally self-motivated and see themselves as lifelong learners, an approach like LeAnn's will be less than effective. As Ramona puts the emphasis on paperwork requirements, she fails to support what she sees as Teacher Lucy's strength. Ramona's actions will unconsciously uphold the lack of creativity she is critical of in most of her teachers. These directors may get staff to perform in compliance with regulations, but this won't usually translate into high-quality work. Everything we know about constructivist theory and adult learning suggests that the kind of learning caregivers need to improve their job performance doesn't come from being told what to do. Rather, staff in our programs need coaching and mentoring, and that implies a different set of staff development activities.

We work in a profession with little public esteem, low wages, and inadequate working conditions. As a result, early childhood programs do not easily attract or retain people eager to learn and develop themselves, let alone think of themselves as qualified professionals. There are certainly a handful of wonderful exceptions, but many people enter this workforce with low self-esteem, and a long history of financial and personal struggle. They often settle on working with children instead of the job they really want. When these folks work alongside our more dedicated and competent staff, the climate is frequently one of tense working relationships. There is a mixture of enthusiasm, victim thinking, blame, and defensiveness.

As we continue to address the external social, economic, and political factors that shape our staffing crisis, our concurrent task is to create a climate that will nurture and stimulate our most skilled and dedicated staff, and mentor and coach those not yet performing as reliably. We have to build self-esteem, confidence, and effective communication skills alongside a working knowledge of child development. This is a pedagogical task, not a management one.

Coaching vs. Managing Staff

We developed the triangle framework to help early childhood program directors understand the difference between their responsibilities as a manager and overseer, and the skills of a coach and mentor. Keeping a clear distinction between these roles requires a commitment to integrity and staff empowerment. To be sure, there are contradictions inherent in having the role of manager and coach in one administrative position. The trust, open communication, and mutual respect required for healthy mentoring relationships are difficult to maintain when one party has the power to hire and fire. However, given the financial resources and organizational limitations of most early childhood programs, these roles are usually combined in one person's job. Directors must and can learn to identify which role they want to work from on which occasion. There are occasions when you will feel that your priority is to immediately step in and exercise your power on behalf of a child or family, overriding a slower learning process for a staff member. In most cases, however, the investment you make on behalf of a teacher's learning process will lead to more meaningful understandings and behavior changes. When you coach staff members to become thinkers rather than rule followers, you are enhancing *their* power to respond on behalf of children and their families. This kind of teacher mentoring requires time and a trusting relationship, more than telling and reminding. It keeps you growing as a director, as you seek to understand your staff as adult learners and invent strategies to help them gain more knowledge.

When we think of a coach, we have in mind not the guy screaming on the field or in the locker room, but the one who takes the team through an analysis of the last game, spotting where the holes were, where things went wrong, and what strengths to build on. We picture the birthing coach who supports mothers through the labor and delivery process—watching; listening; sharing observations, skills, and resources; and providing guidance during the difficult times of giving birth to new life. In many ways this is the work of a director's coaching role—not punishing or admonishing, but focusing on the adult learner and his or her process of birthing new knowledge and skills. As a coach or mentor, your job is to develop strategies that will empower staff members to be autonomous and thoughtful in their work. This may involve addressing their lack of faith in themselves.

Our field has its share of people who see themselves as victims and powerless over their lives. This may translate into passive and/or aggressive behavior and an abundance of "I can't" and "yes, but" thoughts. Being a coach may require you to renew your attitudes and approaches with a given teacher. For instance, instead of responding with irritation, you can be a patient listener, restating what you understand the person feels, and then ask for a story about a time she or he learned how to do something difficult. Point out that even if it is hard to remember, this person has the strength and ability to learn and act on new knowledge. Consistently give the message that you have faith in your staff members and that you are looking forward to hearing their ideas, even if they are different from yours. Whenever you have the opportunity, point out examples of growth and change you see. This helps replace self-doubt with "can do" thoughts.

I hired Neil as an assistant teacher in my program because in our interview he said he really wanted to work with young children and he would especially enjoy doing art projects with them. As I observed him with the children I could see his skills were really lacking and he seemed unfocused. He particularly had trouble guiding children's behavior and taking the initiative in managing a group.

After a number of failed attempts to help Neil improve, I felt I needed to talk with him about finding other work more suited to him. His lack of focus and difficulty in changing suggested to me that he wasn't really that interested in working with children. During our conversation he strongly insisted that he really did want to do this work and just needed more time. I agreed to keep working with him to see if he could realize the potential he saw for himself. I reassigned him to another classroom with a lead teacher who offered him the firm support and encouragement he needed.

It's taken quite a while but he has now blossomed as a teacher. His skills have grown tremendously in many areas and he continues to seek more training to continue his growth. He initiates and tackles complicated projects with children that are so rich and meaningful for all of our program. I am so glad I listened to him and gave him the time and support he needed to reach the potential he saw in himself.

—Jim

There are times you will need to respond to a staff member from the managing side of the triangle framework and we offer suggestions for that role in chapter 5 of this book. As a coach, however, your job is to encourage and provide opportunities for problem definition and problem solving, for self-reflection and collaboration. It is important that you model the kind of behavior you want staff to use with children—providing for self-initiated learning, risk taking, and exploration. When staff are involved in setting goals for themselves and in creating strategies for their professional development, they bring more energy to their work and contribute to the growth of your organization as a learning community.

What Do Adult Learners Need?

Many of us come to director jobs having been classroom teachers ourselves. We have expertise when it comes to providing good learning experiences for children, and this is usually our focus when we seek to improve teachers' behaviors. It is less common for directors to have experience or consolidated thinking about providing good learning experiences for adults. We instinctively think of our job as making sure things go well for the children, and often miss the implications this has for tending to the climate the adults' experience, and the activities we organize for them.

However, the truth is that the better the environment is for the adults involved in the program, the better care the children receive. The link between the quality of experience for the staff and the quality of care for the children has been made clear in a number of research studies in early childhood education. Several of these studies focus on issues of organizational culture and support for the staff, while the studies of Carol Anne Wien and the High/Scope Foundation analyze components of pedagogy and effective in-service training. The findings of these studies forecast the benefits of coaching and mentoring programs that are now receiving more attention across our profession.

For a number of years Paula Jorde Bloom has studied the dimensions of an organizational climate that lead to quality programming for children. Her publication, *A Great Place to Work: Improving Conditions for Staff in Young Children's Programs,* translates these findings into a guidebook for directors. Bloom's studies make it clear that if working conditions aren't suitable for the adults, it is hard for the children to thrive.

This understanding led the Center for the Child Care Workforce to conduct an informal survey and set of focus groups asking child care providers and teachers to describe what they consider to be model work standards. We discuss these standards more fully in the coming chapters, but here it's worth noting that teachers feel their ability to perform well and to continue in their professional development is dependent on their working conditions, and the support and mentoring they receive on the job.

In *Developmentally Appropriate Practice in Real Life: Stories of Teacher Practical Knowledge,* Carol Ann Wien describes her research, which also involved extensive interviews with teachers. Wien's study was designed to learn why teachers educated in developmentally appropriate practice often fail to teach in this way when working in early childhood programs. She suggests that the organizational climate of a teacher's workplace is a significant factor in their ability to follow developmentally appropriate guidelines. Teachers working in programs that use a school-like framework, that emphasize time schedules and top down administrative practices, tend to adopt these same behaviors with children. Wien concludes that when programs promote and provide for observation, reflection, and collaboration, teachers are supported in developmentally appropriate practices and are more likely to carry them out.

An earlier research project conducted by the High/Scope Foundation predicted Wien's findings. To evaluate their extensive teacher training program, High/Scope studied the components of in-service training that resulted in teachers appropriately implementing the High/Scope Curriculum. Their findings, published in *Training for Quality,* are summarized below. Their research demonstrated that effective training

- provided a focus over time, where knowledge was cumulative and followed a consistent theoretical framework,
- actively involved participants through interaction with the trainers and each other,
- allowed time for reflection,
- provided hands-on practice to try out new ideas and strategies, and
- followed up with observation and feedback and more opportunities for peer exchanges.

The study conducted by the Center for the Child Care Workforce and published as *NAEYC Accreditation as a Strategy for Improving Child Care Quality* supports the findings of these earlier studies. The CCW study found that programs who achieved a quality rating of good or better in their accreditation findings also participated in high-intensity support groups. The elements of these support groups included custom-designed training, on-site technical assistance, and regular gatherings for directors and teachers that involved ongoing analysis, dialogue, and collaboration around quality issues. It seems obvious that if these elements were part of the organizational framework of every early childhood program, we would see more consistent quality in accredited early childhood programs. Programs would be closer to our vision of serving as a learning community for both the children and adults.

Finally, it seems important to point out that the engaging projects and complex learning we see with children in the schools of Reggio Emilia, Italy, are directly linked to the conditions provided for the adults in those schools. The organizational culture is centered around attentiveness to children's interest and thinking, and opportunities for the staff to engage in collaborative analysis of their observations of children's work. With the support of a *pedagogista,* whose job is to help the teachers understand children's development, teachers are continually hypothesizing, planning, and evaluating. As any visitor to these schools will tell you, the adults benefit greatly from their debates with each other and from the attitude and role of researcher they take with each other and the children. The experience of learning for the adults in the schools of Reggio parallels the learning experience for the children.

Viewed together, along with the survey of early childhood mentoring programs that we discuss in chapter 6, these studies reinforce the role of a program director as the creator of a learning community, and a coach and mentor for the adults. It's not rocket science to conclude that adults who are engaged in a meaningful learning process for themselves are more likely to be providing a higher-quality experience for children and families. Carol Anne Wien (1995) leaves us with a wonderful vision of teacher empowerment that translates into empowered children:

> Those of us who hope to support the work of teachers (administrators, curriculum consultants, practicum supervisors, teacher educators, and so forth) can help in several ways, beyond simply a better understanding of the context of teacher work in early childhood. Like the support given to teachers in Reggio Emilia, we can work to change systemic constrains so that time is opened up for reflection, for review of practice, for the surfacing of incipient conflicts that the teacher senses but has not had time to address. We can encourage the reflective process by giving teachers opportunities to document children's activity and the development of their curriculum, encourage them to make changes that they themselves

generate, to try out solutions to self-set problems of teaching. Rather than appearing merely as experts with authoritative knowledge, we can encourage a sense of mastery over their work, their sense of agency. Ultimately we must trust teachers to develop the worlds of teaching in which they work, recognizing that their negotiations through two common frameworks for action, teacher dominion, and developmentally appropriate practice are conflicted, frequently contradictory, stressful, exciting, challenging, and that the agency that they can develop in taking action in early childhood settings is ultimately a preferred way to model for children the process of coming to life, of living in a shared social world of responsibility, of care for others, and love of life itself.

The Golden Rule Revisited: Treat Adults as You Want Them to Treat Children

Whether or not you have studied adult learning theory, a director's knowledge of good practices for children can be translated into appropriate practices for educating teachers. How could you justify anything contradictory? Is it fair to require them to attend trainings, ask them to sit and pay attention on small chairs in a cramped hallway, fill their lives with checklists and forms, and then be critical of stagnant and unattractive room arrangements, teachers' use of dittos, and their insistence on teacher-directed activities? The idea of creating an environment and educational activities for adults that parallel what you want them to do with children is not only an ethical issue, but a pedagogical one. Adults who have never experienced, or who have forgotten, the positive elements of childhood and living as part of a community, can hardly be expected to offer this in your program. They need vivid reminders of what this feels like in order to understand its value. Giving your staff a mission statement, a philosophical lecture, or even the criteria for NAEYC accreditation will hardly put a taste of childhood or community in their mouths.

When we get a taste of something we like, we usually long for more. We are motivated to try to find or create it again. When most of our waking hours are spent in programs with groups of children, this actively influences the quality of our lives. Providing adults with experiences that parallel what we want for children should be at the center of a director's thinking.

I believe that professional development works best when it is ongoing and directly connected to what is happening daily in the classroom. It must be free from anxiety. The most consistent time this happens in our program is nap time. While children sleep, teachers talk. This is not a time for announcements, workshops, or other business. We discuss children, their needs, their strengths, strategies for handling difficult behaviors, parents, classroom environments and activities, administrative styles and issues. We also get into personal, political, and social issues. It is a daily processing session. Most certainly we have more formal workshops and staff meetings, but these "professional development seminars" happen almost every day during nap time, informally and without anxiety.

—Margo

Principle

Give Thoughtful Attention to the Environment

If we want caregivers to offer well designed and pleasing learning environments for children, we need to design an environment like that for them. If teachers are to give children choices and opportunities for self-initiated learning, then they deserve that from us. The comparisons of quality learning environments and experiences for children and adults could go on and on.

Strategy

Plan a nurturing environment for the adults

Take a look at the chart at right, which offers some examples of what parallel elements in environments for children and adults might look like. Then choose a couple that you could fairly easily adapt and a couple that could be longer term goals for your program. You might also present this chart at a meeting to see how your staff would prioritize their goals for improvements. Comparing what you and they come up with is another way to assess how closely you understand your staff's view of their needs and work environment.

Environments for Children	Environments for Adults
Children should be surrounded by softness, art, beauty, natural materials, and living things (fabric, paintings, water, rocks, trees, plants, woven baskets, sand, dirt, flowers, animals).	*Strategy:* Put such things as plants, flowers, birds, and aquariums in the office area, staff room, and restrooms. Arrange displays of rocks, shells, and other collections from nature and the seasons in areas where adults can look, touch, and play with them. *Strategy:* Hang attractive photos, paintings, and textures on the walls. Cover hard surfaces with fabric. Provide magazines and books on a variety of topics (nature, science, art, architecture, design) in the office area, staff lounge, and adult bathrooms.
Children need opportunities to be outdoors, and to experience changes in the seasons, light and shadows, weather, animals, plants, and gardens.	*Strategy:* Arrange opportunities for staff to be outdoors when they are not supervising children; encourage walks during breaks; organize staff outings to local nature attractions, art galleries, zoos, and botanical gardens. *Strategy:* Hold staff meetings, retreats, and trainings in beautiful environments reflecting nature, natural elements, design, art, and beauty.
Children need to see their lives, families, cultures, and interests reflected in images, materials, and activities around them	*Strategy:* Have places for adults to display family pictures, collections, or special objects. *Strategy:* Set up a rotating schedule where staff members share special skills, hobbies, or interests—knitting, appliance repair, computer skills, or book discussions.
Children need time and materials to explore, invent, represent, and make-believe.	*Strategy:* Provide adult-oriented, open-ended materials, games, and puzzles in the staff lounge, office area, during meetings, and at gatherings.
Children need a place for their personal things and a place to be away from the group.	*Strategy:* Give each staff member the equivalent of a cubby; create quiet corners with stuffed chairs, soft lighting, and plants.
Children need physical challenges—using muscles, going fast, finding balance and coordination	*Strategy:* Put exercise equipment for staff use somewhere in the building—bicycle, treadmill, chin-up bar, or yoga mat. *Strategy:* Arrange for use of nearby health club or gym.
Children need opportunities to work alone and with others.	*Strategy:* Use staff meeting time for teachers to work on individual goals, have collaborative discussions, or create documentation displays of recent events.

Strategy

Provide time and resources

If you look over the sample Model Work Standards (see appendix 2) developed by teachers and providers across the country, it's obvious that a key ingredient is input on how they spend their time with and away from children. Providing the time for thinking and planning is in and of itself a coaching strategy. It creates room for reflection, for gathering thoughts, and for collaborating with co-workers. This is valuable staff development time, and should not be equated with a break, which teachers also need.

Without adequate resources your staff is likely to experience more frustration than refinement of their skills, more lethargy than learning from their teaching. Stimulate your caregivers' thinking with catalogs outside of the typical early childhood resources. Take a look at ones from garden and landscaping stores, display and craft suppliers, environmental and other groups supporting crafts from developing nations.

As a mentor, make sure to offer tips on time management and organizing the tools they need for efficiently using their time away from children. Keep abreast of how their curriculum is evolving and surprise them with resources you have located from around the center or community.

In chapter 5 we discuss getting yourself organized with systems and resources that enhance your coaching and community-building roles. How you allocate time for you and your staff is a key element in reaching your vision. We're not suggesting you add more work to your packed schedule, but rather that you examine your priorities, organize your work, and develop your skills in the service of creating a learning community. Keeping clear about the difference between your managing and your coaching roles will strengthen your ability to genuinely contribute to growing understandings and expanded skill in your teachers.

Principle

Know Your Adult Learners

Adults bring a complex web of experiences, knowledge, skills, and attitudes to the learning process. They experience a developmental process, just as children do. Their own childhoods and cultural framework have shaped their self-image and how they respond to children and their co-workers. Staff members come to our programs with particular dispositions towards people in positions of authority, and different emotional responses to the idea of making changes. To be effective in staff development, you must take time to discover who your staff members are and, in Carol Ann Wien's words, what their "scripts for action" look like. You must recognize what they already know and what their interests are, and plan training that is relevant and meaningful for their lives. Isn't this just what you hope they will do with the children in their care?

In describing what teachers bring to their work with children, Wien says that "the notion of practical knowledge includes all that the teacher brings of herself to the moment of teaching—beliefs, attitudes, feelings, reflections, gestures, temperament, personal history" (1995). She calls this "practical knowledge" and says this tends to override what may have been learned in any course work, especially when education has been lacking in specific training to become a reflective teacher. Wien describes teachers as needing an adult pedagogy that assists them to think in terms of the power dynamics or developmental process involved in situations they encounter. They benefit from coaching, which helps them analyze their own scripts and those of teachers around them.

Rather than waiting and reacting to issues when they arise, we suggest you periodically devote portions of your staff meetings to uncovering and appreciating the personal and cultural differences that influence teachers' practical knowledge. An activity like the following is not only good for team building, but for shaping your approach to coaching each staff member.

If I am to individualize with my staff the way I want them to individualize with children, I have to invest the time to get to know them personally. This is a big job with nineteen people, plus the children and their families. But what could be more important? My view of mentoring is to be as flexible as possible. I coached one teacher to not be so dedicated, to stop giving her all to the center and start having a life. I coached a very reliable, but mediocre worker with the children to leave the field. Those who need direction from me, get it, while others assume full responsibility for their ongoing development.

—Laura

Strategy

Play true confessions in four corners

To help people talk about their experiences and points of view, tell them it's time for some playful "true confessions." Have people get up and move for this activity. Tell the group that you are going to ask a question and then designate each corner of the room with a possible answer to choose from. There is no "right" answer and everyone gets to determine their own meaning for going to a particular corner.

Learning something new

When it comes to learning something new I usually:

- *read a book or a manual,*
- *seek out advice,*
- *look for a model, or*
- *jump in and try it.*

Once people get to a corner ask them to explain why they are there. They will usually be forthcoming about what works best for them and often have stories that offer an example of why they or their co-workers are standing in a particular spot. This is an easy, playful way to acknowledge differences on your staff. Remind everyone to make a mental note of how each of their co-workers needs to be supported in their learning process.

Follow this first round of "four corners" with one that acknowledges another potential area of difference among staff members. To keep things playful, while encouraging deeper thinking, make use of metaphors. For example, try a category like the following one:

Relating to authority figures

My family or my cultural values have taught me to respond to authority figures like one of the following animals:

- *a German shepherd*
- *a giraffe*
- *a parrot*
- *an ostrich*

The initial response to metaphors is often puzzlement, though some people immediately identify with one and rush to a corner. You may need to again stress that there is no right answer and that their task is to make their own meaning. If they still stand with a confused look, suggest they first think about what their family or culture has taught them about responding to people in authority. Then consider which of these animals might remind them of this way of being.

Ask people to explain why they have chosen a particular animal. If the group is large and your time is limited, you can have them do this in pairs and then ask for highlights to be shared with the whole group. The issue of how people approach someone in a position of authority is very relevant to the relationship you as a supervisor will build with them, even if you don't want to be seen as an authority figure. In the debriefing of this round you will likely discover who has loyalty as a primary value, who has been taught to question, obey, or ignore authority figures. This will give you insight into behaviors you might witness and hopefully spark more self-awareness on the part of staff members themselves.

Finally, try exploring people's dispositions towards change. Again, tell them to make their own meaning and go to the corner that represents what's typically true for them, as you read the following choices.

Responding to requests to change

When I'm asked to make a change, this is the song you'll hear me singing:

- *"Hi Ho, Hi Ho, it's off to work I go"*
- *"Nobody knows the trouble I've seen"*
- *"The itsy-bitsy spider went up the water spout"*
- *"If I had a hammer, I'd hammer in the morning, I'd hammer in the evening, all over this land"*

The debriefing of this final round can bring insight as well as laughter. In any given group there is usually a wide range of how people respond to someone who is bringing about changes. Some find it easy to roll with things, while others have to be dragged kicking and screaming. Many people like the change process to be slow and drawn out, and others want to quickly get on with it. You may discover that some staff members feel you haven't given them the tools with which to make the changes you want. Consider any of the responses that are shared as valuable information for your coaching relationships.

The use of metaphors in this activity makes it clear that there is no right answer you are looking for and no fixed truth to how someone interprets the meaning of, for instance, an animal's behavior or song lyrics. People often have very different reasons why they choose a particular metaphor corner. In the case of the animals above, some may choose German shepherd because, for them, it stands for obedience and loyalty, following an authority figure out of respect for the role. Others may choose German shepherd thinking it represents strong and fierce barking to challenge authority figures trying to control their behavior. Metaphors help us to examine beliefs, values, and behaviors that are not always easy to bring to the surface for discussion.

Try rereading the questions for each round of "four corners" above and practice choosing an answer for yourself. This will help you learn more about yourself and prepare you for the kinds of discussions you can have with an activity like this. Answers to these questions often reflect the concept of "scripts for action" we discussed earlier. They are instinctive responses that are embedded below your consciousness. The metaphors help us examine views and behaviors that are often unconsciously shaped by our childhoods. Most work settings don't acknowledge these scripts in a way that helps us reflect on our behaviors and interactions. Doing so in early childhood settings not only helps us understand the impact we have on children, but it clarifies where our own behaviors come from. Attitudes and behaviors that reflect our instinctive reaction to authority figures, or being asked to make changes often come from unexamined emotions or beliefs that can block our ability to learn and work collaboratively.

A major part of a director's job is to coach staff to examine changes needed. In these efforts it's helpful for everyone to understand how they tend to respond to change. When co-workers discover themselves singing different songs in different corners, they can recognize possible sources of tension between them and gain more empathy. Activities such as these create an acknowledgment and respect for differences, creating a foundation for more productive mentoring relationships.

Principle

Provide Choices for Different Needs and Interests

Take time to remember something important you learned in your adult life, and consider what motivated you to pursue this. Most likely you had a compelling need or particular interest that led you to and sustained your learning. How can you translate this to your coaching of caregivers and staff? They must have an interest or feel a need for the knowledge or skill you are asking them to learn. If your policies or regulations lack meaning for them, teachers are less likely to be consistent in adhering to them.

Some of the behaviors you coach for are related to policies and regulations that none of you had a hand in shaping. They come from an outside regulatory agency or administrative arm of your organization. Most compliance issues are based on behaviors that support your vision, while there are a few that might inhibit it. Each time you find a need to reinforce a regulation, coach teachers in making the connection to how it relates to your vision. You may periodically need to return to some of the vision-building activities we discussed in chapter 1. Explore how your health and safety policies are tied to creating a neighborhood feeling in your program. Why does tardiness undermine your ability to function as a learning community? Sometimes you must be creative in meeting requirements if they are to truly uphold your vision. How can you keep kids safe while encouraging them to take the risks they need for growth and development? Discussions like this are significantly more meaningful than running down a list of regulations. Only after efforts at coaching for these behaviors have failed should you shift to the managing and overseeing side of the triangle framework and seek corrective measures.

Hopefully, most of your coaching and mentoring is individualized for each staff member. You may still have staff meetings focused on a training topic, but these should evolve out of staff input, needs assessments, and interests. Choosing a focus over time, as the High/Scope research highlights, doesn't mean repeating the same training a number of times. Rather, you can come at a topic with a variety of strategies and address goals for different staff members in the same way they are asked to create curriculum that is individualized for children.

Strategy

Think of something you have learned as an adult

To rethink your approach to staff development is to identify something new you have learned in your adult life. Take a minute to remember how that happened:

- *How did you go about this learning?*
- *What motivated you and what barriers did you overcome?*
- *Did anyone else have a role in your learning? If so, how did that relationship work?*
- *If you learned on your own, what strategies did you use?*

Now compare this memory to the typical in-service training you offer in your program. How is it similar or different?

When I moved to Germany to work for the U.S. Army child development programs, I really didn't know how to do my job. I soon found out that it wouldn't work to just tell the teachers what they should be doing. I began to examine my own education to see how I had come to understand things like DAP. What had my mentors done to spark my interest and turn on my "light bulb"? Thinking about these questions helped to form my vision of how to work with the teachers at my center.

I tried adapting what I understand about Piaget's theory to my work with teachers. As I began discussions with staff, I tried to find out their prior knowledge before giving them new information or challenging what I was seeing. I did this with storytelling or concrete examples of children's work. I prompted them with questions so that they would come up with their own answers.

—**Cathy**

Most people's mental image of teacher training is a workshop setting where the director or trainer is in front of the room explaining something to the group. Was this what you remembered in the above activity? Most people say that sitting and listening to someone describe information plays a small role in their learning. Our guess is that the learning process you described above was more involved than that. It probably included such things as experimenting, reading, observing, talking things over with someone, trying out new ideas, making mistakes, and perhaps practicing over and over again. Possibly you were an apprentice to a coach or role model.

Remembering the variety of ways that adults go about learning should help you assess your work with your staff. If your approach to training is limited to "telling" sessions or workshop formats, you might be missing the boat.

Strategy

Train with multiple intelligences *in mind*

Howard Gardner first brought us the term "multiple intelligences," now frequently shortened to MI. In general, keeping the concepts of MI in mind will enhance our teacher development efforts. Gardner outlines seven kinds of intelligence: spatial, logical-mathematical, interpersonal, intrapersonal, musical, kinesthetic, and verbal-linguistic (1983). Finding or creating an MI self-assessment checklist for staff to complete alerts them to these different learning modes for children, themselves, and their co-workers. A sample one is included in the appendix in the back of this book. You can simultaneously focus on an early childhood topic and explore the concept of multiple intelligences by having teachers share their understandings using the different modes of MI. Here's an example. Consider how you might adapt it for a training topic your staff wants to have as a focus for a period of time.

For example, to investigate the concept of the book *The Good Preschool Teacher* by Bill Ayers, set up MI learning stations where staff share what they understand.

- *For spatial intelligence, ask them to draw or paint a representation of the qualities of a good teacher.*
- *For logical-mathematical intelligence, give them the task of creating a step-by-step diagram or description of the qualities of a good teacher.*
- *For interpersonal intelligence, have them explore working with a partner or small group to brainstorm a list of the qualities of a good teacher.*
- *For intrapersonal intelligence, have staff work alone to reflect on a good teacher they have had, considering the qualities that made this teacher so effective.*

- *For kinesthetic intelligence, give them materials to build a 3-D model that represents the qualities of a good teacher.*
- *For musical intelligence, have teachers create a rap or song about the qualities.*
- *For verbal-linguistic intelligence, suggest staff write a short story or poem about a good teacher and then read it aloud.*

Whatever your training focus, you can adapt this activity and use it over time to deepen understandings. You can combine it with other professional resources such as checklists, articles, videos, or books. For instance set up MI learning stations to explore toddler social-emotional, sensory, or motor needs in conjunction with resources such as the video *Time with Toddlers*, the *Toddlers* series from Teaching Strategies, or the infant and toddler videos and training modules from West End Laboratories. Good books to use on this topic include *Multi-Cultural Issues in Child Care*, *Trusting Toddlers* by Anne Stonehouse, and children's books such as *The Runaway Bunny* by Margaret Wise Brown, and *Mama Do You Love Me?* by Barbara Joosse.

As you move between these resources, don't be concerned about repetition or duplication. As long as you keep things lively and meaningful, you will provide a variety of opportunities for staff to construct their understandings in the way that works best for their learning process. Sometimes do the learning stations first, followed by a section from one of the recommended videos. On other occasions, summarize part of a reading as it relates to the video or something uncovered at one of the MI stations. Space permitting, you could even leave the learning stations set up long term in your staff room with ongoing opportunities for self-directed learning.

Strategy

Uncover and cultivate passions

Most directors are inclined to spend precious training dollars on identified weaknesses in staff. But if we heed the theories of adult learning and our principle of providing for different needs and interests, it's important to offer staff opportunities to select training they would like to receive. We tend to worry that they will choose things different from our assessment of their training needs, and indeed, this might sometimes happen. But if you want the adults in your program to be excited about and committed to learning, you need to respect the different directions that might take.

The operative words here are *excited* and *committed.* When emotions get connected to motivation, significant change is more likely to occur. If a staff member wants to really hone expertise in puppetry, but her child guidance skills are lacking, how might learning about puppets improve her guidance of children? It's important to go beyond considerations of how puppets might play a role in her guidance strategies. Assess the potential of how the learning process might influence her work in other arenas. What does it take to really master puppetry? Those who have expertise in this area will tell you that good observation skills and empathy are needed for character development in puppets. If puppets are to go beyond entertainment and address the social, emotional, and learning needs of children, puppeteers need to understand children's issues and ways of thinking.

Create opportunities for each of your staff members to identify passions they want to pursue. Sometimes this requires activities of values clarification, storytelling, and sharing of favorite objects. You might ask teachers to each bring samples of something they are collecting—spoons, shells, buttons, pipes, postcards, antique tools, objects with a frog motif. Discuss what got them interested in this and any stories associated with the collection. On another occasion have them bring a photograph or object that represents a triumph in their life. Spend time in a staff meeting having each person identify one thing they'd really like to understand or be able to do before they die. There are ways for your coaching to continue to stimulate this interest which will enliven you, your staff, and the experiences they offer to the children.

For instance, as you learn about a strong interest a staff member has, keep your eye out for related literature or workshops that you can offer them. Remind the staff member of their individual interests as you engage in other discussion. If someone has a strong attachment to animals, periodically ask them to share an understanding they have from this interest that might offer insights into reading cues from children or their family members. Perhaps there are staff members who like to garden, go biking, quilt, or collect rocks. Find ways for these interests to be brought into discussions and the classroom.

For any of these ideas to work, you must be a suitable model. Spend time with your staff showing them the passion you have about something. Bring in photographs, a poem, story, or article. It might be a volunteer project that has nothing to do with children, something you are collecting, information you are trying to acquire, or a skill you want to master. Work together as a staff to find ways to explore what you care deeply about. Have a space in your staff room where you rotate special things staff members bring from home to share. Don't underestimate this as effective coaching and staff development.

———————————

Our budget allows up to forty hours a year for each staff member to receive some kind of training. Because we recognize that not everybody learns in the same way, most of this money goes to individual training plans, rather than center-wide workshops. We have some teachers who have used the money to improve their literacy skills, while others have attended science or art programs that aren't specifically related to early childhood. My theory is that if you strengthen a passion, you strengthen the teacher.

—Laura

Strategy

Redefine appropriate topics for staff development

Because we have a workforce with limited training in early childhood education, we often have tunnel vision when it comes to thinking about staff development. Teachers typically need training on setting up learning environments, planning curriculum, child development and guidance, working with parents, and a variety of health and safety concerns. It's useful to broaden our notions about topics that are appropriate for our staff development.

If a staff member longs to attend a class to learn skills in bicycle or auto repair, how might that benefit your center? What about plumbing, weaving, contra dancing, or computer software? Are there workshops in your area on community organizing, leadership development, advocacy skills, or facilitating meetings and group dynamics? Perhaps some of your teachers would like to attend or you could go as a whole staff for this month's in-service training.

For example, you might set up a series of workshops with an American Sign Language, Spanish, or Chinese instructor to help your staff work better with more diverse families. Consider scheduling training with a physical therapist on sensory integration activities, with a mental health therapist on eating disorders or addictive behaviors, or an architect, landscaper, or art specialist on principles of design. Attending some cultural performances together also enhances the development of your learning community. Just as we want teachers to break out of the little boxes that confine their thinking about curriculum, you need to expand your definition of appropriate training.

I have been offering a six-hour workshop for teachers to help them understand the value of active, self-initiated, collaborative play and its relationship to self-esteem. We start the day by giving out incentives or door prizes for specific accomplishments. For example, a prize for those people who traveled the furthest or have taught the most years. Everyone gets a prize. After our door prizes are given out we have people measure how it impacted their self-esteem by placing a colored dot on a wall chart.

The workshop continues with teachers visiting a variety of learning centers we have set up. These are adult-oriented with materials such as a large block of ice with hammers, chisels, and drills; plaster, gauze, and collage materials for making face masks; a variety of musical instruments from different cultures; and a section of power tools and wood scraps.

We provide a two-hour free play time with two facilitators to help. Most people move around after about an hour. We do not make people rotate or try every activity. The play becomes more complex and creative. People combine things and use equipment in unusual ways. At the end we again have the participants measure their self-esteem on the wall chart. In every case after the free play, self-esteem measurements go off the charts. Creativity, learning, risk taking all happen without the external rewards and incentives. People feel much better about themselves after the play time then they did when they received the prizes. This is a powerful staff development experience.

—Margo

Principle

Emphasize Dispositions as Much as Skills and Knowledge

Teacher dispositions are as critical to their effectiveness as are skills and knowledge. We first began to think about the idea of teacher dispositions from reading the work of Lilian Katz. She defines disposition as the habit of mind or tendency to respond to situations in certain ways. Katz stresses that teacher educators should be trying to strengthen worthwhile dispositions for their work with children and families and weaken those that are unhelpful dispositions.

This idea proved so useful in our work that in our first book, *Training Teachers: A Harvest of Theory and Practice,* we devoted an entire section to our evolving thinking about the importance of coaching for dispositions. We identified the dispositions we have seen in masterful teachers and reviewed these for teachers to consider in our third book, *Reflecting Teachers Lives: A Handbook for Planning Child-Centered Curriculum.* We believe these dispositions are so central to effective teaching that they are worth restating again here, especially in the context of creating a caring, learning community in your program. As you read through the following list, consider how your approach to in-service training supports or undermines these dispositions.

Master teachers:

- have delight and curiosity about children's development,
- value children's play,
- expect continuous change and challenge,
- are willing to take risks and make mistakes,
- take regular time for reflection and self-examination,
- seek collaboration and peer support, and
- serve as visionary watchdogs and whistle-blowers.

Too often directors say and do things with staff that may unintentionally undermine some of these dispositions. If you keep the staff focused on paperwork, rather than the children, it will be difficult for them to take delight in the play that is unfolding. Requiring teachers to regularly use checklists and assessment tools can quickly take the joy out of observation and documenting children's development. Teachers who are frequently reminded about rules and regulations are unlikely to trust their own thinking or risk trying new things in their work. Like most people, teachers have difficulty sustaining a vision for change if they don't experience support for the risks they take in their daily lives.

On the other hand, some directors behave in ways that support constructive dispositions in the staff members they supervise. For example, when you set up peer mentoring relationships, you encourage collaboration and peer support. If you regularly share observations and hypotheses about children's activities, you model a disposition you want teachers to acquire, that of curiosity. As you devote time in staff meetings to uncovering the elements of childhood and community that you want as the foundation for your program, you strengthen your staff's mind-set to resist pressures from parents for an inappropriate academic curriculum.

If your goal is to strengthen self-confidence and independence and to weaken passivity and dependence in your staff, you will be encouraging and validating staff ideas in all your coaching work. Giving caregivers opportunities to analyze video footage of children in their room will probably promote more self-examination than most verbal feedback you give them. Suggesting that co-workers observe some children at play while you handle their classroom responsibilities has the potential to pique their excitement about child development more than giving them an article to read.

As you develop individual training goals for teachers, consider the dispositions you would like to reinforce in each teacher. Then think through your coaching strategies and consider the underlying dispositions each strategy could strengthen or undermine.

Strategy

Identify how dispositions look in practice

The concept of dispositions can be nothing but an abstract word or personal inference unless you develop shared understandings of how this looks in day-to-day work life. In *Reflecting Children's Lives,* we translated each of the dispositions listed above into general behaviors described on an assessment continuum. An even better staff development strategy is to involve teachers in helping you define the dispositions most

helpful for your program's vision and then together develop
concrete descriptions of what they might look like in practice.
Here's an example from a series of discussions on dispositions
towards mess, risk taking, and schedules.

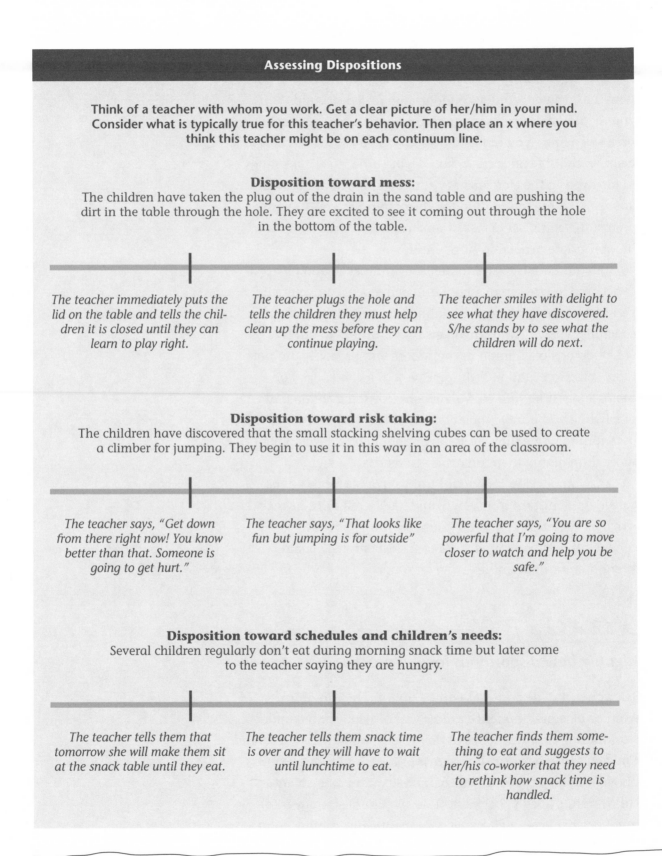

Assessing Dispositions

Think of a teacher with whom you work. Get a clear picture of her/him in your mind. Consider what is typically true for this teacher's behavior. Then place an x where you think this teacher might be on each continuum line.

Disposition toward mess:
The children have taken the plug out of the drain in the sand table and are pushing the dirt in the table through the hole. They are excited to see it coming out through the hole in the bottom of the table.

The teacher immediately puts the lid on the table and tells the children it is closed until they can learn to play right.

The teacher plugs the hole and tells the children they must help clean up the mess before they can continue playing.

The teacher smiles with delight to see what they have discovered. S/he stands by to see what the children will do next.

Disposition toward risk taking:
The children have discovered that the small stacking shelving cubes can be used to create a climber for jumping. They begin to use it in this way in an area of the classroom.

The teacher says, "Get down from there right now! You know better than that. Someone is going to get hurt."

The teacher says, "That looks like fun but jumping is for outside"

The teacher says, "You are so powerful that I'm going to move closer to watch and help you be safe."

Disposition toward schedules and children's needs:
Several children regularly don't eat during morning snack time but later come to the teacher saying they are hungry.

The teacher tells them that tomorrow she will make them sit at the snack table until they eat.

The teacher tells them snack time is over and they will have to wait until lunchtime to eat.

The teacher finds them something to eat and suggests to her/his co-worker that they need to rethink how snack time is handled.

To connect dispositions with behaviors under discussion, you can represent a continuum across the floor and ask teachers to stand next to the response that best represents what they would do. This usually uncovers differences that can lead to tension and conflict among the staff. A coaching process that helps teachers collaboratively identify their underlying habits of mind in typical early childhood situations will lead to more self-reflection and fewer knee-jerk reactions.

Strategy

Discover with dots

When they have more expertise and child development knowledge than a given caregiver, it's often easy for directors to identify problems in their practices. Sometimes you can walk in a room and immediately see something that needs "fixing." As a coach who is focused on cultivating dispositions, resist the urge to immediately offer suggestions. Instead, invent strategies that will promote reflection and self-examination.

For instance, rather than tell caregivers that their room arrangement is a setup for continual conflicts between children, give them a way to discover this for themselves. We've supplied teachers with dots to stick in the area of the room where and when they see conflict disrupting engaged play. At the end of the week, they discover a pattern. An activity like this may take a bit longer to solve a problem, but the results tend to be more substantial because effective dispositions are being cultivated.

Principle

Promote Observation, Collaboration, and Mentoring

A learning community has a very different feel than a typical school setting where people are expected to learn and master things for themselves. The organizational culture of our programs must counter the dominant culture's message of survival of the fittest and everyone for themselves. Most of us agree that rivalry, jealousy, victim thinking, and passive-aggressive behaviors are self-destructive to individuals and organizations. But that doesn't mean people know how to behave differently. They need coaching and structures which make it clear that together we're better and any weak link in the program deserves all the collective support we can muster.

Listening and observation skills are also central to developing a learning community. Again, active listening and objective observation aren't skills that come naturally to most of us. On the contrary, most adults need coaching to develop the consistent habit of paraphrasing and acknowledging what they hear in order to build trust and identify misunderstandings. Likewise, adults need to give equally careful attention to what children say, restating and affirming what they say to garner a feeling of respect as well as language development.

Strategy

Set up a peer-coaching system

Ideally you will work to get a peer-coaching process in place, one that works well for your program. Hopefully, it will also then contribute to other programs in your early childhood community. This involves identifying staff members who want to make a career of this work with children, and who show signs of mastering the needed dispositions, skills, and knowledge to do so. You can offer them opportunities to nurture new teachers in your program as well as exploring adult learning and human development theories.

As a director, start with yourself, enhancing your own understandings of adult pedagogy and empowerment. Practice your mentoring skills with your most able staff members so that before long, you can have a peer coaching system in place. From there you could join with other directors or training institutions in your area to set up a wider exchange of mentor teachers who receive training and compensation for coaching staff members in other programs. These kinds of mentoring programs are emerging across the country and are helping to both improve the quality of programs and stabilize our workforce. A resource for learning about these initiatives is listed at the end of this chapter.

I learned from one of my board members who lived in the corporate world that I should think of myself as a CEO and mentor my lead teachers as my vice presidents. Strange as that sounded at first, it became a good strategy. I directed most of my mentoring energy to them and told them to do likewise with the staff in their rooms. I brought them current research, ideas, articles, and information from the community. We went as a group together to conferences and to Worthy Wage Day activities. And we continually talked about what we were learning and what we still needed to know. I was responsive to their ideas and issues while continually requiring them to take one more step to grow.

—Julie

Strategy

Build collaborative and mentoring relationships

As a group, take time to identify the strengths of each staff member and each room. For each, probe to discover what might be called the "signature feature," a particular attribute or skill that contributes something unique to your program. Begin an inquiry as to who wants to be known for what expertise. Whether you develop a formal or informal peer mentoring system, this recognition will strengthen your learning community. Pairing people for collaborative tasks that cross rooms and age groups can keep the learning mutual. The following list of tips will help you move toward these mentoring relationships in your program.

- *Choose a mutual focus for learning and set individual goals.*
- *Visit each other's rooms and rooms in other programs.*
- *Read and discuss relevant literature together.*
- *Tell stories of things you've observed related to your focus.*
- *Observe a child together and share notes.*
- *Examine children's portfolio collections together.*
- *Facilitate a staff meeting together on your topic.*
- *Submit a workshop proposal together for a conference.*
- *Write articles together for your program and other professional newsletters.*

We are a group of diverse individuals in our program who have learned to collaborate, sustain momentum, and flourish over time. Here are the key elements that have been instrumental in our continued progress:

Passion

Our passion for what we do goes way beyond our commitment to the work. Commitments seem to drain us, but our passion continues to fuel us. We are a group of individuals who came together already passionate about our work with children. Joining together with others who shared this level of devotion offers us an unstoppable degree of momentum.

Shared Vision

We want our mission statement to be more than words on a paper. It serves to keep our group's energy focused. Our shared vision of purpose and philosophy is a continual resource to reaffirm our individual contributions and actions. It has helped us turn our individual differences into strengths over time.

Self-Reflection/Lifelong Learning

Our team has access to our fullest potential because each of us possess a willingness to self-reflect on personal strengths and challenges. Looking inward provides us opportunities to continually discover our emerging talents and growing edges. We all believe that learning is a lifelong process and we are all "works in progress" along this continuum.

Creative Energy

Our team thrives because we create an atmosphere that values free-flowing exchanges, fosters vision, and limits judgment. Our members share a spirit of creative thought, feeding off each other's ideas and building on our own ideas. This environment provides a scaffold for learning, originality, and energy.

Risk Taking

The challenges of our work have presented a different degree of risk for each of us. The willingness to take on these risks and others has been crucial to our longevity. For us to succeed as individuals, our group has offered us the support and security that encourages our risk taking. Our members feel comfortable with the connections and in the trusting environment that we co-create.

I've noticed that when we are all out together, we've developed a unique way of walking. We tend to have a constant flow in and out of smaller conversations—a sort of drifting and shifting from group to group as we all move in the same direction. You have your choice of discussions about different ideas, projects, and visions. You can put your ten cents in one exchange and then just speed up or slow down your walking pace to join another group. It's really pretty amazing.

—Wendy

Strategy

Become a community of listeners and observers

A director has a unique opportunity to help teachers become more acute and discriminating observers of children's work and play, and of each other. With each visit to a room you have opportunities to coach caregivers and teachers by describing even a small conversation or activity you have witnessed. You can informally share detailed descriptions in quick conversations in the hallways and in staff meetings. This modeling shows staff that you value stories that come from listening and observing and gives them a sense of how to do it themselves.

Every so often I use staff meetings to practice sharing our different views. I choose topics that may initially seem unrelated to our work with children, but they help us sharpen analytic skills and clarify our values. For instance, I brought in copies of a newspaper article about a strike at a nursing home where some of our parents work. We discussed the issues that were raised in the article and shared our own opinions. As the discussion became heated, we had great practice in sharing different perspectives and learning how to disagree. The experience of examining the social, political, and economic interests behind events in our community ultimately enhances our ability to be an anti-bias program.

—Ellen

Strategy

Practice active listening, informally and formally

When your regular communications include active listening skills you are providing experiential learning for others in your program. People feel heard and respected and come to recognize the value of natural paraphrasing as a way of acknowledging that they understand what is being said.

It's useful to take time in staff meetings to specifically outline and practice active listening skills. Have people practice in pairs with role-plays or topics you know to be full of emotion for the staff.

As a coach, your job is to remind people to first paraphrase what they are hearing before offering a response. Using paraphrasing may not be a way people normally want to conduct conversations, but it's a useful skill to call on when faced with tension, conflict, or miscommunication with a co-worker or parent.

Strategy

Cultivate observation as a skill and an art

Most teachers come to our programs with no formal training in observation skills. Some come having taken course work that made the process tedious and boring. Your coaching must address both of these possibilities, helping teachers acquire the ability to gather objective data and to become curious about what they are seeing. When observation skills are refined, teachers can learn more about child development as they cultivate the art of interpretation of what they are seeing.

Provide ongoing opportunities in meetings for your staff to practice their observation skill. Use photographs and video clips with the following questions to guide your discussions. As the staff share their observations and analyses, you can point out the expanded set of possibilities to consider when the process is a collaborative one.

Questions for observing children:

- *What did I specifically see?*
- *What do I think is most significant about this experience for the child? Why?*
- *What does my data reveal about what the child knows and can do?*
- *What can I say about how this child feels about her/himself?*

Strategy

Learn to observe in many ways

Teachers will grow in their observation skills when you coach them to look closely at the world around them. As they learn to stop and smell the flowers, their eyes get sharper, their hearts become softer, and they begin to see the world as children do. The following activities are playful and useful for skill building:

- *Try putting pictures or relevant books in the staff room and restrooms—"spot-the-difference," "find the hidden object," or 3-D Magic Eye children's books are great ways to build observation skills.*

- *Offer magnifying glasses, telescopes, color paddles, kaleidoscopes, and other optical "toys" for teachers to play with in the staff room. Bring them to staff meetings and have teachers use them and talk about new ways they are seeing the world.*

- *Include books in your staff library and signs around the building with quotes from naturalists and artists using beautiful detailed descriptions of nature and animals.*

- *Display engaging descriptive observations and quotes about children written by some of our profession's best observers and writers, such as Vivian Paley, Jim Greenman, Elizabeth Jones, and Loris Malagucci. These further expose staff to the power of the skill and art of descriptive observation.*

- *Do your own observations and storytelling about children's activities, sharing your excitement, delight, and curiosity with staff and families. Model the value of visual documentation stories by sharing written notes, photographs, and children's work samples on bulletin boards and in homemade books. These can be a coaching system to enhance your staff's observation skills and their ability to analyze and use descriptive language.*

One of my best coaching strategies is to personally get to know every child so that I have stories to bring to our conversations. When I share stories about individual children with my staff it puts us on the same side of the table. It alerts them to what I value and they start gathering stories to share with me.

—Laura

Principle

Create a Culture of Curiosity, Research, and Storytelling

Rather than portraying staff development as a process where teachers learn from "experts," cultivating a disposition of inquisitiveness and a desire to analyze activities will support teachers in their self-development. When they are encouraged to develop and pursue questions about what they are seeing and hearing, teachers become participatory researchers. The stories of their discoveries can generate learning and excitement in others.

"Researching" the significance of children's activities encourages teachers to see children's play and their own work as more valuable. Informal research projects strengthen observation, documentation, and collaboration skills. Paying closer attention to the seemingly ordinary events of the classroom helps teachers see things in a new light. They are motivated to reflect on their previously unexamined responses to children.

Strategy

Launch a research project

Identify a topic about children's behavior that seems to generate a lot of teacher attention, if not discussion. Consider a question related to this that teachers could focus some observations on. Perhaps provide some simple observation forms for them to document each instance related to the question that they notice. You may need to coach them in initially recognizing the details of children's conversation and play. You can collaborate in analyzing and hypothesizing about its significance. Here's an example of how one research project evolved, excerpted from a lovely documentation display.

In the fall of this year, our program was growing an emergent curriculum project around children's interests in firefighters. As we discussed our observations we became fascinated with the variety of sounds children used in their firefighter play. There were sounds of sirens, water squirting, fire burning, and rescue efforts. As teachers, we kept wanting the children to use their "inside voices" to keep the noise down. But the more we listened and watched we noticed the children seemed to use sounds very purposefully, not just to represent the sounds of fire fighting. These were intense and repetitive sounds. It was as if these sounds helped them more fully experience the emotions of their drama and helped them feel more powerful and in control of their fear of fire.

On the way to work on one of these fire fighting days I happened to hear a gospel singer interviewed on the radio. He said his favorite songs were the old Negro spirituals that slaves sang as they worked in the fields. He described the sounds he used to sing the music as even more powerful than the words. They resonated throughout his body, filling him with an understanding of the meaning of the words and the experiences they described. As I heard him singing the deep, earthy sounds, I was reminded of the children's play. His description matched our hypothesis about the meaning of the sounds the children had been making.

As I shared this interview and the insight it confirmed for me with the other teachers, our curiosity surged and we wanted to know more about the role of sounds in children's play. We decided to launch an informal research project to collect data on the noise in our room. We kept observation notes for a month and then met to discuss the significance of what we observed.

The purpose of our study was not to create curriculum or intervene in children's activities, but to deepen our own understandings and ability to respond appropriately. Our observations, collaboration, and analysis of the children's play offered us an opportunity for intellectual stimulation and added meaning to our work. We began to notice things about children that we never paid attention to before. Before starting this little research project we would often stop noisy play without realizing its significance. Our research helped us develop a different relationship to the "noise" in our room. Rather than always getting annoyed, we now try to watch and listen to decide on its meaning and the best response.

—Deborah

Strategy

Provide regular contact and descriptive feedback

With busy schedules and long "to do" lists, it's easy for a director to neglect staff when things seem to be going okay. You might even find yourself trying to slip in the door unnoticed so that you can get right to the tasks on your desk.

Teachers need more than annual evaluations to get a sense of how you see their work at the center. A manager does performance evaluations, but a coach consistently offers encouragement and descriptive feedback. As the ship's captain, your leadership is like a magnet to stay on course. Ask each staff member for an aspect of their work in which they would like some coaching and feedback from you. On the managing and overseeing side of your triangle framework, schedule time to do this and treat it as importantly as you do the other mandates on your calendar. Then on the coaching side, devise some observation and feedback strategies that are specific and supportive. And don't forget to just check in with everyone each day with personal greetings. How would you feel if someone in your family was home all day but never spoke with you?

I'm a fairly task-oriented person. Not long after I started working at our center, the cook took me aside and told me I needed to be sure to go around and greet each teacher every day before I start on other tasks. I had been afraid of getting sucked into problems and not tending to the list of things to do on my desk. But the teachers are stuck in a room all day and don't have the mobility to come and go as I do. This simple reminder from our cook made sense and when I began doing it, it made a huge difference in my relationship with the staff. Now I talk to everybody all of the time. These personal connections reinforce why we are here and my vision for how it feels to be in our program.

—Laura

Strategy

Develop questions to guide your own observations

It's helpful to have a set of mental questions to guide your observations of teachers. These questions can parallel those that you want caregivers to be using with their observations of children. They will help you clarify what you are seeing in relationship to the focus the teacher has requested for your feedback. Ask yourself the following questions:

- *What am I specifically seeing?*
- *What is my first reaction or judgment?*
- *How would I name the essence of this experience for this teacher?*
- *How can I account for what I am seeing? Why might she be behaving in this way?*
- *What strengths do I see in this teacher?*
- *What could he do differently to be more successful?*
- *What understanding about child development would be helpful?*
- *What disposition do I want to strengthen or weaken?*

I get energy around my work on interpersonal relationships with people. It's especially challenging for me to stick with relationships when people are not pulling their weight. I get annoyed, believing I am letting these people hang on when they really should leave. What I have realized is that the first place I need to start is with my own attitude. When I take the viewpoint that we are a community trying to make this work together, then one person's difficulties impact us all. Rather than always seeing what's wrong about a staff person, I work to promote their growth and create a climate where each person is recognized for the contribution they make to the larger group. I've found that the investment this takes is well worth it because we learn how to get through the rough times together and come out a stronger team in the long run.

—Ellen

Strategy

Practice your feedback with Cassandra

Consider this scene and the possible responses you might make. Then bring the scenario to your staff meeting and ask how each response would be received. You will get valuable information for developing yourself as a coach.

Cassandra is a new teacher in your young three-year-old room. She recently graduated with a two-year degree in early childhood educa-tion and has lots of enthusiasm and good ideas, especially for curriculum activities. Her good ideas often end up in chaos, however, with you having to go in and help her gain control of the kids and the classroom activities. During small group time today the activity she has planned is fingerpainting on the tabletops. As you enter you see her pleading with a couple of kids to stay in time-out chairs, as she chases others to keep them from getting paint on the walls and toys.

How would you respond?

a) You say, "Cassandra, remember we don't use time out in this program."

b) You jump in and take control, saying, "What a mess! Things are out of control. You get these three kids to the sink to wash up, and I'll get the paint cleaned off the table."

c) You say, "Wow, Cassandra. What a wonderful sensory activity you've planned. The children really like getting into paint, but you look frazzled. How can I help?"

d) You say, "Oh, you look too busy to talk. I'll come back later," and you leave immediately.

e) Other responses you might make:

Consider how each response might make Cassandra feel. What disposition might be strengthened or weakened by each response?

Strategy

Practice with stories

As a final strategy for this side of the triangle framework, read the following stories about two directors, Becky Brown and Yolanda Young. Analyze the nuances of their approaches with the questions that follow. Then review the comparative charts we offer, which highlight the difference between a manager and a coach.

Becky's Story

Director Becky Brown is having her regular meeting with one of her teachers, Juanita, to go over curriculum plans and individualizing for children of concern. She brought the performance standard checklist to review that all requirements are being met.

Juanita knows how to complete all her paperwork and each week dutifully fills in all the boxes on the planning form. As she and Becky talk, Juanita feels a bit guilty when Becky compliments her for the variety of finger plays included for her circle times. The truth is that Juanita never got to those finger plays because during circle time this week the kids were all excited to tell new baby stories after Jami told everybody he had a new sister. They just didn't seem interested in doing what she had planned for circle time. Juanita wonders if she's really a good teacher.

Becky asks Juanita how this month's weekly themes around transportation went. She compliments Juanita on all the transportation activities her plans indicate. Again, Juanita doesn't know what to say. The truth is, the kids weren't very interested in most of the transportation projects she offered. She put boats in the water table, trucks in the block area, and each day a new art project with the transportation theme. Many of the kids stayed in the house area, feeding doll babies, burping them, and putting them to bed. Juanita wishes she had more dolls because there's a lot of competition for them.

Becky reminds Juanita that she doesn't have much documentation of her individual planning and this is a requirement. Juanita says this is something she has a hard time with. Should she admit that she really doesn't get why this is such a big deal and she can't find time to write all this stuff? She keeps quiet. Becky reminds Juanita that this requirement is so very important and she'll review again how to do it. She tells Juanita to get out one child's assessment records, find an area of weakness, and plan an activity around that to do with the child. Juanita dutifully complies by writing down that she will work with Jami on his colors. She smiles to communicate she now understands, but this paperwork still doesn't have much meaning for her teaching. She thinks it will be hard to get Jami interested in colors when all he wants to do is put the doll babies to sleep.

Finally, Becky pulls out the list of this year's curriculum themes and gives Juanita the suggested activities for the upcoming month. She reminds her to get a list of any supplies she needs turned in by the fifteenth. Becky suggests Juanita talk to the other teachers about what they're planning to see if materials can be shared. As she leaves, Becky reminds Juanita about next week's required training on "Math Their Way" and also to get her parent newsletter article turned in on time.

Yolanda's Story

Director Yolanda Young is looking forward to dropping in on the teachers in the Rainbow Room during their planning time today. She's excited to show them the photos and observation notes from her visit to their classroom this week. The children used tape and string to invent an amazing crane to lift the blocks as they played in the block area.

During the meeting they read and delight in the things they heard the children say during the play. Yolanda asks what learning and development they think was involved. They report complex problem solving, classification, math, spatial relations, and fabulous social skills to name a few. She asks if they have any ideas about individual planning from watching the play. They make notes to build on Amanda and Ryan's interest in the cranes and to address Amanda's language needs and Ryan's small motor skills.

Yolanda shares that two families are leaving the center next month. She suggests the moving theme might be linked to the children's emerging interests in moving blocks. The group brainstorms a list of books, props, pictures, and songs and hypothesizes how the children might respond to these. Yolanda offers to find a couple of luggage carts and boxes and suggests they watch what unfolds and share more at their next meeting. The teachers eagerly agree.

Yolanda asks to see documentation of this month's curriculum activities and notes on individual children. She looks at their photographs and samples of children's work. Teacher Jane has made a handmade book telling the story of play in the dress up area. There is also a set of anecdotal notes on Eric's emerging writing skills. Yolanda loves to look at these collections. She feels they help her learn so much about the children's development as well as the teachers' thinking.

Jane expresses some concerns about how much instruction to give around writing skills. Yolanda and the teachers talk for a few minutes uncovering some differing opinions. One teacher thinks that children gain self-esteem and confidence when they know they are writing letters adults can read. Another thinks that when children's invented printing is respected this confidence and positive self-image grows naturally. Yolanda inserts clarifying questions into the discussion to discover how specific observations of Eric can lead them to the answers they are seeking. "What clues does Eric give you about his confidence or frustration with writing? Does he seek help or seem concerned about adult approval? How is he involving others in his literacy play?" Yolanda offers to look for helpful resources in her files and any training opportunities in the community. She suggests they focus on this area by watching the children and comparing notes to see if they can get more insight.

The team shows Yolanda a curriculum web of activities they may offer around a bicycle race happening in their community. Yolanda says she knows that Teacher Phyllis is an avid biker and she'll be sharing her interest with children. She thinks a number of parents will also be involved. The teachers ask Yolanda if they need to transfer all of their ideas onto the standard curriculum form or if they can just use the web as their plan. Yolanda is cautious, reminding them of the elements needed in a plan:

- There should be attention to arranging the learning environment so that children's curiosity is stimulated.
- Props should be added to sustain individual and group interests the teachers have noticed.
- Different materials should be made available for children to represent their ideas.
- Provision should be made for all the developmental tasks children need to pursue (such as social, emotional, large- and small-motor, language, and literacy skills).

Yolanda says if the teachers can invent something that addresses these elements but better meets their needs, she'll advocate for its use.

Compare the approach of these directors by answering the following questions:

- What goals do Becky and Yolanda seem to have for their programs (for curriculum, for children and families, for staff development)?
- What specific strategies and approaches are they each using to reach their goals?

- How do Becky and Yolanda's approaches encourage or undermine teacher dispositions needed for a caring and learning community?

Consider your approach in light of Becky and Yolanda

As you spent time examining the approach Becky and Yolanda take in directing their programs, did you see yourself in one of them? Becky is a highly organized, efficient director who has developed and mastered systems to guide her program. She operates primarily from the managing and overseeing side of our triangle framework. As she conferences with Juanita, we see her using techniques that are taught in management courses—using checklists, giving descriptive feedback, offering praise and concrete assistance in addressing a weakness. But how effective has she been in coaching a promising teacher like Juanita?

In some ways Becky's approach actually undermines her goal of supporting Juanita. She reinforces the dispositions of distrusting one's own ideas and intuition and relying on authority outside oneself. Her approach encourages Juanita to focus more attention on the rules and regulations than on the children.

Yolanda, on the other hand, operates more clearly from the coaching and mentoring side of the triangle framework. She keeps herself attuned to the real happenings of her program and builds her coaching activities and interactions around meaningful events taking place. In fact, the unfolding events and the daily lives of the people in her program are the foundation for her guidance. We see a glimpse of her thinking about managing and overseeing in her response to the teachers about requirements in documenting curriculum plans. She is clear about standards and elements for quality, but flexible in giving teachers autonomy in how they meet these. Yolanda mentors with genuine interests, ideas, and resources rather than rules and regulations.

If you were to do a comparative analysis of Becky and Yolanda's approach to directing, here's how it might look. As you read the items in each column, put check marks beside the ones that are closest to your thinking and behavior. Then decide if you are satisfied with the balance in the roles you play in the triangle framework.

Becky	Yolanda
Goals	
• Meeting standards through compliance and conformity. Relies on checklists and paperwork to demonstrate goals are being met.	• Creating a learning community through active involvement of children, families, and staff. Evaluating progress toward goals based on people's relationships and self-initiated involvement.
• Weekly pre-planned curriculum activities coordinated around yearly themes.	• Teacher-initiated curriculum planning based on observation, unfolding events, and knowledge of children and families.
• Having parents see their children participating in posted activities. Keeping parents informed with newsletter.	• Reflect the lives and events of children and their families in the curriculum. Parents are central to the evolution of what is planned for the curriculum and environment.
• Assessing and individualizing focused on children's deficiencies.	• Assessments and plans for individualizing done in the context of emerging interests.
• Requiring all staff to attend training on information she deems important.	• Autonomous, self-reflective thinkers, collaborating in self-identified staff development activities to improve their practice.
Specific approaches and strategies	
• Reviews plans with teachers, reminding, and looking for evidence of compliance.	• Observes in classrooms and contributes to planning with ideas and resources.
• Requires standardized planning forms and a list of supplies turned in by a specific date.	• Encourages teacher collaboration to invent planning forms that reflect the quality elements and their needs.
• Gives feedback and praise based on forms; little knowledge or inquiry as to what really occurred or how the teacher felt about it.	• Engages in dialogue with teachers based on what she saw and heard; coaches by seeking their ideas and encourages deeper understandings.

Adopting the mind-set of a coach

Your personal style of directing might be different than either Becky or Yolanda's. The issue here is not one of style, but of a mind-set that translates into effective coaching strategies. When you are working with caregivers to enhance their understandings and nurture certain dispositions and skills, you will be most effective if you take off your manager's hat. If you invest in cultivating mentoring skills, you set the stage for staff members to become more autonomous, self-initiated learners.

Whether she is aware of it or not, Becky's behavior reveals a strong goal to have a staff that is in compliance and adhering to standard practices. Yolanda goes beyond that with the goal of having a staff that is thoughtful and creative in responding to the ever-changing demands of their work. She knows that teachers who are able to analyze, hypothesize, and consider diverse points of view will individualize more appropriately for children. Yolanda is coaching her staff to be reflective thinkers, not rule followers.

Setting goals and wanting teachers to be reflective doesn't automatically translate into coaching behavior. Yolanda employs specific strategies to model and nurture this goal along. She takes notes and photographs and brings them as concrete data to launch staff discussion. Her contributions in staff meetings set the tone for a reflective planning process, one that generates excitement and engagement on the part of others. She offers not only current information relevant to the children's lives, but specific resources to help the staff grow curriculum from that.

Notice the listening and communication strategies that are part of Yolanda's interactions. She restates what she hears, identifies potential conflicts, and expects there will be discussion and learning from them. When a teacher expresses a learning need, she takes it seriously and commits herself to following through with specific resources. She encourages her staff, not just to see and do things her way, but to see themselves as researchers, self-evaluators, and inventors. Yolanda communicates respect and support as she mentors her staff in upholding her high standards for quality.

Practice Assessing Your Approach

As you consider the approaches of Becky and Yolanda, are there any new insights for your own work? Make a two column chart for yourself. On the left write the heading "Current Approach" and on the right, "New Things to Try." As you fill in the chart, refer to your weekly calendar, agendas for staff meetings, and conferences with individual teachers. Be specific and honest, setting aside any excuses or hesitations. After you have filled your paper, go down the right column and set some priorities for yourself.

Working as a coach can be as rewarding for you as it is for your staff. When you encounter bouts of discouragement, remember the tenacity of the midwife and the coach who brings a team to the Olympics.

Resources for Coaching and Mentoring

This list represents a selection of titles that all reflect the notion of empowerment and transformative education. Some are titles from within the early childhood field, while other are from coaches in the world of theater improvisation, storytelling, science and literary arts, and community organizing. Each of these titles has informed our understanding of the mentoring process.

Boal, A. *Games for Actors and Non-Actors.* New York: Routledge, 1993.

Bellm, D., M. Whitebook, and P. Hnatiuk. *The Early Childhood Mentoring Curriculum and Trainers Guide.* Washington, DC: Center for the Child Care Workforce, 1997.

Breunig, G., and D. Bellm. *Early Childhood Mentoring Programs: A Survey of Community Initiatives.* Washington, DC: Center for the Early Childhood Workforce, 1996.

Carter, Margie, and Deb Curtis. *Training Teachers: A Harvest of Theory and Practice.* St. Paul: Redleaf, 1994.

Gardner, Howard. *Frames of Mind: The Theory of Multiple Intelligences.* New York: Basic Books, 1983.

————. *Multiple Intelligences: The Theory in Practice.* New York: Basic Books, 1993.

Jones, Elizabeth. *Growing Teachers: Partnerships in Staff Development.* Washington, DC: NAEYC, 1993.

Lipman, D. *The Storytelling Coach: How to Listen, Praise, and Bring Out People's Best.* Little Rock: August House, 1995.

Ruef, Kerry. *The Private Eye: Looking/Thinking by Analogy.* Seattle: Private Eye Project, 1992.

Tatum, B. *Why Are All the Black Kids Sitting Together in the Cafeteria?* New York: Basic, 1997.

Vella, J. *Learning to Listen, Learning to Teach: The Power of Dialogue in Educating Adults.* San Francisco: Jossey-Bass, 1994.

Wien, Carol Ann. *Developmentally Appropriate Practice in Real Life: Stories of Teacher Practical Knowledge.* New York: Teachers College Press, 1995.

Chapter 5

Your Role of Managing and Overseeing

Could this be your story?

Director Paula is very responsive to staff, parents, and children. She can often be found sharing a story of delight about a child, or the vision she has of her program as one big happy family. Wanting to always be available to staff and parents, Paula has an open door policy. When anyone comes to her office, she waves them in, whether she's on the phone or at the computer. Paula always says she's eager to hear what's on someone's mind, but she frequently shuffles through papers or continues to answer the phone as they set out to tell her why they've come.

The staff really like Paula, appreciating her warmth and genuine praise of their work. She often tells them, "You teachers know what you are doing and it's my job to back you up with the parents." Paula doesn't want to impose on the teachers' time and avoids scheduling meetings if there isn't some important decision pending. Teachers are glad Paula has trust in them, but you can't help notice their comments about feeling isolated and rarely having time to talk with their co-workers. Privately staff members reveal their discouragement about Paula's lack of follow-through on ideas or needs they have brought her: "She always has a good excuse, but she is continually forgetting things or misplacing papers. I'm not really sure I can count on her to do what she says."

There is also disgruntlement brewing over not knowing how they should respond to parents who are raising concerns about a teacher introducing the topic of AIDS to their children. "What does Paula think about this?" one of them asked a co-worker passing in the hall. "Are we supposed to just say what we think or wait for Paula to handle it? I wish she would provide some leadership around here!"

Managing to Make Your Vision a Reality

Paula, the director in the above story, is well liked by those in her program. Her good intentions and convincing talk paint a picture of a quality workplace. She has the notion of staff empowerment and the desire for a family feeling in her program, but ultimately, the intentional leadership required to make this a reality is missing. It's not even clear if there is a competent manager at the helm.

Throughout this book we've encouraged you to think of your work as going beyond mere management tasks. This is key if you are trying to lead your program with a vision. When you function only as a manager you are misunderstanding the coaching and community-building process so essential to your vision. However, if you neglect the managing and overseeing side of your job and operate primarily with good intentions and intuition, you soon create a credibility gap between the vision you espouse and your ability to follow through in creating it. Failing to be clear about standards and policies, or neglecting to organize all your tasks into workable systems will surely jeopardize the survival of your program, not to mention your sanity.

Picture again our triangle framework. If any side is not strong, the imbalance created can easily lead to the collapse of quality. Perhaps you are creative in developing strategies for coaching and mentoring, or excel in building and sustaining community. But for every strategy on those sides of the triangle, you need to be clear about compatible standards, systems, and resources on the management side. Without these, your good ideas are not likely to bear fruit.

There is a growing body of resources to help you with the day-to-day tasks of managing your program. You can find articles, books, and seminars to help you with such things as fund-raising, budget development, computer software, time management, and hiring and firing staff. Our intent is not to duplicate those resources here, but rather to offer a way of thinking about your managing responsibilities so that your policies and systems support, not undermine, the vision of your program as a caring and learning community. This chapter offers some principles and approaches to consider in developing policies and systems. In no way is it intended to be comprehensive, but rather to give you a taste of possibility. For more and how-to information on management see the resources listed at the end of this chapter.

Director

Cultivating the Organizational Culture You Want

Begin your managing and overseeing work by looking at the current climate in your program. Examine how you approach your tasks, and the values and priorities that your behaviors and management systems convey to the staff and families. In *A Great Place to Work,* Paula Jorde Bloom discusses her research on how the interplay between people and the environment, and between work attitudes and group dynamics, supports the professionalism of an organization. In discussing the concept of organizational climate she says, "Although it is not clear whether climate or satisfaction comes first, job satisfaction seems to be higher in schools with relatively open climates. These climates are characterized by a sense of belonging, many opportunities to interact, autonomy, and upward influence" (1988).

With our vision of early childhood programs as places for childhoods and learning communities for the adults and children alike, we might expand on the dimensions she has identified as influencing an organization's climate. We use the term "organizational culture" to describe how people live and express themselves together in that setting, while the term "climate" suggests the conditions that influence our feelings and ability to work. Obviously the concepts are interrelated, and we are grateful to both Paula Jorde Bloom and Jim Greenman for the contributions they have made in adding these components to the assessment of early childhood settings.

More recently, through the efforts of the Center for the Child Care Workforce, early childhood program staff themselves have been developing an assessment tool, the Model Work Standards, which highlights the components of work environments that are linked to quality for children in our programs. This tool is a welcome addition to our work and substantiates Bloom's point:

One valuable insight gained during an assessment of employee attitudes about their work environment is the sharper understanding of where perceptions differ between administrators and employees. One of the more common findings, for example, is that directors often believe they give far more feedback to their staff than

their teachers perceive they get. Another common difference is found in the directors' and staff's perceptions
regarding staff involvement in decisions about practices to
be followed in the center...directors typically rate the
climate more favorably than do teachers. (1985)

Bloom goes on to describe the benefits of having a systematic method to measure staff perceptions of the organizational
climate. Sometimes directors are reluctant to do this because
they fear that staff will complain about things there are no
resources to fix. However, when you welcome staff feedback on
how the work environment feels, you unlock the potential for
creative problem solving. A tool such as the Model Work
Standards helps us see clearly where we should be headed. As
with accreditation criteria, it can serve as a weather gauge and
concrete reference point for budgeting and/or grant writing.

Your organizational climate is created by a number of
factors that fall on the managing and overseeing side of the
triangle, as well as being affected by your work on the other
two sides. As a manager, you formulate long-range goals that
guide the development of your program toward your vision
over time. You are responsible for creating and upholding standards and policies that support your long-range goals. You
establish the systems that ensure and document a quality
program, embodied in the daily procedures, routines, and
schedules through which everyone involved in the program
experiences its values. You can see these tasks as a burden, as a
distraction from the work of building community, or you can
develop policies, systems, and routines that are compatible
with your vision.

When we think of principles to guide this side of our
triangle, our goal is to have them reflect our values of
embracing diversity, empowerment, and participatory democracy, as well as our vision of early childhood programs as
caring and learning communities.

To develop your thinking and help you move into action,
we recommend further study of related resources recommended
at the end of this book. In the meantime, here are some
guiding principles and a sampling of strategies to move them
into practice. Many require boldly diving in, while others allow
you to dabble, just getting your toes wet. All encourage you to
color outside the lines, to see yourself as an able player, not
helpless in the face of barriers before you. These principles

suggest a new way of seeing and acting, a reinventing of your own power on behalf of a vision for children, families, teachers, and caregivers.

Formulating Long-Range Goals to Support Your Vision

Most significant changes desired for a program require a strategic planning process. Form a commitment with staff, parent, and community involvement, and call on a consultant or agency like United Way to help design the process. Strategic plans often involve a three- to five-year time line, and that can seem daunting for a transient early childhood program. Consider entering into collaboration with other early childhood or related programs in your community to mobilize a critical mass of colleagues to share resources and support each other. When you adopt a strategic plan you have specific goals, time lines, and people responsible for action plans. This moves your managing and overseeing role to a new level of professionalism and your vision within closer reach.

Principle

Create a Continuous Cycle of Evaluation and Planning

Planning and evaluating go together like salt and pepper or peanut butter and jelly. In between is the everyday work of acting on your plans. Far too often, directors act without planning or evaluating, or they make elaborate plans that they never act on. Here are some basic strategies to keep in mind:

Because I had served on so many monitor and review teams for Head Start, I had insight into the process. When it came time for my own program review, I decided to take an active approach. Rather than sitting back and waiting for the review team to tell us about how we were doing, I wanted us to take the lead.

I began to meet regularly with the staff to determine the areas we would like feedback on. We choose those areas that we saw as our strengths and those that we wanted to improve upon. This was a powerful process because we felt more invested in the review than ever before. It meant we were requesting specific help that would be meaningful to us rather than waiting defensively for the bad news.

This process changed the way we thought about evaluation. We became less defensive about our weaknesses and more able to really utilize the feedback we received to create changes in our program. Our staff now actually looks forward to review time each year.

—Louise

Strategy

Conduct regular program evaluations

Each year your managing and overseeing work should include a method for evaluating your program. You could design your own form, survey, or interview questions, or you could use one of the standard program review assessment tools, such as the NAEYC Accreditation Criteria or the Environmental Rating Scales developed by Thelma Harms. These evaluations deserve more than a passing glance. Tally the responses and look for patterns in your strengths and areas needing improvement. Then use your strategic planning process to address the weaknesses. The annual evaluation and planning processes should complement each other, with the evaluation giving you the information to help guide strategic planning and also acting to provide milestones along the way to let you know how far toward your goals you've come.

Strategy

Develop a clear understanding of the planning process

Most libraries and bookstores have resources that outline how a business undertakes a strategic planning process and many communities have organizational development consultants that can be hired to get you started, if not guide you through the entire process. Typically a strategic plan involves these components:

- *clarity on values and vision,*
- *assessment of current needs and operations,*
- *identification of specific goals,*

- *analysis of barriers to overcome,*
- *measurable objectives with a time frame,*
- *action steps with designated people responsible, and*
- *evaluation and adjustments (see the discussion of the annual program evaluation above).*

There are both elaborate and simple strategic planning forms you can use to document your plans, decisions, and accomplishments. A simple one that works for most small to moderate-sized early childhood programs looks something like the following. Without trying to be comprehensive, we've noted an example of how the planning chart might begin to look.

VISION	Children and families in our program come from a range of cultures and economic groups		
GOALS	Diversify our population	Revamp any policies that may be barriers	Year-long staff training on anti-bias, culturally relevant programming
BARRIERS & ISSUES	Current staff homogenous	Environment only reflects Euro-American culture	Materials all in English
SPECIFIC OBJECTIVES	Hire staff of color for next 3 openings Recruit bilingual staff	One in-service workshop each month	Target relevant workshops at conferences
ACTION STEPS	Contact community organizations Attend meetings like Black Child Development and Asian Refugee Alliance. Send notices to college classes	Research training options	Write grant for additional training funds
WHO & WHEN	John, Elise by March board meeting Director and 2 lead teachers Director	Director and 2 leads; June 96	Aug 96

Strategy

Take time to plan the planning process

For a strategic planning process to be effective, it has to be thought out carefully. The planning begins long before the first meeting is held. Here are some steps to consider:

- *Decide how to make the planning process as inclusive as possible.*
- *Identify key groups to have represented.*
- *Outline elements of process, needed resources, and tools.*
- *Project the possible time line and frequency of meetings.*
- *Review helpful facilitation and group process skills.*
- *Create folders or notebooks for each planning member to keep related notes and resources organized.*
- *Begin the process with a purpose statement and review of history.*
- *Build into initial meetings activities for the planning group to get to know each other's strengths, assumptions, and hopes.*
- *Give as much attention to process as to end goals.*

When I came to direct our program I felt it had the basis to be much more than it was. The day in, day out tasks of directing are a treadmill that is difficult to get off. I knew that if we didn't formalize a plan for big changes, it would never happen. We formed a strategic planning committee of parents and staff who began to ask, "who do you think we are" in a series of focus group discussions to assess our strengths and weaknesses, our opportunities and threats. We included the kids in this. We set some priorities for our facilities, financial health, staff compensation, and strengthening our anti-bias practices. Our plan has clear goals, action steps, and a timeline so I am confident we are on the road to greatness.

—Laura

Principle

Refuse to Adopt a Scarcity Mentality

We can address both short- and long-term program needs by refusing to have a scarcity mentality. Most certainly current resources for our programs don't match our needs, let alone our dreams. However, the attitude we develop toward resources can become a self-fulfilling prophecy. If we confine our vision to the current limitations of our budget, we put policies and systems in place that can actually lower our standards, erode the quality of our programs, and lead us farther from our vision of a learning community.

As a director, your greatest challenge is to let your vision, not your current resources, drive your decision-making process. Our intent in this book is to awaken in you an active commitment to a vision that goes beyond how things are. To keep this vision alive you must regularly stir up the soil, add fertilizer, and plant new seeds. Otherwise you will find yourself drifting down the road to accommodation, adopting a scarcity mentality, and accepting the limitations of your current situation.

Carl Sussman puts it well: "Providers need to cultivate the cognitive dissonance of living with inadequate facilities while harboring an ambitious vision that could sustain a greatly enhanced program" (1998). He writes about Sandy Waddell, an inspiring director, in his article "Out of the Basement: Discovering the Value of Child Care Facilities." She decided to break out of the classic scarcity mentality of an early childhood program director and undertake an ambitious renovation of her facility.

The drive and determination necessary for such an undertaking usually leaves some disgruntled souls in its wake. When you step outside of the passive, nurturing, and accommodating roles typically assigned to females, and to those in the early childhood field, some may criticize and label you. But if your vision and principles propel you, your efforts will not only serve your program well, but uplift our profession as a whole. Each time a program breaks through the barriers placed in its path, we have another model to emulate, and momentum grows toward refusing to accept the limited vision and resources we've been given.

Perhaps you are unsure of where the energy for such determination will come from. Directors typically say they want to be realistic as they consider policies and resources for their program. "It costs too much" comes from our lips too easily in response to visionary ideas. Consider again, these concepts of being realistic and costing too much. What's the real picture of quality in your program? Is it close to your vision? What is being sacrificed? Are you or any of your staff members reaching burnout?

Remember the Langston Hughes poem "What Happens to a Dream Deferred"? What are the costs of deferring your dreams—to your energy and your physical and emotional well-being, and to that of the children, families, and staff in your program? Have you considered that this cost might be too much? We have a growing body of research and literature that is confirming this point. Until we shift how we think about the full costs of providing quality child care, we will continue to incapacitate ourselves. In the introductory chapter to her book *Reaching the Full Cost of Quality,* Barbara Willer says, "The full cost of quality therefore holds a dual meaning. It refers to the costs of program provision while fully meeting professional recommendations for high quality, while also implying the social costs that are incurred when quality is lacking" (1990).

Strategy

Move your budget toward the full cost of care

In 1990 NAEYC published *Reaching the Full Cost of Quality,* a handbook that added information and tools to their accreditation criteria to help directors compute the dollar figures of what providing quality child care really costs. Use the worksheets in appendix 4 of this book to help you build your budget around your quality needs, not your parent fees. Once you have a realistic picture of what it really costs to provide a quality program, you can use this data to challenge your own scarcity mentality.

Next use your full cost of care data to determine how your budget priorities and policies need to be refocused. To begin developing a strategic plan to address the changes you want to make, use the worksheets offered in *Reaching the Full Cost of Quality.*

Make use of all the communication systems you have in place to educate parents, board members, the general public, and policy makers about the actual dollars required to provide quality child care. Put displays on bulletin boards, articles in your parent newsletters, and letters in the mail to newspapers and legislators. In the appendix of this book you will find an example used by many programs on the annual Worthy Wage Day for child care workers—a mock invoice given to parents showing how low teacher wages are making

up the balance between parent fees and the full cost of
providing quality child care.

A previous director in our center realized that we would never get
parent involvement in the Worthy Wage Campaign until they
knew the hard, cold facts of what our teachers made. They were
absolutely shocked. As a result, we began to get a wage scale in
place, immediately invested in our lead teachers with a 50 percent
increase each year. We then began to step up our assistants and
part-time staff. This created a much stronger commitment on the
part of both the parents and our staff and took away some of the
initial antagonism that came from the huge disparity in their
economic circumstances.

—Julie

Strategy

Invest in your staff

A centerpiece of your short- and long-term goals must be
investing in teachers and caregivers. Consider ways you can
move your program along the following lines:

- *Create policies and budget line items to pay for and reward
  staff for ongoing training.*
- *Transfer some of the time and money you spend each year
  on continually recruiting and training new staff directly
  into the existing staff who want to make early childhood a
  career.*
- *Build your budget with a salary scale that goes beyond the
  high end of what is typically paid in your community.*
- *Design a career path system to help you stabilize a core of
  excellent teachers who are paid well to mentor others.*

I am a strong believer in training. I know that in order for my
program to retain excellent staff and keep them dynamic in the
classroom, I must provide opportunities for professional development. To ensure that there is a strong system in place, I protect 1
percent of my program's budget each year for training. This
includes not only training that I plan and provide in-house, but

also college classes and seminars that teachers might want to attend outside of our program, as well as the NAEYC conference. This commitment truly sets our program apart from other small ones that say they believe in training yet don't institute a formal system or budgetary support for it.

—Jim

Strategy

Be generous with your nickels and dimes

A scarcity mentality often leads directors to rationing basic tools, supplies, and paid time staff need to do their job well. Generosity in this department will build staff morale as well as competency. It will save you money and heartache in the long run.

- *Put money into carving out some kind of staff room with comfortable chairs, lighting, and a work space. Furnish it with tools teachers need: a telephone, computer, copy machine, cameras, film.*
- *Make it a policy to pay staff for time spent thinking, planning, organizing, and collaborating.*
- *Nourish caregivers and teachers with plants, flowers, and healthy treats on a regular basis.*
- *Give teachers autonomy and concrete assistance in getting the supplies they need for their work. Long delays in getting film developed or materials for a project can undermine their best efforts.*
- *Set up efficient purchasing and petty-cash systems to accompany each room's budget so that caregivers can have the things they need in a timely fashion.*

Strategy

Involve others in expanding your nickels and dimes

All centers need a budgeting system that goes beyond the families you serve for the big dollars you need. Nonprofit programs tend to write grants and hold fundraisers, while large for-profit ones can now be found seeking investors on Wall Street. Whatever your larger plan for financing your center, don't overlook the sources for your nickel and dime items right in your own community.

- *Ask parents to turn in rolls of film along with their immunization records and enrollment forms. When they regularly see photos of how their children are spending time in your center, most will gladly donate cameras, film, or time to get photos developed.*
- *Develop a system to solicit parent contributions of time, resources, and services. This could include getting film developed, donating paper, or desktop publishing services.*
- *Contact local businesses in your community. They are often glad to donate space or refreshments for events, scrap lumber for children's carpentry, remnant fabric, paper, mat board, or foam core for documentation displays.*

The secret to soliciting these donations is to build relationships and have ongoing conversations with people about your needs. It is also important to have a system in place for retrieving and storing material donations. Families and members of your business community are often more than willing to make a contribution to a program they know firsthand.

Strategy

Adopt a business mind-set when big funds are needed

This advice comes from Carl Sussman, who reminds us to adopt the core strategy of business when funds for a major project are needed—use other people's money. Traditionally, nonprofit early childhood programs have been reluctant to take out bank loans, something our counterparts in the for-profit sector do all the time. When you consider the tangible, indirect, and marketing payoffs of a major capital improvement, taking out a loan may be one of the most effective strategies for improving the learning and work environment of your program. Get someone experienced to help you crunch the numbers and then contact one of the community development loan funds listed at the end of this chapter.

Creating the Experience of Community with Your Systems

The experience people have working with an organization's systems can either alienate them or give them a sense of belonging. This is especially true when it comes to upholding rules and regulations. Your vision of a learning community can be significantly undermined by top-down systems that are rule-, not people-oriented, and that fail to involve others in a democratic process. Many organizations proudly display anti-discrimination statements and claim to embrace an anti-bias approach. But a closer look at their policies and procedures reveals cultural blinders and practices that limit who will feel at home in the program. In your efforts to simultaneously comply with standards and regulations, and grow a healthy community for your organization, consider these principles and strategies.

Principle

Involve Staff and Families in Active Exploration of Standards

Within the reach of every director is an array of carefully thought out and field-tested materials promoting professional performance standards, best practices, quality criteria, and assessment tools. Our profession has clarified the components of quality experiences for children, and efforts are underway to provide a comparable set of component standards for the staff work environment. Keeping these quality components in front of everyone is a major part of your managing and overseeing work. What systems can you put in place to involve everyone in that task and make them active players and keepers of the standards?

Strategy

Form task groups

As you undertake introducing your program to assessment tools like the Accreditation Self-Study or Model Work Standards (see appendix 2 for a sample of this latter tool), call for volunteers from your staff and families to take on different sections to study, assess, and advocate for.

This will engage them far more than being told or given all the components to read. If you present these as tools for data collecting, discussion, and decision making, the process itself will be a pedagogical strategy to help others internalize the standards of our profession. Here are some tips to help the focus groups run smoothly:

- Ask the task groups to discover what is working and what is really needed, rather than who is in compliance and who isn't.

- Ask each task group to be the eyes, ears, and mouth of its component area. Guide them to take pride in becoming an advocate for this aspect of quality, rather than adopting a complaining or policing mentality.

- Make it known that, as the director, you count on them to keep needed improvements or praise for this component area in the limelight.

- Have the task groups examine how the program policies and procedures related to their component area are affecting your organizational culture. For example, ask them to consider questions like the following:

  a) Does the paperwork system for tracking individual children support teachers' work with children or detract from it?

  b) Are the daily staffing patterns and schedules meeting the needs for consistency and communication between children, families, and staff?

  c) Are efforts underway to reduce staff turnover and appropriately reward teachers and caregivers?

As we worked toward NAEYC Accreditation, one of the biggest areas of concern was our high child-staff ratios. We knew we needed more staff at certain times of the day but it was difficult to figure out how to accomplish this with the resources we had and the lack of qualified staff willing to work with the inconsistent schedule we had to offer. We organized a group made up of board and staff volunteers to wrestle through the issues. We had five intense planning sessions where we explored options from utopia to minimal changes. We discussed the pros and cons of using volunteers, part-time staff, and combining groups of children. We decided on a plan that would work best for the staff and still provide quality for the children. We developed a floating system of four lead teachers who divided the schedule and alternated staying and taking the overflow of the children into the gross motor room. The teachers could decide to receive comp time or extra pay.

The whole process of developing this system has been great for our program. Rather than me, the director, coming up with a solution, the staff was able to create the system and in the process gain more understanding and investment in larger program operation issues.

We all came to see this collaborative process and the entire accreditation process as a way we could control quality for children. This was a powerful new way for us to think about our work. Rather than victims of the social and economic ills that impact our work, our program and classrooms provided us the opportunity to overcome negative external factors in children's lives. We successfully worked together and solved the basic but most critical of issues—ratios. The whole experience made us all into critical thinkers, ready to tackle any difficult issue.

—Mary

Strategy

Create games to enliven discussions of standards

If your goal is to solidify understandings among teachers and parents about quality learning and work environments, try turning the standards into games to play.

Sorting and matching games

These work especially well with tools formatted into comparative columns like NAEYC's *Developmentally Appropriate Practices* book, the *Essentials* book from the Council for Early Childhood Professional Recognition, or the *Caring For* or *Creative Curriculum* series from Teaching Strategies. Use the following general steps:

- *Copy the column headings onto large pieces of paper, for instance, "Appropriate/Inappropriate" for the* Developmentally Appropriate Practices *book, or "When Children Do This/They are Learning" from the* Creative Curriculum *parent booklet.*
- *Photo-enlarge and cut up the lines of text under each column and have people sort and match them into the column where they belong.*
- *As they work in this playful manner, encourage discussions about your own program.*

- *Create a third blank column for them to add what your program does in each area.*
- *When they are done give them the intact tool to compare with their columns.*

Drawing games

A version of the popular drawing game Pictionary can be another fun way for staff and parents to internalize certain quality components or procedures required in your program. The following strategy works well for visual learners and offers everyone a new memory tag for important regulations in your program (you can also turn this game into "Sculptionary" by using playdough to represent the concepts):

- *Make up slips of paper or file cards, each with one concept or quality element written on it.*
- *Divide the group into two teams.*
- *Ask one person on each team to pick a piece of paper or file card and then draw the concept on easel paper or a white board while the other team tries to guess what they are representing.*
- *Have a discussion about the concept or quality component after the answer has been guessed.*

Principle

Seek to Counter Inequities of Power and Privilege

Whether in developing your personnel or enrollment policies or setting up systems for communication, tuition collection, or health and nutrition, this principle can guide your thinking. Ask yourself questions like these: If I create a policy that all tuition must be paid by the fifth of the month, who might I be excluding from our community? When our communication systems are primarily based on handbooks, memos, and notices, are we putting anyone at a disadvantage in our program? What assumptions in our health and nutrition systems might be biased? If we extend benefits to spouses, how does that impact gay or lesbian staff who are legally not allowed to marry?

It will never be possible to address all the possible variables that diversity might bring to your program, but this principle will keep you alert to unintended bias and perpetuation of injustices that you don't want as part of your program. In many cases, it will provoke discussions that need to take place in a democracy and unearth new awareness and creativity.

It's not enough to just believe in something. I've learned over the years as a director that I have to create management systems to support the philosophy we have of being inclusive of many different types of families. One way I have done this is to have a flexible system for how families can pay their tuition. I've developed work trades where a parent works for us in the office or the classroom evenings or weekends to accomplish something I would have had to pay someone else to do. I first set up payment plans when I saw someone getting behind in their tuition. I want to ensure that we serve a variety of families, so I need to keep thinking of formal yet flexible ways respond to different needs.

—Paul

Strategy

Seek feedback from all segments of your community

Who is a part of your community? Sit down and identify all the different groups of people who might potentially be involved in your center as families, staff members, volunteers, or board members. At the very least, consider diversity along the following lines: culture and race, class, disability, gender, religion, and sexual preference. Ask three people from each of the communities you identify to review your personnel, enrollment, health, and nutrition policies, procedures, and forms.

Strategy

Expand your approach to communication

To make your program information and functions accessible to a wide variety of people, use a variety of communication systems to reach the people in your program. Consider some or all of the following alternatives: one-on-one conversations, buddy systems, phone trees, group meetings, written notices, and visual displays. In addition, take the initiative to translate key written materials into one or more other languages as a way to reach out to other potential staff and families for your program. Consider simultaneous translation for parent meetings if a number of your families speak home languages other than English.

Strategy

Make diversity and anti-bias work part of your orientations

When you do interviews or orientations for new families and staff, walk them through visual examples of how your anti-bias policies look in practice—have a variety of images on the walls, show them documentation notebooks of past curriculum projects, let them look over books, dolls, and materials to get a flavor of how you approach diversity. Also, ask prospective new families and staff what diversity they might bring to your program and how you might actively support that.

Strategy

Formulate personnel policies and systems to encourage diversity on staff

Consider the needs not only of current staff, but of the potential staff members in your community when developing personnel policies and systems. Develop flexible policies, benefit packages, and floating holidays to accommodate the diversity of staff needs.

Designing Systems to Promote Reflection and Problem Solving

If your policies provide the structure to support your vision of community, the systems that grow from them directly control people's experience of community in your program. Systems organize the many responsibilities you have as a director and shape the way staff members feel about the workplace and about themselves. Indirectly, they are a pedagogical tool, along with the specific coaching and mentoring strategies you employ. For instance, you can create procedures, paperwork, and accountability systems that foster reflection, collaboration, and active participation, rather than ones that emphasize meeting the requirements, checking off boxes, and not asking why. Inherent in this approach is the notion that people should participate in developing systems that they will be responsible for following.

Directors deal with mounds of paperwork. Some trees are sacrificed for regulatory bodies outside their programs, while others are sacrificed in order to meet their own requirements for documentation and accountability. The paperwork systems you develop and require also have a big impact on how your staff see the priorities of their work. No one likes or genuinely benefits from meaningless paperwork.

The goal of record keeping and documentation should be to support and provide evidence of progress toward your vision. You can design accountability systems that encourage particular dispositions in staff and families and enhance everyone's experience of the community you dream of creating. Make a commitment to yourself and to your vision that all documentation systems you invent encourage people to think, assess, and offer solutions to problems encountered.

Principle

Develop Child Assessment Systems that Enlist Teachers' Excitement

Across the country supervisors, special education staff, and teachers in Head Start and other early intervention programs express frustration over meeting assessment and individual planning regulations. Most admit that the systems they're using have little real meaning for them or the children. The joy of observing and following the amazing process of child development has been replaced by an accountability system that teachers dread. In contrast, when teachers are actively involved in creative and useful ways to observe, record, assess, and plan for children, they find this one of the most affirming parts of their job.

If your attention is primarily on whether your staff has their paperwork done, teachers will come to dread rather than treasure this aspect of their work. As you model and offer feedback around assessments of children, also encourage staff members' curiosity about and delight in the children's development by emphasizing your own. Share your observations, notes, and questions about children's play. Arrange for teachers to observe children as they engage in self-chosen activities (often called "play-based assessment") rather than activities directed by teachers. This encourages teachers to see that attention to children's daily activities is critical to knowing their developmental progress.

Strategy

Design forms that encourage curiosity and delight

When teachers have minimal skills in observing and individualizing for children, systems that require them to check boxes and answer "yes or no" questions retard their professional development. Instead, they need assessment systems that foster thinking and analysis and include reflective questions, problem posing, hypothesizing, interviewing, and personal reflection. Here are some examples of questions that you might put on an assessment form:

- *What did you specifically see the child(ren) doing?*
- *What is your reaction to this child and what may be influencing this in you?*
- *What is the child trying to figure out in this situation?*
- *What experiences, knowledge, or skill is the child building?*
- *What questions, inventions, or problems is the child encountering?*
- *What does this child find meaningful? challenging? frustrating?*

Strategy

Arrange for collaborative discussion among teachers

If you include collaboration as central to your formal system of assessment, teachers will learn to analyze, hypothesize, and plan next steps together. When systems encourage teachers to see themselves as researchers engaged in the process of learning about each child, they are more alive in their work and appropriate in their planning for children. Use some or all of the following suggestions to make room for collaboration:

- *Rotate teacher and/or substitute schedules to give teachers regular time to meet together.*
- *Include time in regular staff meetings for sharing highlights of an observation and collaborative hypothesizing.*
- *Post or circulate examples of collaborative discussions for teachers to learn from each other.*

I am always looking for ways to access grant money to open up some more possibilities for staff development. Oftentimes there is grant money available for particular topics or issues. When I write the proposal I try to frame our specific interests and needs around the requirements the grant is asking for. My goal is to have extra funds from grants free up staff time for planning and meeting, as well as help us acquire new resources. I know that whatever the topic or focus, the process of thinking and planning together builds a collaborative, supportive climate for all of the work we do.

We entitled one of our most successful projects "Culture, Conflict Resolution and Kids." The funds we got for this enabled us to strengthen our basic philosophical approach to staff development, curriculum development, and participation project. The extra money helped pay for staff to document real life conflicts for discussion and problem solving, as well as training on cross-cultural communications and conflict resolution. We had extra paid staff time to develop case studies with accompanying narratives, to work with children's stories and plays about setting disputes, and to set up a workshop series.

—Lisa

Principle

Involve Staff in All Phases of Evaluating Their Job Performance

In addition to the coaching and mentoring roles so important to directing work, your managing and overseeing responsibilities call for you to conduct a performance evaluation of each staff member, at least once, but preferably twice a year. You should view these functions as separate and distinct and provide that clarity for your staff. Some directors are quite comfortable with this task, while others feel awkward and avoid its formality. Evaluations are not only important for marginal or mediocre staff members. Without them, the ongoing development of experienced and master teachers can languish or stagnate.

All evaluations should include self-assessment, a focus on strengths and the development process, and clear goals and action plans for the next area of growth identified. Evaluations should be based on observable evidence gathered over time, not just the week before you conference with a caregiver. This means you must devise a system for observing as well as evaluation forms that cover the data that is important for your discussion and goal setting with staff members. Samples of forms we've developed are in appendix 6.

Strategy

Supplement checklists with observational narratives

Most approaches to staff evaluations involve using a standard form with a checklist as a quick way to rate how well the staff member is performing. This can make performance reviews efficient and fair, but quite often renders them meaningless when it comes to genuine growth and development. Checklists help make things that feel intangible more solid, but if they aren't accompanied by some narrative comments or specific observations, they can become very subjective. You might include anecdotal notes in your performance evaluation files, or consider using video or photos as tools for discussing specific considerations. These techniques capture the flavor and tone of a caregiver's performance, which are lacking in a checklist.

Strategy

Plan the cycle of supervision and evaluation

Particularly with a large staff, it's easier for you to keep track of evaluations if they fall in a regular cycle. It's also less anxiety-producing for staff if they know when they can expect to be evaluated. You may want to consider designating certain times of the year for evaluative, as opposed to coaching, observation sessions. Establish a clear cycle of supervision where you observe, document, conference, set goals, practice, observe again, document, and so forth. This practice keeps evaluation in its proper context as just one point in an ongoing cycle of growth and discovery.

Strategy

Experiment with different forms

No standard evaluation form will meet your specific needs as well as one you've designed yourself. In addition, it's important to see forms as flexible, able to change for different purposes and situations. Try developing evaluation forms together as a whole staff to ensure you've taken into account cultural differences and other issues that are important to staff members. Develop different observation forms and strategies to cover different areas of focus. Create separate evaluation forms for each position on your career ladder, acknowledging different levels of knowing and growing. Finally, experiment with different methods for staff to regularly evaluate *your* performance—anonymous feedback, direct feedback, forms from books, forms created by you and staff.

Strategy

Acknowledge the power differential in the evaluation process

Performance evaluations always reflect issues of power relationships in a workplace. You should not pretend this doesn't exist, but rather see your role as providing a mirror or snapshot for each staff member to see themselves more clearly. From this side of the triangle, your responsibility with staff is to uphold professional standards, but as with your mentoring and coaching role, your ultimate goal is to enhance teachers' power to develop. Meet together to compare their self-assessment with the one you did and discuss possible goals for the coming period. Together, create action steps toward that goal and make sure you have systems in place to follow through with these plans. On your form designate a place for staff members to sign their agreement or disagreement with your evaluation, make sure it is dated, and make sure they get a copy and a copy stays in their files.

One of the toddler teachers came to us with a background in family child care as opposed to center-based child care. She had been with the center two years when I became the director and was a highly dependable, valued employee, the kind who stays extra hours to set up or clean up, sweeps the playground, takes care of the library books, and so on. But as the head teacher, the stress of responsibility for guidance and discipline with toddlers was getting to her. During her evaluation she told me she really didn't want to be the head teacher and asked several times for a less stressful position. I gave her the option of becoming an assistant in our kindergarten program and she worked there for a year with moderate success, still having difficulty with guidance and group management.

We discussed these continuing concerns and I offered her the position as our cook. She dived into the job and was the best cook we ever had, rounding out our philosophy perfectly. Menus began to reflect what was happening in the program as well as in the larger community. The kindergarten children began writing her letters requesting specific menu items. She wrote back and told them when they could expect their requests to appear at lunch or breakfast. One of the toddlers who was fascinated with trucks of any kind was invited to the kitchen every Wednesday to "help unload" the food delivery truck. He always managed to carry something off the truck, often the large containers of spices.

One morning I arrived to find a two year old sitting on the prep table stirring a large bowl of eggs. She had a difficult separation that morning and had been invited to the kitchen to help make French toast for breakfast. This wonderful cook kept a corner of the kitchen readied for any child who needed special attention to get through the day. She knew all of the children by name, and they all knew her. She readily left the kitchen to give a helping hand to any teacher or administrator who needed it.

But alas, as budgets tend to do, ours became tight. The only way to give the teachers a raise was to do away with the lunch program and have the children bring their own lunches. As these budgetary discussions were underway, I talked to the cook and reassured her that her job was not in jeopardy, but it would likely change. She asked me if she could return to the classroom. She thought she was ready. I thought she was ready too. As we start a new year, our center cook is once again a classroom teacher. She is doing a wonderful job, even with guidance and discipline.

—Margo

Principle

Plan Training to Reflect Your Vision of a Learning Community

Along with a budget line item for in-service training, you need a careful plan for how you will spend your precious training dollars. As consultants often called upon to provide training to programs, we're discouraged by the lack of thought that goes into many of these training requests. Directors sometimes ask what topics we'd like to focus on, rather than addressing a particular training need in their program. Even those who call with a specific focus in mind seldom view our training as part of an overall plan.

To develop an effective in-service training program, it's helpful to have a focus for each individual staff member and also the program as a whole. The focus should be drawn from conducting training needs assessments and using individual performance evaluations and program tools such as those mentioned above. Mandates generated from outside agencies requiring such things as first aid, AIDS, and sexual abuse prevention training should be integrated into individual plans so that staff members are not required to attend this training more often than necessary.

Ongoing professional development should be a require-ment for everyone working in early childhood education, with a specified minimum number of hours per year which the program budget covers. However, caregivers should choose the training they want to attend within the agreed upon focus and goals that have been outlined.

Make mandatory attendance at a given training the exception rather than the rule. Isn't this the approach we want teachers to take with children? On the whole, we've seen a significant difference in the eagerness to learn of teachers who choose our training, compared with those required to attend. What a waste of limited resources to mandate attendance without ever asking what teachers need or want!

Strategy

Develop individualized training plans

In order to provide meaningful training, have staff conduct self-assessments to determine their needs and interests. Then, develop individual training plans on a specific focus. For each, identify goals, a time line, and an evaluation process. Keep track of local training opportunities, and notify teachers of ones that are relevant to their training focus. Research specific resources for them as well. Be sure to formalize some time spent observing in other rooms, reflecting, problem solving, and collaborating with a mentor as legitimate in-service training. Consider designing a portfolio system for teachers to document and show evidence of their growing understandings and skills within their training focus. Finally, don't forget to celebrate and reward achievements.

Strategy

Expand your approach to program-wide training

With individual training plans underway, it is also important to establish a focus for program-wide training to enhance your learning community as a whole. Involve families and staff in choosing a focus for a year, using information from program evaluation tools, group interests, or problems encountered. Perhaps you want to create more opportunities for children to feel powerful in your program and decide to pursue training relevant to that goal. If a child in your program is Deaf, that might be an opportunity for everyone to learn American Sign Language. Maybe there are persistent conflicts between children or the adults and everyone could benefit from training to improve listening, paraphrasing, and conflict negotiation skills. If parents repeatedly express concerns about school readiness skills, you could study how children learn to read and write and focus on developmentally appropriate ways to foster literacy skills.

Learning happens when you have a variety of strategies focusing on a topic over a period of time. Once the program-wide focus is determined, the manager's role is to design the time, resources, and delivery systems.

I was so excited to learn about emergent curriculum approaches that I couldn't wait to help my staff learn how to do this. My excitement led me to try many things and thus tend to overlook the small steps the staff were making toward my main goal. When one of the teachers accused me of wanting to have "little Adinas" running around, I thought about that statement and realized that I didn't want clones of myself. What I *did* want was my teaching staff to be the most creative teachers they could be.

I began to realize how important it is to find out from what areas the teachers feel they need training. As I began to involve them in the training process and in our work toward accreditation I saw much more sharing between classrooms and individuals. During the accreditation process I saw staff become more comfortable in speaking out in the group and even delivering presentations to others. From these experiences I realized the most important piece to working with adults in child care is to help them feel they are important in so many ways—from actually caring for the children to working as a team. Most of all my job is to help them to realize their own special talents in working with young children.

—Adina

Strategy

Provide many ways of exploring an annual focus

Think of a good early childhood classroom, where the teacher provides many ways of exploring the same concepts. Adults, too, need diverse opportunities to play and experiment with new thinking. Consider some or all of the following: arrange for classes to be held on site or locate offerings in the wider community; hire a consultant to offer a training series on the topic, with periodic visits to observe and coach; attend relevant conference sessions as a group and schedule follow-up discussions (see sample conference planning form in appendix 7); arrange for group visits to other programs known for strength in your area of focus (see appendix 8 for example of observation form designed for this purpose); identify in-house staff members to acquire the expertise and then mentor others; focus a portion of each staff meeting time for storytelling related to the focus; have a parent and teacher lead a book discussion group together; collect and display related resources, books, and articles in the staff lounge, bathrooms, office areas, and on bulletin boards.

Strategy

Acknowledge and celebrate progress toward your training goals

One of the manager's critical tasks is to make the program's growth visible to staff members and parents, who may be so deeply involved in the program that progress is invisible to them, and to the community at large, which may be completely ignorant of the strengths of the program. Consider some of these techniques: create visual displays with photos and observation notes to document progress and make it visible to all; invite visitors from the community to see what you are doing; solicit recognition in the media; celebrate accomplishments with social events and a significant purchase for the center.

Principle

View Time as a Building Block

How we think about time in our programs is directly related to the growth available for the people there. Consider time a worthy investment, not something to rush through. In *The Fifth Discipline,* Peter Senge asks, "If a meeting takes only fifteen minutes, are we really going to learn anything?" In *Developmentally Appropriate Practice in Real Life,* Carol Anne Wien, an early childhood education college instructor, writes of the dangers of structuring our child care centers around a school-like time schedule for activities and routines. She says, "Typically there is an industrial notion of time as scarce, with strictly kept time schedules and fixed purposes for activities that begin and end when the teacher specifies (often these are determined by events outside the classroom). There is a routine to be accomplished by the teacher that includes shepherding her group of children through basic needs such as toileting, eating, and napping. Conformity to teacher purposes in carrying out the routine is paramount" (1995).

Bringing these two voices together leads us to question the way we structure time for both the children and the adults in our programs. If our systems require the adults to chop their time into little blocks, what will this do for their thinking process and the way they behave with children and their families? If we organize staff meetings as a series of disjointed announcements and trainings, is it realistic to call this staff development?

Viewing time as an investment will help us guard against the fast food or artificial flower mentality. Time invested in relationships, and in sowing and growing new seeds doesn't always show immediate results or bring relief to your bottom line. But with time on their side, teachers and children in your program get more nourishment and opportunities to bloom.

Jim Greenman reminds us, "Avoiding rigid and narrow schedules that choke, or loose schedules that frighten or intoxicate, generally requires a thoughtful and complete analysis of how all the program structural elements interact—time, space, goals, organization, and people—and creative problem solving to minimize negative side effects" (1996).

The time schedules established for children and adults have a huge effect on their experience of quality. When directors look to increasing ratios or group sizes and altering staffing patterns as cost cutting or profit margin enhancement strategies, they are putting consistency and continuity for children on the chopping block. If you expect staff to use their break time for planning, or require them to plan, do paperwork, conference, and attend meetings on their own time, we will never stem the turnover crisis. Staff members need paid time to think, evaluate, and plan. This is a prerequisite for doing their job well. They need time to be together for discussions and trainings of interest, and time for visiting each other's classrooms and other environments for children out in the community. This is a building block for quality.

How you organize time in your program grows or defeats the vision you hold. Here are some strategies to consider.

Strategy

Use colored dots for analyzing how time is spent in your program

As a director, first do your own analysis of the balance of your time that is spent working on each side of the triangle framework. Take your calendar from the last couple of weeks and first, add to it anything you did that isn't noted for each day. Then use a package of colored adhesive dots or different colored pens to code each item as follows:

- *Put a red dot in front of activities that are about managing and overseeing.*
- *Put a blue dot for each item that involves coaching or mentoring.*
- *Put a green dot for the times you were intentionally working to build or support an experience of community in your program.*

Now, count the number of red, blue, and green dots you have. Are you satisfied with the balance in how you are spending your time? If there are changes you would like to make, stop here and develop some priorities and plans for yourself.

Have your staff do a similar assessment of how time is spent in their classroom. Ask them to write out their daily schedule, including all the things between the lines that they do with the children. Suggest they do the following:

- *Put a red dot beside each time block where they are making the choices or directing the children in what to do.*
- *Put a yellow dot for times when children are in a transition, a holding pattern, getting ready or waiting for the next thing.*
- *Put a green dot for times when children are free to make their own choices and initiate their own play activities.*

Similar to what you did in evaluating your time, ask teachers to look at the overall balance of dots. Encourage them to find ways to reduce the number of red and yellow dots in order to expand the blocks of time children have to engage in their self-chosen activities.

What I have found works best in building a sense of community in my program is to make sure I do the simple things like saying hello and good-bye to everyone, every day. Simple things matter, such as spending at least a few minutes in each room every day; responding to complaints and difficulties quickly; and making sure we rarely cancel or postpone regular staff meetings. When I let paperwork take precedence over human contact, the whole program suffers.

—Ellen

Strategy

Reclaim time on behalf of your vision

We have never met a director who didn't fret over not having enough time to do their job. The question is, who's running the show, you or your unfinished tasks? As the director, you have the opportunity to create systems and organize time to lead your program in the direction of your vision. Here are ideas that help keep time in line with where you want to be:

- *Rotate your schedule so as to have regular contact with all families and staff.*
- *Create specific time blocks for you to be in rooms coaching teachers.*
- *Designate a portion of your schedule each week for reading and thinking.*
- *Have regular all-staff meetings, alternately used for training, problem solving, and community building.*
- *Utilize a floating teacher for weekly team meetings, mentoring, and parent conferences.*
- *Schedule quarterly professional development days and annual retreats for all staff, preferably on weekdays with the center closed.*

Principle

Design Meetings Around Community Building and Staff Development

With busy lives and tired bodies, there's nothing worse than sitting in a boring meeting at the end of a long work day. Whatever frequency and time frame you use to schedule staff meetings, make it consistent, reliable, and something to look forward to because they are an engaging, important part of the satisfaction they get from their work. This means holding it in a comfortable setting, having refreshments, time for community building, and a clear agenda.

Some people find it helpful to hold several shorter meetings in a month, while others prefer a monthly three hour evening meeting. Whatever format you use, designate some time for staff development and other time for problem solving and decision making. Limit announcements and information sharing that can be more efficiently handled through written notes or other means which don't eat into precious time together.

For the problem-solving and decision-making portion of your meeting, designate a method of advance sign-up for the agenda and design a process for addressing issues from meeting to meeting. This will provide consistency and opportunity to experience and learn effective communication, facilitation, and problem-solving skills. Chapters 3 and 4 of this book have further specific strategies that can be used in staff meetings.

I decided to do a couple of presentations and show slides of Reggio at our staff meetings. I knew it wouldn't work to try to require the staff to move in this direction. In fact, that would defeat my whole purpose and undermine the real meaning of what the Reggio approach has to offer. My excitement about Reggio did spark an interest among a couple of staff members who approached me saying they wanted to try it. This got us on the road and forced me to make a commitment to support their growth in exploring Reggio. This is an example to me of how one important sense of direction for our program comes from the staff. That year seven teams of teachers voluntarily joined in a commitment to explore the Reggio approach. As others saw their changes, ten more teams joined.

We chose areas of focus for exploration, using discussions, planning and evaluation, and some hands-on activities to provoke our thinking. For instance, we actually explored different art media to discover how they can be used by the children to represent ideas. We also explored what skills, strategies, and support are needed to use them effectively. When a new idea or activity seems risky to pursue, I ask for volunteers to be our pioneers to go out and explore, experiment, and come back to the rest of us to share their discoveries. For example, we realized we needed to do something different in our relationships with parents. Our pioneers tried a new approach with home visits, asking the parents to tell them about their hopes and dreams for their children and what kinds of adults they wanted them to be. What we heard totally changed our views of the parents.

—Karen

Strategy

Devote staff meetings to enhancing teacher development

You can provide effective staff training during staff meetings if your primary goal is to provide a learning process for the adults rather than trying to convey information. Time devoted to active learning in staff meetings conveys the importance you place on thinking and growing and develops your program as a learning community for adults as well as children.

Our earlier book, *Training Teachers: A Harvest of Theory and Practice,* discusses at length the components of adult learning and offers scores of constructivist training strategies. Here we want to review again our thoughts about conducting workshops and revisit the sample one-hour format we learned from the High/Scope Training of Teacher Trainers model:

- *Start your planning process for a training by brainstorming an overview of the core ideas on the topic.*
- *Prioritize and narrow the ideas you want to work with so that they fit the particular goals and time frame you have.*
- *Design an opening activity to spark initial thinking on the topic. This is similar to what some call an icebreaker. However, it is designed specifically to give the group a common experience around the ideas to be taken up.*
- *Debrief this activity with a minilecture connecting the ideas to the reflections teachers have on the experience they just had.*
- *Design or choose one or more activities for practice in applying the core ideas to be explored.*
- *Conclude with some brief discussion of next steps and a summary and evaluation. Next steps might call for further training, taking up other ideas on your brainstorm, or practical things caregivers want to begin doing.*

Sample workshop format:

- Training Overview (5 minutes)
- Opening Activity to Reflect on Topic (10 minutes)
- Debriefing and Discussion of Core Ideas (15 to 20 minutes)
- Practice Applying Ideas (15 to 20 minutes)
- Next Steps and Follow-Up (5 minutes)
- Summary and Evaluation (5 minutes)

For example, if you want to spend an hour exploring sources of emergent curriculum for teachers to consider in their planning, an hour's workshop might look like this:

Training overview

If we want to use an emergent approach to curriculum, that doesn't mean just standing around waiting for something to happen. Teachers can create what the Italians call a "provocation," arranging for a discovery or activity that might spark children's interests.

Opening activity

Have a selection of interesting boxes or bags displayed, each with a different object or picture that isn't immediately identifiable as to what it is. This might be things like dried seed pods or other things from nature, diagrams or x-rays, kitchen gadgets, hardware, or Styrofoam packing shapes from shipping boxes. Ask people to form pairs or small groups around one that intrigues them. They should generate a list of questions or ideas they might have about the picture or object.

Debriefing and discussion of core ideas

Initial questions might include:

- What intrigued you about the picture or object?
- What would make it possible for you to pursue this interest?

Points to cover in discussion:

- Emergent curriculum can come from something in the lives of children, their families, the wider community, or your own interest.
- If you want to introduce something as a possible topic to explore, initiate interest by arranging for a discovery or interesting way for children to explore what they might find interesting about it.
- Observe with attention to their interests and ideas, rather than something you want to teach them about the topic.
- Based on what you discover seems engaging to the children, plan further opportunities for their exploration.
- Consider a number of ways they might represent their ideas about this topic with different media.

Practice applying the ideas

Pass out a few short scenarios for teachers to discuss in small groups, considering the following questions:

- How could you provide a provocation to capture the children's attention?
- What are possible questions, ideas, or misinformation they might have?
- How might you provide different opportunities for them to explore and represent their thinking?

Next steps and follow-up

Ask each teaching team to identify something of excitement in the their own life, in the children's life, or the families' lives that might be a source of curriculum. Tell them to make this the focus of their next team planning meeting, going through the same questions just used in the practice session.

Summary and evaluation

- Ask if there were any new insights from today's discussion.
- Ask if there are there any outstanding questions that need to be taken up in the next meeting.
- Ask if there are any suggestions for how time could have been better used in exploring the topic.

Staff members become motivated to learn when their appetite has been whetted through active engagement with ideas that relate to their real-life experience. Thus, even for an hour-long training, we recommend devoting at least half of the time to exercises that have participants actively involved. In longer workshops the sample time frames can be expanded, but the bulk of the additional time should still be spent in the practice of applying the workshop ideas.

Paid time for the adults to gather away from children to pursue their own problem solving and learning is a precious commodity. It is foolish, not to mention unethical for us to waste it out of carelessness, poor planning, or facilitation skills. If you feel you need more skills in facilitating meetings, managing group dynamics, or conducting workshops, make that a professional development goal for yourself. There are numerous print resources, workshops, and classes you can draw upon. You can also begin to study those who you think have good skills in this area. Be systematic about learning this important management skill.

Making Good Use of Your Power and Influence

Because there are so many forces that seem out of our control, it's common for directors to see themselves as having very little power and influence to make change. The truth is, through the organizational climate you create, you have far more influence than you may imagine. The approach you take in developing your policies and systems makes an enormous impact on how things unfold in your program. Unless you work under the umbrella of a larger organization, you have direct decision-making power over these areas and can use them in the service of your vision. We've found that even directors who are bound by larger agency policies can creatively work around most of those constraints. You can access a powerful resource when you approach your work with a "can do" rather than "no way" attitude. Supporting this attitude with additional skill development and know-how will enhance your leadership in ways that spread beyond your program.

Thus, we end this chapter where we began, stressing the importance of cultivating the kind of organizational culture that supports your vision. These pages have offered you a number of principles and strategies to build on for the managing and overseeing side of your work. However, before you jump in and make use of them in an arbitrary fashion that may appeal to you, we suggest you first get some honest input from those you work with.

Practice Assessing Your Organizational Climate

Wise managers periodically play the role of meteorologist, checking out any possible clouds or storms brewing with staff, children, and families in your program. You can easily turn the Model Work Standards or Bloom's "Ten Dimensions of Organizational Climate" into a weather report of your program. (See appendices 2 and 10 for excerpts.) Consider including additional dimensions that reflect an experience of community.

To use the "Ten Dimensions of Organizational Climate" for a quick assessment tool, create a large graph on chart paper by listing each of the dimensions (collegiality, professional growth, supervisor support, clarity, reward system, decision making, goal consensus, task orientation, physical setting, innovation) along the side of the paper and three possible ratings, for instance, sunny/no sign of clouds, partly cloudy, and dark clouds, across the top of the paper so that it looks something like this:

Ten Dimensions of Organizational Climate			
	☀	☁	⛈
collegiality			
professional growth			
supervisor support			
clarity			
reward system			
decision making			
goal consensus			
task orientation			
physical setting			
innovation			

- Ask each person to plot a rating for each of the dimensions, using a colored adhesive dot or marker in line with their rating for each category.
- Have each person connect their dots with a single line.
- Leave the completed chart posted in your lounge for a week and see what you have in the way of a climate.

Sometimes there are surprises, like finding yourself in the eye of the storm. This suggests you may need to pursue a more formal, in-depth assessment of your organizational climate, perhaps with the aid of a consultant. On other occasions the results are an affirmation of the good things about your organizational culture. We recommend you hone your skills as a meteorologist rather than avoiding or denying the possibility of bad weather.

Resources for Managing Policies and Systems with a Vision

This list includes resources primarily drawn from the early childhood field because our settings are unique to most management systems. Readers should be aware that *Child Care Information Exchange*, the magazine listed below, regularly reports on valuable new management developments and has a number of booklets that organize past articles into topical issues, such as budget and finance, working with boards, and staff evaluations.

Bloom, Paula Jorde. *A Great Place to Work: Improving Conditions for Staff in Young Children's Programs* (revised edition). Washington, DC: NAEYC, 1977.

———. *Early Childhood Work Environment Survey*. Wheeling, IL: National-Louis University, 1985.

Capital Investment Fund, a new type of development lender emerging in many areas of the country, offering loans to early childhood programs. For information, contact National Association of Community Development Loan Funds, 924 Cherry Street, 3rd Floor, Philadelphia, PA 19107-2405.

Carter, Margie. "Honoring Diversity: Problems and Possibilities for Staff and Organization" in Neugebauer, B., ed. *Alike and Different: Exploring Our Humanity with Young Children.* Washington, DC: NAEYC, 1992.

Child Care Information Exchange, a Magazine for Directors, published by Exchange Press, Redmond, Washington.

Center for the Child Care Workforce. *Creating Better Child Care Jobs: Model Work Standards for Teaching Staff in Center-Based Child Care.* Washington, DC: Center for the Child Care Workforce, 1998.

Diffily, D., and K. Morrison. *Family-Friendly Communication for Early Childhood Programs.* Washington, DC: NAEYC, 1996.

Doyle, M., and D. Straus. *How to Make Meetings Work—The New Interaction Method.* New York: Jove, 1982.

The Director's Link, a newsletter published by the Center for Early Childhood Leadership, National-Louis University, and distributed free to directors in Illinois. The Center's web site is www.nl.edu/cecl.

Eiselen, S. *The Human Side of Child Care Administration: A How-to Manual.* Washington, DC: NAEYC, 1992 (revised edition).

Greenman, Jim, and Anne Stonehouse. *Prime Times: A Handbook for Excellence in Infant and Toddler Programs.* St. Paul: Redleaf, 1996.

Sussman, Carl. "Out of the Basement: Discovering the Value of Child Care Facilities." *Young Children,* January, 1998.

Taking the Lead, a national leadership initiative coordinated by the Center for Career Development at Wheelock College now has a web site (www.wheelock.edu) that has regular information about seminars in child care administration, director credentials, and other leadership development projects. You can reach them at the Center for Career Developement in Early Care and Education, Wheelock College, 200 The Riverway, Boston, MA 02215; Phone 617-734-5200, ext. 211; Fax 617-738-0643.

Willer, Barbara, ed. *Reaching the Full Cost of Quality in Early Childhood Programs.* Washington, DC: NAEYC, 1990.

Chapter 6

Moving From Surviving to Thriving— The Need for Nourishment and Activism

Take a look at

the roles you play. Say "I am a..." before each word in the following list:

broker	detective
firefighter	horticulturist
beekeeper	mechanic
judge	plumber
meter maid	star gazer
archivist	archaeologist
fortune-teller	flight attendant
meteorologist	bureaucrat
air traffic controller	journalist
hostess	guardian angel
carpenter	traffic cop

Now consider which of these roles drain you. Which sustain you?

Periodically the media features a story reporting on the most stressful jobs in the country. Don't we have a thing or two we could tell them! Early childhood program directors never make their surveys or lists, but that doesn't mean your work is any less stressful than that of an air traffic controller.

As we've discussed elsewhere in this book, metaphors can give us new insights and perspectives on ourselves and others. They can help relieve the strain we feel with a few good laughs. But more importantly, metaphors offer a way to transform our thinking, especially when we feel stuck, bruised, burned out, or on the horns of a dilemma. For instance, during one of our seminars a director described how discouraged he feels by having to continually start things over and over again in his job—hiring and training new staff, resolving a budget crisis, getting the walls painted, redoing his parent handbook. When we asked him to think of himself as a gardener, a smile spread across his face. "I love gardening," Jim said. "It never bothers me to turn over the soil again and plant my seeds each spring. I know I'll have to weed throughout the summer, but there'll be that taste of fresh green beans and then tomatoes to savor. As fall approaches I always put my garden to bed and look forward to planting again next year."

Metaphors can help you refocus when you run into a barrier or find yourself discouraged over some aspect of your work. But as you strain through the difficulties of your job, day after day, and week after week, you will need more than a laugh or magic word. Pacing and sustaining yourself will take some self-awareness and planning. As you say yes to your vision and move full speed ahead, there will be times when you need to say no, to pull back, catch up with yourself, and do some replenishing.

The Visionary Director has suggested a number of things you can do on behalf of a vision that more fully addresses our human needs for community and justice in the world. As the pages of this book draw to a close, we would be remiss if we didn't ask you to consider your own human needs. We've suggested a variety of strategies you can use to nourish others around you, and now we must ask what strategies nourish and sustain you. This is not a question to be taken lightly. We want you to work as diligently with questions here, as you have in earlier chapters focused on responsibilities for others. This is the time to consider your responsibility to yourself.

Finding Energy and Determination

In *The Heart Aroused*, poet-turned-business-consultant David Whyte says, "The split between what is nourishing at work and what is agonizing is the very chasm from which our personal destiny emerges" (1994). Facing that chasm makes more sense than griping about it. In it we can find a source of new energy and determination. We know this to be true because we have undertaken this confrontation on numerous occasions, most recently while writing this book.

The ideas for our book have grown and been tested in working with directors around the country over the last six years. When our publisher approached us about expanding our well-received seminar into a book, we responded with confidence. We enjoy the writing process and set about the task with excitement. However, as we moved through the months of writing we found ourselves struggling with bouts of thirst and uncertainty.

Continuing our weekly visits to programs kept us faced with the statistics that 86 percent of child care services are empirically judged to be poor or mediocre. Even the ones that have risen above these grim statistics seem to be dangling on a thin thread of security. We faced self-doubt about the feasibility of our book because it moves between the world of visionary ideas and the daily life of program directors. Will we be taken for Pollyannas with our vision of communities forming around early childhood programs? How could directors possibly try all these strategies when each day presents them with challenges as basic as staff illness and no substitutes, broken equipment, and families beset by divorce, violence, or economic hardship?

Then the birthday of Martin Luther King, Jr. was upon us. In our celebration we were reminded that people can unite and overcome what once seemed impossible to change. Leaving the computer, we took walks and noticed the promise of spring as buds pushed through what seemed like barren branches. We supported our writing partnership by instinctively taking turns calling each other with an inspiring passage from a favorite book or comments from directors on our workshop evaluation forms. Our own experience began to confirm the message of this book—a well-conceived vision can serve as a compass and guide you through those difficult days. Organizing complex tasks and challenges into a conceptual framework strengthens your ability to respond.

Our resolve to get this book to the publisher ultimately came from remembering the inspiring stories that directors around the country have brought us. We've heard about disasters and ordinary difficult days that directors addressed with tenacity, passion, and oftentimes, a terrific sense of humor. In spite of the barriers you face, directors are moving ahead, creating a way out of no way with precarious budgets, another round of head lice, and continual staff turnover. Your stories have become a powerful resource for our work and our sense of possibility for early childhood programs.

As we have experienced, witnessed, and heard about triumph over bouts of discouragement and exhaustion, some guiding principles have come into focus. We offer them here as sources of energy and determination in your efforts to stay nourished and thrive.

One of the most valuable things we provide for staff is an occasional retreat, where an individual can spend an extended time reflecting on our mission. We have time for meeting and time to be alone for thinking and writing. These retreats help me to keep in touch with why I do the work I do. They keep me grounded in my vision as it intersects with the reality of my day-to-day work in the program.

—Jim

Principle

Know Yourself and Act on What You Know

How often have you found yourself getting sick on the heels of a demanding fundraiser? Have you ever had a car accident while eating your lunch and rushing to the next meeting? Perhaps there are days when you find you've shown a prospective family around your center and not noticed a thing they said. These are messages, not from the universe at large, but from your own body and spirit. It's tempting to point the finger elsewhere when these kinds of incidents occur. Instead, stopping to notice and wonder will usually alert you to read these as clues. You'll discover you haven't been paying attention to yourself or the things that nourish you.

Sometimes people can get so out of touch with themselves that they need the help of a professional counselor to get them back on track. But in most cases, one can train oneself to pay more attention and learn how to take better care of oneself. There are oodles of self-help books on the market and we've listed a few at the end of this chapter. Most of the strategies we offer here seem like good, common sense, but living in today's world, it's remarkable how easy it is to stray from them. We recommend becoming more intentional about ordinary self-care strategies. They will make an extraordinary difference in your life.

Strategy

Listen to your body

Self-awareness is a key ingredient for self-care. Learn to recognize clues your body gives you, be they headaches, stiff necks, indigestion, or back spasms. As you start or end a work week, take a few minutes to close your eyes and ask yourself these questions:

- *As I've been walking, do my feet have energy or are they dragging?*
- *Have my eyes been eager for or irritated by the things around me?*
- *Am I sitting with my weight equally balanced over my buttocks and my spine?*
- *Are my shoulders and head aligned and free of tension?*
- *Where is my breath and how is it moving in my body?*

Even the act of closing your eyes can bring your attention inward to assess how you are doing. Most of us are besieged with overwhelming external stimuli and it's often difficult to hear what our body is telling us. A few moments to regularly check in with yourself will help you take care of yourself on a more consistent basis. If you discover you are typically tense, without energy, or irritable, it might be time for a stress reduction, exercise, or new nutritional plan for yourself. One assistant director we know keeps a sign over her desk which reads, "Your body is a better home than your house, a better vehicle than your car. *Invest!*"

Strategy

Be clear about your best time of day and healthy energy boosters

Directors have an advantage over teachers in that you can set and rearrange your own schedule at will. Consider your daily, weekly, and monthly tasks and how you can match them with the ebb and flow of your energy. Some people do best early in the morning, while others can't creatively function until almost noon. Most people slump at some point during the afternoon. Assess yourself and plan accordingly. Ask yourself questions like these:

- *When are you at your peak to tackle difficult questions or tasks?*
- *What routine tasks can be done when you aren't at your best?*
- *Is there something else besides sugar or caffeine that you can turn to in your low times of the day?*

Finding answers to these questions is the first step. The next one involves arranging your time and tasks accordingly. If midmorning is your best time of day, turn on your answering machine and put a "do not disturb" sign on the door. Perhaps your peak time is first thing in the morning, but by early afternoon you have a brain-dead period. In that case consider using those early morning hours to do your most demanding tasks, in the quiet of your office, at home, or in a coffee shop. Then catch up with your personal errands after lunch when you can't get your brain to focus steadily.

Try limiting how often you turn to chocolate or coffee for energy and instead, take a brisk walk or swim, practice yoga, or take an aerobics class during your low-energy time blocks. Or go to a room where the children are and sit on the floor with them for twenty minutes. You'll be amazed at the fresh energy routines like these will bring you.

Strategy

Be intentional when you doodle

Many of us idly doodle while talking on the phone, in a meeting or class. Sometimes this reflects boredom, but often it is an unconscious way of trying to access our kinesthetic learning needs. Turn your doodles into self-awareness opportunities. On your paper draw symbols or words that answer questions like the following:

- *What keeps you lively and enthusiastic?*
- *What makes you angry?*
- *Who brings you inspiration?*
- *What's worth celebrating today?*

Keep a collection of your doodles and periodically look them over. You may find there are some themes or patterns that merit your attention.

Principle

Know Your Resources and Access Them Regularly

The scarcity mentality that directors sometimes bring to their programs can also seep into your self-image as well. The "I don't have what it takes" feeling can rear its head when you try to manage your program without adequate staff and your substitute teacher list has totally vaporized. Perhaps you see yourself as a resourceful person, but there are times when we each find ourselves at the bottom of a dry well.

Bringing a vision to life takes strong, dedicated people who are thinking outside the checklists, inspiring and empowering others, forming coalitions and collaborative projects, and, when all else fails, raising hell and regrouping. Director work is for resourceful people, not martyrs or scaredy-cats. As you share your vision and move toward new possibilities, others will tell you, "It can't be done," "The money isn't there," "You're being unrealistic." It does no good to beat your head against the wall. You have to step back, figure out how to go around or over, tunnel underneath, or dismantle the wall.

Strategy

Reflect on your experiences and values

You can hold on to yourself and stay the course when you are clear about your values and personal resources. In the foreword to *Developmentally Appropriate Practice in Real Life*, Elizabeth Jones says, "Professionalism is defined by reflection on practice. To reflect, we must tell our stories and give names to our experience, names that connect it with the values we hold and the theories that inform our work" (1995). Begin an informal self-inventory by answering questions like these:

- *What stories have confirmed your understandings, fueled your passion, or served as an inspiration to keep on keeping on?*
- *What qualities in yourself can you count on when the going gets rough?*
- *Who or what can you turn to when you find yourself weary or in muddy waters.*

Consider the answers you came up with as resources you can return to again and again. You can formalize this inventory with the strategy which follows below, adapted from one in Katrina Shields' book, *In the Tiger's Mouth*. She quotes John Sanford as saying, "It is not rest that restores, except temporarily, but tapping into energies within us that we have not yet used" (1994).

As you come to name your passions and values, they will provide sustenance for your life, as well as those around you. Initially you may need to remind yourself to do seemingly simple things like slowing down, taking time to enjoy the children, staff, and families around you. As you cultivate yourself as a reflective person, this will start to happen organically.

To become more mindful and reflective, surround yourself with simple beauty and inspiring words. Seek the company of those who do the same. Care for your spirit, your mind, and your body. Make a commitment to be physically active and to eat well.

A menudo escucho a otros profesionales quejarse del trabajo y de la necesidad de buscar otras opciones profesionales. Cuando se me han presentado nuevas oportunidades, he tratado de dejar mi posición como Directora para seguir nuevos horizontes. ¿Porqué no cambio despues de 18 años? La respuesta a esta pregunta se hace clara cuando reflexiono sobre los siguientes aspectos de mi trabajo.

La estabilidad, seguridad y respeto cuando entro por las puertas de La Escuelita, como siento solo en mi hogar.

La afinidad que tengo con las trabajadoras, la solidaridad y el acuerdo mutuo que no he podido encontrar en otro lugar.

El amor que brindan los niños y mi devoción incondicional para ellos.

El orgullo y la tristeza cuando los niños de Kinder se van todos los años. El orgullo por todo lo que han realizado y la tristeza porque no sere parte de su vida diaria.

La satisfacción cuando una de mis empleadas llega a un nuevo nivel en su desarrollo profesional.

Mi visión se realiza cuando uno de mis estudiantes graduados viene a decime que lo han aceptado en *Drew University* y que quiere compartir la noticia conmigo.

El sentirme orgulloza cuando mis hijos me ayudan en la Escuelita y ellos son el resultado de criarse en este ambiente.

Siempre me sorprende que trabajo mas de diez horas y nunca me parece que es un trabajo.

Esta Primavera tendre el honor de matricular el hijo de una de mis primeras estudiantes pre-escolar.

Siempre hay nuevas pruebas y tribulaciones, la vida seria monotona sin ellas. Estas las veo como un desafio y como un trampolín para aprender cosas nuevas. No he encontrado otro lugar que me provoque sentimientos tan positivos y me valide de una manera tan significativa.

—**Carmen**

I often hear professionals in the field discuss the issue of burn out and the need to move in new directions. As opportunities have become available, I have also considered leaving my job as director to pursue new horizons. Why *not* change after eighteen years? The answer to this question becomes clear to me as I ponder on the following aspects of my job.

There is a feeling of belonging, security, and respect as I enter the doors of La Escuelita that only my home can compete with.

There is the kinship that I have with the staff, a sense of joint commitment and purpose that I have yet to find elsewhere.

There is the love that is offered by the children and my own unconditional devotion to them.

There is the feeling of pride and sadness when my kindergarten children leave every year. Pride in their great accomplishments and sadness for I will no longer be a part of their everyday lives.

There is that great sense of accomplishment whenever one of my staff reaches a new milestone in their professional development.

My vision is validated when one of my students returned to tell me that he got accepted at Drew University and he just had to share this news with me.

There is the sense of pride when my own children assist me at La Escuelita and model the values they have learned here.

It always amazes me that I can put in a ten-hour day and not feel like it's a job.

This spring I will have the honor of enrolling the child of one of our school's first preschool students.

There are always trials and tribulations. Life would be monotonous without them. I take them as a challenge and as a springboard to new levels of understanding. I have yet to find another place that can evoke so many positive feelings while validating and empowering me in such significant ways.

—Carmen

Strategy

Create a visual map of your resources

Begin the process of concretely naming the resources you know you have. This may seem tedious at first, but think of it as a treasure hunt. It helps to remember the words of David Whyte: "We have to crack that door only slightly for the swift breezes alive in the imagination to swing it completely open" (1994).

If you are a linear thinker, you can make your list in two columns divided horizontally to create four boxes. Intuitive thinkers can web out your answers starting from four circles with spokes. (See sample Resource Map at top of next page.)

The two big ideas to explore here are your internal resources and external ones. Put those as headers over each of two columns or in the center of two circles on a paper. Under "internal," first consider your passions and values. When you've generated a list or spun out spokes with words for these, then move to the bottom quadrant and write notes about your skills, things you're good at, and tools you have to use. Be specific, write things that may seem insignificant, as well as major within yourself.

Then under the next column or circle consider your external resources. First make notes about the concrete people, places, activities, and things that you draw on for inspiration and renewal. Name them and write them down. Keep probing before you move on. Finally, for the last quadrant or series of spokes, consider challenges and ideas that keep you thinking

My Resource Map	
Internal Resources	**External Resources**
Passions and Values	*Places, People, Activities for Inspiration and Renewal*
Skills, Things I'm Good At, Tools I Have to Use	*Ideas and Challenges That Keep Me Thinking and Growing*

and growing. Again, be specific, writing words and phrases to describe these.

Carefully look over what you've written, perhaps returning to it after a cup of tea, a walk, or talk with a friend. Are there things you want to add? When you are satisfied with the ideas you have written, your next task is to represent them again in a visual way.

Invest the time to do this. Using some basic art materials, create a representation of your resources that is visually interesting and pleasing to you. Think of this as a map to accompany you on an unknown journey, a touchstone to keep you safe from pirates.

Principle

Know Your Own Goals and Pursue Them with Vigor

Throughout this book we have stressed the importance of having a vision for what you want. A vision can not only serve as a tremendous source of inspiration, but can be breathed into life as you set concrete goals and develop action plans to reach them. Directing work requires you to have goals for your program and for the individual staff members you supervise. But you must also set goals for yourself, for your personal and professional development. Too often directors are so busy tending to the goals they have for others that they neglect their own needs.

Determining your own personal and professional goals involves defining what will make you successful and satisfied. Allocating time and resources for your own needs doesn't come easily for the typical director. As you prioritize and focus yourself you will periodically need to evaluate and adjust where you are headed. You may discover that focus on your personal goals will enhance your professional life. Here are some strategies to consider.

Strategy

Cultivate personal goals that will round out your development

Keep in mind that your goals don't have to be limited to early childhood topics. Here are some skills and arts we have found directors pursuing as we've moved around the country:

computer graphics	photography
bicycle repair	Japanese flower arranging
aromatherapy	furniture refinishing
ice sculpting	soccer coaching
playing the flute	quilting
Swedish massage	astrology
landscape design	speaking Spanish
dream interpretation	

These directors found these pursuits relevant to their overall mental health, growth, and development. Setting a goal and approaching it with discipline will give you more insights into the learning process itself. This will no doubt expand your self-confidence, deepen your reflective insights, and refine your ability to communicate with others. Directly or indirectly, achieving your goals will also make a tremendous contribution to your workplace.

Strategy

Join a sports team, reading circle, or support group

In your work as a director, you are in the leadership position, with many people turning to you for guidance and support. Make sure you are part of at least one other group where you have someone else offering you leadership and support. Again, this doesn't have to be within the early childhood domain. Even if you just meet once a month, find a group to be part of that will keep your body alive, your mind stimulated, and your spirit replenished.

I am personally and professionally committed to anti-bias issues, but there are times when I'm not sure how best to respond. What do you do when you hear children on a field trip refer to someone as a bum, when you encounter someone speculating about someone's ethnicity for no apparent reason, or when a parent doesn't want his son to play with dolls? What if countering a bias goes against someone's cultural or religious teachings? These are things I need help thinking about.

To both ease and stimulate my mind I became part of a support group in the larger early childhood community helping each other think through anti-bias issues. Our group meets monthly and we spend time talking through our issues and incidents, and possible ways to respond. We've started reading and discussing books and articles together as well. This group has been a powerful support for positive changes related to anti-bias approaches in my program. It has an additional benefit that I did not anticipate. As my staff has seen how this support group has helped me, they've been sparked to create support groups for themselves.

—Ellen

Principle

Be Aware of Your Friends and Your Foes

There is a delicate balance between being an accepting, flexible person, and allowing your compassion and empathy to keep you from the road you want to travel. We find it helpful to think in terms of surrounding yourself with friends, some of whom are humans, while others can be environments, experiences, and tools to make your journey more sane. In the friends category we would include people with whom you can spin out dreams and collaborate and those who can give you a balanced perspective or spot any unacknowledged assumptions or biases that may be getting in your way. Experiences that keep your senses awake and alive, fresh air, natural light, flowers, and exercise can also all be considered friends. We would also add some technology like voice mail, e-mail, cellular phones, and laptop computers, all of which help you do your work efficiently, stay in touch with others, and make clear choices about when to take a break from contact.

It's useful to consider who or what your foes might be. For instance, you may want to avoid sharing your wildest dreams with people who always either throw caution to the wind or never let you get to first base with your excitement. Those who influence you to avoid physical activity, or who are narrow minded or bigoted are also likely to serve as your foes. Limit your intake of these folks, along with other unhealthy substances or activities.

Enslavement to the telephone or television won't serve you well or keep your mind creative and moving forward. Neither will time bandits like procrastination, distractions, interruptions, or disorganization. Think of bad habits as your enemy, intent on keeping you from what you really want.

Keeping clear about your friends and foes requires that you cultivate presence of mind, or what Buddhists call mindfulness. Cultivate mindfulness in everyday moments. Whether you live in a big city, small town, or rural area, life in today's world often requires us to numb ourselves to noise, air pollution, traffic, and bad news. Here are some strategies that are adapted from our favorite Buddhist activist, Thich Nhat Hanh, and writer-therapist Ruth Baetz.

Strategy

Spill out your worries instead of allowing them to pile up

Take some time each day to spill out your worries and "to do" lists. Put your fingers to your lips and say them one at a time. As you name each worry or thing you need, have your fingers throw it away from you. Then transfer your attention to close examination of a detailed object like a coin, leaf, or blossom. A jeweler's loupe or strong magnifying glass helps you really concentrate on what's there. Give it a word of thanks.

Strategy

Practice observation and stillness by doing nothing

Go to a busy public place, stand still, and do nothing for ten minutes. Do not pretend that you are waiting for someone or sightseeing. You might try a quick self-hypnosis exercise. For example, be still in one place and name four sights, four sounds, and four physical sensations. Then name three of each, then two of each, then one. Or instead of watching television, spend fifteen minutes watching someone else who is watching television.

Strategy

Use focused meditation techniques to bring you back in touch with yourself

There are many possible variations of these, but here are some that have worked for us:

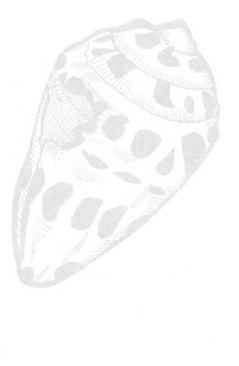

- *Look deeply into the palm of your hand for ten minutes and see your parents and all generations of your ancestors.*
- *When you wash your hands or bathe, try to mentally trace the origin of the water that comes out of your tap as far back to its source as you can. Every time you use the water, be aware of its journey to reach you. You can try the same exercise in reverse, trying to mentally trace what happens to your garbage and waste as it leaves your hands.*
- *Adopt the word* soften *as your mantra. Take three slow breaths and quietly say the word to yourself, noticing the air as it crosses your lips. Take another three breaths and say the word again. Repeat this pattern until it takes on its own rhythm. Begin to add a new word to each repetition. For example, "Soften jaws [three breaths], soften shoulders [three breaths], soften belly [three breaths]."*
- *Observe yourself in the mirror for twenty minutes. See what you see. Don't do anything, just be there. Advanced practice is to observe yourself naked for twenty minutes!*

Principle

Organize Yourself, Your Time, and Your Stuff

Self-care also requires getting organized. There are any number of popular books to help with this task, but people have to find their own way of getting organized. It's useful to consider how other people organize themselves. We recommend informational interviews and keeping a watchful eye with those who are good at it. Whatever you devise, consider including these basic strategies.

Strategy

Create and maintain systems for nearly everything

Remember that time devoted to organizing is time gained, not lost. Consider breaking projects into steps, lists, and flow charts for regular use.

Strategy

Have a place for everything

A place for everything helps you control clutter to keep your mind free and creative. It also ensures that when you need something for a task or project, you can find it quickly and easily, saving you valuable time. It's also helpful to have different places for different kinds of work, since you need different kinds of space for typing on a computer keyboard, a messy art project, and a quiet meeting with a staff member or parent.

Strategy

Plan each week and day before it begins

Establish and guard some time blocks that are free of distraction and interruption for concentrated work on demanding tasks. Treat tasks like appointments and put them in your calendar. Use your best time of day for the most difficult tasks. Don't forget to build in time for self-development and self-care, and devote some time each week to system maintenance.

Strategy

Utilize the trash and recycling bins regularly

Try using the "4-D" strategy to sort papers each day. As you go through the mountains of mail you receive and paperwork waiting to be accomplished, sort them immediately into four piles with the following purposes:

Discard
Delegate
Defer (for reading or filing)
Decide today (act and do)

Don't be hesitant to put things in the discard pile, and get rid of them right away! If something is to be delegated, try to get it off your desk that day as well.

I knew things were not going well when I looked out from underneath the stack of papers on my desk to see the inspector on the other side. She said she could tell that my staff was being trained, but my paperwork did not reflect this. In the world of Army child care, this was not a good thing. Later, as I was crying, driving around in the car with my boss, I thought to myself, "I have to change."

After the shock wore off I began to do research in time management. I took a couple of classes on the subject, I got a planner and wrote down everything I did for a whole week. From my research I found out several interesting things. I spent too much time doing things for people that they could do for themselves. I had a problem saying no to people, and difficulty delegating items to others. In addition, I was a procrastinator. It seemed at times that I was trying to do everyone else's job instead of my own.

In the end I decided to turn things around by empowering my teachers to do more for themselves. I made as many things available as possible, such as articles and paperwork. I started an appointment book so that the staff could sign up for times to see me. I organized my office so I knew where everything was.

Now I have freed up a lot of my time and I am able to focus more. I make a commitment every day to clear my desk so I will never have to hide from an inspector again! A friend of mine once said that "doing paperwork" is like being a zookeeper. If you don't clean out the cages every day, the animals will get restless and all of the stuff will start to pile up and smell. This thought is always in my mind.

—Cathy

Principle

Get Active Beyond Your Program

To move from surviving to thriving, we need to discover our own internal strength and connect with others around us. These connections not only provide support for your individual efforts, but they enhance muscle and vocal power for the larger socioeconomic and political changes that must be made if you are to reach your vision. Involving yourself in a local directors' group is an obvious way to build connections, as is work with affiliates of the National Association for the Education of Young Children or other professional groups, organizations focused on the needs of different populations, and advocacy groups like the Worthy Wage Campaign, who are working to make change on behalf of children, caregivers, and families. The formal and informal ties that grow from your activities with these groups can strengthen the tapestry you are weaving with your vision.

Getting together with others has to go beyond griping and complaining. When we gather to describe how things are, we must also paint a picture of how it could be. This mobilizes vitality, creative ideas, and problem solving. In her foreword to *Developmentally Appropriate Practice in Real Life,* Betty Jones describes it this way: "We gain power to make changes in our lives as we learn to name our experiences…We make changes when we experience the moral pain of conscious acknowledgment that things are not as we want them to be. In this process the role of the educator, mentor, pastor, therapist, researcher is to invite us to name the discrepancies and examine new possibilities for action…Moral pain is a fruitful source of energy for change" (1995).

As you move out into your community, find for yourself that educator, mentor, or pastor or rabbi who will spur you into action. In turn, play that role for others in groups you work with. When you speak your mind and share your vision, you become a beacon for those ready to contribute their leadership. You may form a caucus, or task group to solidify your connections, educate yourselves, and generate energy and a plan for action. Joan Lombardi has provided us with valuable resources for getting groups organized into action. Her chapter, "Developing a Coalition to Reach the Full Cost of Quality" in *Reaching the Full Cost of Quality,* and the NAEYC book she co-authored with Stacie Goffin, *Speaking Out: Early Childhood Advocacy,* offer detailed guidance on working in coalitions and taking action. Part of our city's story of growing political clout for child care illustrates the results of Lombardi's advice.

In Seattle a small group of directors in geographic proximity began meeting informally to share staff training strategies. We went on to write a grant for collaborative in-service training and the accreditation process, and within a year joined forces with other directors building connections to start a citywide directors' association. We began to build ties with folks in other agencies who led us to political figures in our city and state. With allies mobilizing their allies, our directors' group launched a worthy wages task force and began a five-year public education process which included rallies, an annual symbolic day of closing centers, and a city government commission which leveraged local businesses to provide ongoing technical assistance for child care.

This is but one small story of activism that a dedicated group of directors successfully undertook. Child care salaries have risen significantly in many programs in Seattle and early childhood education has been put on the private sector and public policy agenda. Years of dedicated activism have led to a number of promising initiatives in cities and states across the country. We mention a very few examples in the afterword of this book and their numbers will no doubt be multiplied by the time of your reading.

Stories of children's champions and activism in early childhood education circles remind us of the well-known Margaret Mead quote: "Never doubt that a small group of thoughtful, committed citizens can change the world. Indeed, it's the only thing that ever has." If you don't move out into activism beyond your program, you won't experience how true this is. You'll miss out on the energy, good ideas, and empowerment that comes from collaborative action.

Strategy

Learn from I Dream a World

When we think of social change, most of us have monumental images from our modern history books—efforts to enact child labor laws, the civil rights, antiwar, farm worker, environmental, and women's movements, to name a few. Changes brought about by these large-scale efforts started with the steady, courageous work of individuals and small groups which began to link together. For a reminder of how simple acts can lead to the building of a mighty force take a look at Brian Lanker's book *I Dream a World: Portraits of Black Women Who Changed America.* The book features photographs and autobiographical stories of ordinary African-American women who became extraordinary leaders for change, each in her own way. In these photos and stories you will find women in the arts, politics, and church. Social workers, athletes, and healers are included, as are women who are famous and women who are relatively unknown. You can look through this book time and time again for inspiration.

Selections from *I Dream a World* are now printed in calendar form each year. We have saved those photos for doing the following activity with groups:

- *Glue each photo on a piece of cardstock or mat board with the accompanying autobiographical story glued on the back.*
- *Place the photos around the room so that people can see them.*
- *Ask each person to choose a photo that they are drawn to and return with it to their seat to read the story on the back.*
- *In pairs, introduce the women in the photographs and share what you learned and what first drew you to the photograph.*
- *As a whole group, discuss the themes of the inspiration and lessons we can draw from these women.*

Strategy

Identify the components of real social change

Reaching out strengthens us individually and collectively. It gives us opportunities to connect our issues with others, for instance, addressing the dynamics of racism, power, and privilege. This is work you might not fully grasp or take on alone, but in working with others, you gain the courage to begin. For collective action to sustain, not drain you, you need to pick and choose your battles. We see promise in initiatives which have the following components:

- *making a vision visible by providing a taste of how it could be,*
- *connecting people in collaborative relationships,*
- *practicing consensus building, democratic and egalitarian principles,*
- *developing leadership in those historically denied access to power,*
- *committing to the hard work of overcoming bias and oppression, and*
- *addressing systemic, interconnected issues.*

A group that you choose to be part of may find it overwhelming to take on all the pertinent issues related to the kind of social change you'd like to see. Indeed, it is usually important for groups to stay focused on a clear set of attainable goals. The point is to see this work in a larger context, to understand the interconnections between how things work to maintain or change the inequities of power and resource distribution. It is equally critical to pay as much attention to the means of change, the processes you use for coming together and taking on challenges, as to the goals you have in mind. In the words of Myles Horton and Paulo Freire, "We have to make the road by walking."

Strategy

Think in terms of zoysia plugs

In *Community Building: Renewing Spirit and Learning in Business* (1995), business consultants Brown and Isaacs suggest finding and cultivating "zoysia plugs." They explain:

"Zoysia is a grass, originally indigenous to Asia, which people sometimes use to start lawns. You water and fertilize plugs of grass scattered far apart. Eventually they find each other and meld into a beautiful carpet covering the whole lawn. In organizations, 'zoysia plugs' are people who share your passion. They are also the informal leaders who know how to make things happen. Find them, wherever they might be, and support them however you can. Eventually, when you reach a level of critical mass, you may feel the atmosphere of the entire enterprise shift."

Make a list of possible people that might serve as your "zoysia plugs." Where might you find them? Perhaps in a directors' organization, community association, synagogue, church, or other affinity group. You might also explore discussion groups on the Internet. Make a plan for some initial contact and discussion which centers on shared passion and longing for things to be different. Use this and other books of interest as your fertilizer. Put the quotes at the end of this chapter in your watering can.

There was a time when I thought if I lost yet another staff member I'd really have to quit. It's too heartbreaking, not to mention exhausting to have to lose such good teachers because they can't afford to stay. I realized it was useless to just hope things would get better. I had to get involved to start forcing this issue out into the public. There's no way I was going to solve it alone in my own little center.

What amazes me is how much energy and hope the Worthy Wage Campaign has given me. Seeing my letters to the editor published, showing my city councilman around my center—this stuff gives me a real charge. But more importantly, it has gotten our staffing crisis on the agenda to be dealt with.

—Leslie

Living Your Way into a Vision

If you've come to this book looking for answers, we hope you've come to your senses! By now you know that it is our belief that the work of an early childhood program director will only get easier when you mobilize people around a common vision. We've offered you principles, strategies, models and inspiring words from directors to consider. Your job is to live your way into the answers and resources you need.

We hope you'll keep the triangle framework in mind as you go through your days. Consider starting a study group of this book to help you internalize this way of work and create a support system with others trying to do the same. You might want to create a triangle graphic as a totem for yourself and put it in a prominent place along with your resource map.

We often sense whether directors are working with a vision when we first meet in their offices. Typically there are books on the shelves that differ from those found in early childhood press catalogs. We notice inspirational quotes taped above the desk, the copy machine, or coffee pot in the staff lounge. Here's a sampler of some of our favorites. We'll let them have the last word in this book:

> Having a vision is different than having a plan. A vision inspires creativity while a plan dictates action…A vision catches the spirit of a people.
>
> —GEORGE LAND AND BETH JARMAN

> You don't get far without a dream to lure. A dream keeps you looking forward, whereas the dreamless are inclined to look backward on some former dream defused. Dreams are a living picture in the mind generating energy. They are at once direction finders and a source of power. A dream makes a life worthwhile. Life takes its quality from the glow of a dream.
>
> —SYLVIA ASHTON-WARNER

> What we need is neither optimism nor pessimism, but commitment to a vision
>
> —ROSEMARY RADFORD RUETHER

> We first design our structures, then they design our lives.
>
> —WINSTON CHURCHILL

> First in the heart is the dream
> Then the mind starts seeking a way.
>
> —LANGSTON HUGHES

> Whatever you can dream or dare to imagine, begin it. Boldness has power, vision, and magic in it.
>
> —GOETHE

A vision without a task is a dream.
A task without a vision is drudgery.
But a vision with a task is the hope of the future.

—SOURCE UNKNOWN

When we talk about community, we are not referring to
any aggregate of people, but to the quality of communication among them.

—M. SCOTT PECK

We have here children and adults who are looking for the
pleasure of playing, working, talking, thinking and
inventing things together. They are trying to get to know
both each other and themselves, to understand how the
world works and how it could be made to work better, and
be enjoyed in friendship.

—THE SCHOOLS OF REGGIO EMILIA, ITALY

Children are our hope; they embody our dreams...As
places and as institutions, child care programs shape
future visions of what society is and should be.

—JIM GREENMAN

Resources for Thriving

Here are books from teachers, writers, artists, business consultants, and social activists, each of whom has touched our lives
in important ways.

Ayers, W. *To Teach*. New York: Teachers College Press, 1993.

Baetz, R. *Wild Communion: Experiencing Peace in Nature*. Center
City, MN: Hazelden, 1997.

Bateson, M. C. *Composing a Life*. New York: Penguin, 1990.

Bolman, L., and T. Deal. *Leading with Soul: An Uncommon
Journey of Spirit*. San Francisco: Jossey-Bass, 1995.

Fried, R. *Passionate Teacher*. Boston: Beacon Press, 1995.

Gozdz, Kazimierz, ed. *Community Building: Renewing Spirit and
Learning in Business*. San Francisco: New Leaders Press,
1995.

Goffin, S., and J. Lombardi. *Speaking Out: Early Childhood Advocacy.* Washington, DC: NAEYC, 1988.

Horton, Myles, and Paulo Freire. *We Make the Road by Walking.* Philadelphia: Temple University Press, 1991.

Kent, C., and J. Steward. *Learning by Heart: Teachings to Free the Creative Spirit.* New York: Bantam, 1992.

Lanker, B. *I Dream a World: Portraits of Black Women Who Changed America.* New York: Stewart, Tabori & Chang, 1989.

Lamott, A. *Bird by Bird: Lessons on Writing and Life.* New York: Bantam/Doubleday, 1994.

Manz, C. *Mastering Self-Leadership: Empowering Yourself for Personal Excellence.* New York: Prentice-Hall, 1992.

McMakin, J., and S. Dyer. *Working from the Heart: For Those Who Hunger for Meaning and Satisfaction in Their Work.* San Diego: LuraMedia, 1989.

Shields, Katrina. *In the Tiger's Mouth: An Empowerment Guide for Social Action.* Gabriola Island, British Columbia, Canada: New Society, 1994.

Stout, L. *Bridging the Class Divide and Other Lessons for Grassroots Organizing.* Boston: Beacon, 1996.

Thich Nhat Hanh. *Present Moment, Wonderful Moment.* San Francisco: Parallax, 1996.

Whelan, Mary Steiner, and Jean Steiner. *For the Love of Children: Daily Affirmations for People Who Care for Children.* St. Paul: Redleaf, 1995.

Whyte, David. *The Heart Aroused: Poetry and the Preservation of the Soul in Corporate America.* New York: Doubleday, 1994.

Afterword

Take heart.

Promising initiatives are growing. Around the country there are a growing number of early childhood alliances, community collaboration projects, and organizing efforts that are showing promise to move us out of the current crisis in early childhood education. These projects have a range that includes providing support and resources for NAEYC Accreditation, supplying leadership development and credentialing directors, training teachers to be mentors and leaders, efforts to ensure developmentally and culturally appropriate practices, and financing quality child care and improved compensation. Some are small, local efforts that do not have outside funding, while others have generated grant money to launch their projects.

Because many directors might not be aware of these efforts we offer a sampling of descriptions here to whet your appetite for involvement and action. This is in no way intended to be a comprehensive list, but rather some different snapshots of where dedicated hard work can lead. Publications which review a wider scope of promising initiatives are listed at the end of this afterword.

Montgomery Child Care Training Institute

Directors and teachers in this organization describe it as a very simple story. In 1985, Montgomery Child Care Association (MCCA) had a problem. They had eight child care centers and were dissatisfied with the quality of outside training available for their staff. The education director, Pat Scully, began organizing a group of her most promising teachers, guiding them to share specific stories of things they were proud of in their classrooms. As they worked to reflect on their practice, Pat cultivated this expertise into workshop leadership, coaching them in a training style that was hands-on, practical, and interactive. Gradually they began offering workshops for their program and then went on to develop classes, and teacher visitations in their wider community.

Today, long after Pat has left the program, MCCA Training Institute is one of the most respected sources of child care training in the metropolitan area of Washington, DC. In 1997 they decided to take their story to the NAEYC Professional Development Institute, selling 2,016 candy bars to cover their costs. At this conference, they found an enthusiastic response to the model they had developed. It keeps skilled teachers working with children while using their own class-rooms as demonstration sites. They are offered a career path which brings them additional salary and recognition without having to leave the work they love best—being with children. Thanks to their collaborative candy bar and reflective training efforts, there is now widespread interest in this model and other programs are beginning to adapt it as an approach to training and staff retention. For their reflections on how they have been able to achieve their goals and thrive in the process, see Wendy's director story in chapter 4. For more information about the MCCA Training Institute model contact them at 2730 University Boulevard West, Suite 616, Wheaton, Maryland 20902; Phone 301-949-3561; Fax 301-949-6726.

Early Childhood Mentoring Programs

Unbeknownst to Pat Scully or the Montgomery Child Care Association, for more than a decade the Center for the Child Care Workforce (CCW, formerly called the National Center for the Early Childhood Workforce) has been actively studying and developing mentoring program models. At the time of their 1996 publication, *Early Childhood Mentoring Programs: A Survey of Community Initiatives,* there were nineteen programs surveyed throughout the country. Mentoring efforts continue to grow, often independently and with limited knowledge of each other. Nevertheless, program developers have reached remarkably similar conclusions about the core training needs of mentors and apprentices. These include learning about adult develop-ment and learning styles, reflective practice, culturally relevant and anti-bias education, the process of change, and leadership and advocacy.

As the Montgomery Child Care Association learned, expanding an internal mentoring program in your community has a multitude of paybacks for your own program and broader professional efforts. To learn more about the variety of structures and funding that mentor programs have adopted, see the above mentioned survey of community initiatives. You might also want to get the *Early Childhood Mentoring Curriculum* handbooks that are listed in the resource section at the back of this section of the book. To order these handbooks or learn more about the Mentoring Alliance, contact CCW at 733 15th Street NW, Suite 1037, Washington, DC 20005; Phone 202-737-7700; Fax 202-737-0370.

North Shore Community Action Head Start Program (NSCAP)

If you haven't read the story of how Head Start director Sandy Waddell transformed a former high-school cafeteria into an architectural dream of an early childhood space, rush right now to the January 1998 story in *Young Children*. Sandy is described as a strong-willed leader with a vision, and though we aren't personally familiar with her work, it served as a model for the inspiring article Carl Sussman wrote and we have quoted elsewhere in this book.

We've seen many Head Start programs making do with the dreary space NSCAP started with. Sandy's story could be duplicated all across the country if you follow her example of cultivating a vision, seeking out design and development professionals, and refusing to give up even in the face of a $290,000 price tag. This is a story of determination, risk taking, and collaboration. It could be yours!

To learn more about the Capital Investment Fund, a new type of development lender emerging in many areas of the country that offers loans to early childhood programs, among others, contact the National Association of Community Development Loan Funds, 924 Cherry Street, 3rd Floor, Philadelphia, PA 19107-2405.

Model Work Standards Project

While working with groups in many cities to coordinate the Worthy Wage Campaign, the Center for the Child Care Workforce (CCW) has also begun to coordinate a multi-year effort led by child care teachers and providers to define the working conditions needed to create quality programs. Around the country they raised two key questions: "What is a high-quality work environment?" and "What needs to be changed to improve your job and your capacity to be a good teacher?" Through a national postcard campaign, house parties, workshops, and community-based consensus-building efforts, CCW began to compile answers and compare them with research findings on best practices in early childhood education. A draft was then developed and circulated for feedback and efforts are now underway to put this tool to work in center-based programs around the country.

The development and implementation process of the Model Work Standards are instructive for directors to consider. As mentioned earlier, Paula Jorde Bloom writes that there is often a discrepancy between director and staff perceptions of a work environment. The director frequently judges things to be more favorable. In our view there are a number of probable reasons for this: lack of open communications in a program, differing standards and expectations, and directors accommodating their expectations to the limitations in their budget and facility.

Rather than view the Model Work Standards as out of reach or a threat to your relationship with staff, directors can welcome the assessment and discussion that the Standards generate. You might view working with the Standards as the equivalent of the self-study for accreditation, generating the same kind of creativity and commitment to a set of quality criteria for a work environment. In appendix 2 you will find sample pages from the Model Work Standards along with a recommended process for using them. To order the Model Work Standards, contact CCW at 733 15th Street, NW Suite 1037, Washington, DC 20005; Phone 202-737-7700; Fax 202-737-0370.

California Tomorrow's "Looking In, Looking Out" Project

Sometimes hearing the data collected by another group helps early childhood educators recognize and use their individual and collective influence to take specific action. This has been happening with the growing mentor teacher programs and the Model Work Standards Project described above, and this intent was at the heart of an effort undertaken by California

Tomorrow, a nonprofit organization that works on issues of multicultural equity.

Beginning in the spring of 1994, California Tomorrow began an action research project to redefine what is needed for child care and early education in a diverse society. Their premise was that knowledge of families, practitioners, and programs should be documented, that practitioners should be involved in analyzing data, and that diverse perspectives should always be sought. The collaborative research efforts of Hedy Chang, Amy Muckelroy, Dora Pulido-Tobiassen, and scores of families, providers, teachers, and agency directors, gathered views and experiences across great diversity. They then engaged early childhood practitioners in analyzing this data.

From this broad-based, participatory action project a new vision for the early childhood field emerged, representing the voices of those directly involved rather than the more distant regulatory agencies or policy makers. This kind of process left people feeling more powerful and hopeful about collaborative work across the difficult arenas of race, language, and culture. They went on to publish a remarkable book detailing their work and findings, offering a vision to guide the thinking of all of us who work on behalf of culturally relevant, anti-bias programming. You can contact California Tomorrow at Fort Mason Center, Building B, San Francisco, CA 94123; Phone 415-441-7631; Fax 415-441-7635.

Massachusetts Open Forum on Early Education and Care

The Open Forum on Early Education and Care initiative emerged from a discussion group that the Child Care Resource Center in Massachusetts convened in 1992 to respond to proposed legislation to restructure the child care delivery system. During a painstaking four-year process they developed consensus on a vision for early education and care that had a single goal: the creation of universally accessible, high-quality, and affordable programs that meet the diverse needs of all children and families in their state.

Rather than confine their thinking to the limitations of the existing "non-system" of education and care, they spoke the truth of the uneven quality and the way it is failing children, families, those who work in programs, employers, and their communities at large. This group not only articulated the current problems in graphic terms, but went on to devise four possible models of state infrastructure to create a new system of universal care. They went on to do a presentation at the national NAEYC Conference, and their model and call for a universal early education and care system is spreading to states across this land. For information about the Open Forum, contact The Child Care Resource Center, 130 Bishop Allen Drive, Cambridge, MA 02139; Phone 617-547-1063; Fax 617-547-3340.

Taking the Lead/The Center for Career Development in Early Care and Education

Taking the Lead is a 2.4 million dollar national initiative sponsored by The Early Childhood Funders Collaborative, a group of foundations that has united to improve the quality of early care and education that the children of the United States receive. Taking the Lead is designed to build capacity to increase program quality by expanding the skills of new and existing leaders within the field, to generate increased public support and private and public investment in early care and education, and to advance the development of a director's credential for program directors of early care and education programs.

A major emphasis of Taking the Lead will be to enhance the pool of a diverse and new generation of leaders, while simultaneously assisting those leaders already in the field to develop an understanding of institutional and personal barriers that may impede their leadership. Many of these will be women, people of color, and people with low incomes, who at present may not have full access to the information and resources necessary to move into the field's leadership roles.

Taking the Lead has a number of activities underway. They are conducting a national information gathering and dissemination activity designed to amass and share data on existing leadership initiatives, materials, and program. Focus groups will be held throughout the country, particularly in areas and communities underserved or underrepresented in the leadership dialogue. A series of pilot projects will focus on promising strategies for recruiting, training, supporting, and retaining a diverse group of emerging leaders. For information on Taking the Lead activities, contact them at the Center for

Career Development in Early Care and Education, Wheelock College, 200 The Riverway, Boston, MA 02215; Phone 617-734-5200, ext. 211; Fax 617-738-0643; Web: www.wheelock.edu.

The Center for Early Childhood Leadership

Formerly known as the Early Childhood Professional Development Project, this is the newest Midwest initiative established to promote professional development of directors of early childhood programs. While the Early Childhood Professional Development Project has been providing grant-funded training and technical assistance to directors for over ten years, the new name comes as the result of a year-long data-gathering and strategic-planning process. The findings from the Illinois Directors' Study highlighted the need for director training and support and a coordinated system to deliver these services. Future plans of the Center include the establishment of a network of administrators of early child-hood programs and the development of an Illinois Director Credential to raise the level of administrative competence among directors in the state and to recognize the important work they do each day. The Center has a new, practical, and informative newsletter, *The Director's Link,* and a web site and promises to spread their good work far beyond their state. Contact them at the National-Louis University, 1000 Capital Drive, Wheeling, IL 60090; Phone 847-475-1100, ext. 5252; Web: www.nl.edu/cecl.

National Culturally Relevant and Anti-Bias Education Network (CRAB)

In 1991, Louise Derman-Sparks received a grant from the Kellogg Foundation to further the enormous interest in promoting anti-bias education generated by her book, *Anti-Bias Curriculum: Tools for Empowering Young Children.* The grant provided for the development of a network of educators and leaders in three states who received support and resources to become master trainers and organizers on behalf of culturally relevant, anti-bias efforts in the early childhood programs, schools, and organizations in their communities. These pilot projects led to sister networks across the country. In the last five years, members of the Culturally Relevant Anti-Bias Leadership Project have been working at the local, state, and national level to get issues of racism, power, privilege, and other biases addressed in the early childhood field and its wider community. In Seattle this effort led to a collaboration between city, county, and state regulatory and training divisions. They held a two-day conference for their agency members "to get on the same page" with their understandings, requirements, and messages to child care programs about the need for culturally relevant, anti-bias programming.

As this book goes to press a further planning grant from the Van Leer Foundation has been researching how to forward anti-bias education into the next century. A national network will be established to further this work, coordinate the dissemination of information about training, leadership, and resource development, and possibly expand this work to include parents and older children. For further information about the work of the National CRAB Network, contact their office at Pacific Oaks College, 5 & 6 Westmoreland Place, Pasadena, CA 91103; Phone 626-397-1306; Fax 626-397-1304.

City Task Forces on Child Care Compensation and Business/Child Care Partnerships

One of the most exciting outcomes of work to address Worthy Wage issues in Seattle, Washington, and Berkeley, California, has been the formation of local government task forces to explore ways to improve child care quality and address the issues of compensation and turnover. In Berkeley advocates have been developing proposals for a stipend or wage supplement system, and a plan is to be approved as this book goes to press.

In Seattle the City Child Care Task Force resulted in the funding of the Business/Child Care Partnership, established with a mission of improving the quality of child care by facilitating partnerships and the exchange of resources between business and child care. A project manager with an office at the local resource and referral agency connects local companies' employees, equipment, and skills with centers that need all of that and more. In accepting assistance the child care programs have to follow one main rule: money saved through receiving donations and services must be redirected to improve the pay or training of the staff.

Many other states have government task forces and business child care partnerships in the works as well. Business journals have been featuring the efforts in Indiana, Texas, and Colorado to teach businesses how to help child care programs with such things as scholarships for teachers, improving facilities, and contributions of money and services. To learn more about the Business/Child Care Partnership in Seattle, contact Bill Larrabee at Child Care Resources, 1265 S. Main Street, Suite 210, Seattle, WA 98144-2030; Phone 206-461-3213, ext. 216; Fax 206-461-3726.

Child Care Union Projects

Over the years child care workers in some communities have made efforts to organize themselves into unions. These union drives have met with varying results. Programs that are part of larger agencies have found ways to tap into existing unions that are in place, but for the most part, the working arrangements of small to moderately sized nonprofit early childhood programs don't easily lend themselves to traditional union setups. Typically, staff and directors of early childhood programs like to view themselves as one big family or working team and fear that unionizing would insert an element of antagonism with unrealistic demands. Most directors want their staff to see them as committed to doing what they can to improve wages and working conditions, within the current limitations. Directors call for recognition that they have no more power than teachers to change the economic exploitation. Where would the money come from?

In the early childhood field the point of unionizing is to force the issue outside of the current limitations. It is about directors sharing power and moving to action beyond tolerance, patience, and maintaining the status quo. Contracts negotiated through collective bargaining insist that we enlarge the concept of "fair" beyond what parents can afford to pay to include a reasonable wage and working conditions for staff. It forces the issue of larger social and economic responsibility needed from government and the private sector.

Bob Peterson of *Rethinking Schools* has proposed that we need a new vision of teacher unionism. He says, "Industrial models of collective bargaining agreements are not sufficient in education. Teachers are not building widgets or processing beef, but teaching children who have a broad range of social and cultural needs." Peterson calls for a social justice union model, moving the scope of accountability out into the community. A child care union drive underway in King County of Washington State is drawing on Peterson's ideas. They are developing four components to their project: 1) a worker organization for negotiating contracts, 2) a public education and awareness campaign to mobilize greater private and public commitment and pressure for change, 3) a legislative and political agenda that includes compensation and quality issues in child care bills, and 4) an employer organization for care programs to purchase group benefits, retirement plans, and so on. This model is worth watching for its potential to push the agenda for a social justice union and universal child care system. You can contact *Rethinking Schools* at 1001 East Keefe Avenue, Milwaukee, WI 53212; Phone 414-964-9646; Fax 414-964-7220. The King Country Child Care Union Project can be reached at 2900 Eastlake Avenue East, Suite 230, Seattle, WA 98102; Phone 206-328-7275.

Resources for Tracking Promising Initiatives

Early Childhood Mentoring Programs: A Survey of Community Initiatives, the National Center for the Early Childhood Workforce (now CCW), 1997. Available from CCW at 733 15th Street NW, Suite 1037, Washington, DC 20005. Phone 202-737-7700; Fax 202-737-0370.

The Future of Children: Financing Child Care. Volume 6, Number 2, Summer/Fall 1996. Center for the Future of Children, The David and Lucile Packard Foundation, 300 Second Street, Suite 102, Los Altos, CA 94044. Fax 415-948-6498. You can also read the executive summary of this publication on-line at http://www.futureofchildren.org.

Making Work Pay in the Child Care Industry: Promising Practices for Improving Compensation. A report by the National Center for the Early Childhood Workforce (now CCW), 1997. Available from CCW at 733 15th Street NW, Suite 1037, Washington, DC 20005. Phone 202-737-7700; Fax 202-737-0370.

News and Notes for Child Care Professionals A quarterly publication with a compilation of stories and clips from the nation's newspapers and wire services about children and the child care profession. Available from the Alliance of

Early Childhood Professionals, 1600 Lake Street, Minneapolis, MN 55407. Phone 612-721-4246.

Rethinking Schools. A nonprofit, independent quarterly newspaper with an emphasis on reporting efforts toward equity and social justice reforms in urban elementary and secondary public schools. They are beginning to report on early childhood education initiatives as well. Subscriptions available from *Rethinking Schools*, 1001 East Keefe Avenue, Milwaukee, WI 53212. Phone 414-964-9646; Fax 414-964-7220; E-mail RSBusiness@aol.com.

Prayer for the Future

May our spring gardens flourish
may love old and new develop
may children blossom

may each of us find a balance
between work and play
may we be fulfilled by our work
and nurtured by our play

may we hold sacred the earth
and our bodies

we will mourn many times
sorrow strengthens us
sharpens our awareness of life

we rise each morning with joy
we stand in this doorway with hope

MIRIAM YARFITZ

Appendices

Conflict Resolution

Here are examples of statements developed by two programs in their efforts to work with conflict. Written statements of assumptions and processes about conflict can serve as a reference point for learning to work through disagreements.

Cambridgeport Children's Center

At Cambridgeport Children's Center, we assume that...

1. Conflict can be healthy and can foster growth, learning, responsibility, and trust.

2. Helping children resolve conflict gives children control of their environment and their relationships with others. It also fosters their social and personal growth and maintains self-respect and respect for other children.

3. Children's ability to resolve conflict is influenced by multiple factors, including developmental stages, cultural expectations, models from family and significant others, experience, and the media.

4. Teachers' approaches to conflict are influenced by their knowledge of their students through observations, parental input, previous experiences, and the understanding that each child learns in a different way over time.

5. Children are capable of taking responsibility for their actions, and they are able to come up with creative, positive solutions. They can be empathetic to peers and are able to understand the consequences of their actions.

These are the implications of these assumptions:

1. Classroom curriculum must include multifaceted approaches to meaningfully address and readdress conflicts over time for each child. Children can revisit a painful conflict through books, drama, drawing, songs, writing, and empathetic dialogue with peers and teachers.

2. Our classroom will be a safe place where everyday conflict is used as a "teachable moment" to build children's self-reliance, self-esteem, problem-solving skills, trust in peers, empathy, and compassion. Teachers participate as facilitators, allowing children to practice their evolving conflict-resolution skills in varied ways.

(Cambridgeport Child Care, Inc., 65R Chestnut Street, Cambridge, MA 02139; Phone 617-868-4275)

Multnomah Playschool

The Background of Our Conflict Resolution Procedure

It is essential that confidentiality is maintained at a high level throughout conflict resolution.

This process is based on a proven, innovative, and cooperative procedure developed by a cooperative preschool association.

It is also based on a proactive, positive, problem-solving model developed by "Resolutions Northwest."

This process incorporates a method to document the evolution of a conflict and the attempts made at resolution.

Follow up communication is an integral part of the procedure to ensure that the issue is being satisfactorily resolved and that all parties' needs are being met.

Conflict Resolution Model:

1. Listen actively to each person.
Paraphrase what was said and clarify your understanding.
Acknowledge the person's feelings.
2. Ask each person in turn what his or her needs are in the situation.
3. Jointly brainstorm many possible solutions to meet the needs.
Accept all suggestions as possibilities.
Do not evaluate at this point.
4. Evaluate possible solutions and select one.
5. Make an action plan together.
Distribute copies of the action plan to those involved.
6. Implement the action plan.
7. Check back.
Phone the conflicting parties in one week to see how they are doing.
Phone back one week after that.
Modify the action plan and/or call additional meetings as necessary.

Conflict Resolution Agreement

If I have a concern, complaint, conflict, issue, or problem with any member of the Multnomah Playschool community, I agree to follow the steps of conflict resolution outlined below.

1. I will contact the person with whom I have a conflict or concern directly, respectfully, and in a timely manner. We will attempt to use the "Conflict Resolution Model" as a guide to help resolve the problem. Discussing the conflict with anyone other than those directly involved or the class representative is not appropriate.

2. If the issue is not resolved, I will contact the class representative, who will mediate for us using the *Conflict Resolution Model.*

3. If the issue remains unresolved or if the class representative or I feel it would be beneficial, Multnomah Playschool's Resolution Team will meet with the parties involved to help resolve the issue to our mutual satisfaction.

4. If concerns remain after meeting with the Resolution Team, a professionally trained mediator will be called in to mediate.

Signed_____   Date_____

Signed_____   Date_____

(Multnomah Playschool, PO Box 19001, Portland OR 97280; Phone 507-244-9141)

The Model Work Standards Assessment Tool

With the input of hundreds of teachers, directors, and providers from around the country, the Model Work Standards have been developed to complete the picture of a high-quality early care and education program by articulating the components of an adult work environment that enables teachers to do their jobs well. The Standards are divided into thirteen categories, ranging from Wages and Benefits to Professional Development, Diversity, and the Physical Setting. You can use the Standards as an assessment tool, rating each item as Consistently Met, Partially Met or Unmet/High Priority, or Partially Met or Unmet/Low Priority. A fuller description of the complete Model Work Standards assessment tool along with guidelines for its use can be found in the publication *Creating Better Child Care Jobs: Model Work Standards for Teaching Staff in Center-Based Child Care*, available for $10.00 from the Center for the Child Care Workforce.

The following pages offer a few extracts from the Model Work Standards to give you a flavor of only the first few of the standards in two of the thirteen categories. Guidelines for their use include these ideas:

1. Look at each Standard area and determine if all staff agree that your program adequately addresses this issue. Identify what you currently have that satisfies staff and what you want to work for right now. If not everyone agrees, it will be important to work toward understanding why the staff have varying perspectives on this subject.

2. Ask each staff person to identify one or more of the Standards that they want to achieve. Rank the top one to three priorities that are agreed upon by all staff members. Taking your top priority, use the worksheet provided to develop your plan of action. You may want to start with a Standard that will be fairly easy to achieve but important to you. For example, increasing your number of paid sick days. For those child care teachers who are represented by a union, this process can be used to improve the current union contract.

3. Determine the cost for each of your top priorities. It is important to place a dollar amount on the various goals you have set. Some programs decide how much money they can allocate or will raise to make changes (for example, $5,000 for the coming year) and then select their top priority.

4. Develop a plan and a time line. This will include whose support and what resources you will need to accomplish your goal.

5. Document progress. This will help you evaluate, learn from, and adapt strategies to sustain continued efforts.

6. Celebrate and broadcast your accomplishments. Every victory, no matter how large or small, moves us closer to our goal of achieving good child care jobs.

(Used with permission from the Center for the Child Care Workforce, 733 15th Street NW, Suite 1037, Washington, DC 20005; Phone 202-737-7700; Fax 202-737-0370; E-mail MWS@ccw.org.)

Consistently Met	Partially Met or Unmet/High Priority	Partially Met or Unmet/Low Priority	**Category: Communication, Team Building, and Staff Meetings**	Essential
			Proposed changes in policies and procedures are circulated in writing to all staff, and a sufficient period is allowed for meaningful staff input and response before changes are adopted or implemented.	
			Paid staff meetings engaging all staff are held at least once a month. Staff meetings are primarily for improving program quality, enhancing staff communication, and promoting professional development of staff.	
			Staff have input into the agenda of staff meetings, the agenda is distributed in advance of meetings, and a written record of the meeting is kept and posted.	
			Opportunities exist for teachers to work collaboratively on projects, share resources, and solve problems together.	

Consistently Met	Partially Met or Unmet/High Priority	Partially Met or Unmet/Low Priority	Category: Decision Making and Problem Solving	Essential
			Teaching staff make decisions regarding daily activities, room arrangements, and other matters that affect their day-to-day practice.	
			Teaching staff share decision making with the administration in situations where decisions impact their work life. These decisions include but are not limited to staffing for paid leave time, scheduling, rotation of responsibilities, ordering materials for the classroom, screening and interviewing new staff, and managing staff turnover with consideration for the needs of children and staff.	
			Staff are engaged in setting program goals, identifying priorities to meet the goals, and measuring progress.	

Consistently Met	Partially Met or Unmet/High Priority	Partially Met or Unmet/Low Priority	Category: Professional Support	Essential
			Staff have access to petty cash funds for immediate consumable supplies, and a system is in place for requesting funds when needs are apparent.	
			Staff have input in determining the program's operating budget for supplies and equipment. Professional development plans, as well as recruitment and promotion practices, ensure that peer support is available to all staff from entry level to those with the greatest education and experience.	

Consistently Met	Partially Met or Unmet/High Priority	Partially Met or Unmet/Low Priority	Category: Physical Setting	Essential
			There is adequate classroom space that is designed with the developmental needs of children in mind. Staff have input into room arrangements and are provided resources, training, and support to improve classroom space.	
			Classrooms have comfortable places for adults to sit and be with children. Staff are encouraged to add artifacts, photographs, and other objects that reflect their lives as well as the lives of the children. A staff room or designated area is available which allows for staff interaction and a relatively quiet place for reflection and breaks.	
			Staff have a safe place to put personal belongings and a work area for preparation and planning.	

Multiple Intelligences Checklists

These abbreviated checklists have been adapted from the ideas of Howard Gardner and other educators using his work on multiple intelligences. As referred to in chapter 4, these can be used as a self-assessment for staff.

Logical/Mathematical Intelligence

Often called "scientific thinking," this intelligence deals with inductive and deductive reasoning/thinking, numbers, and the recognition of abstract patterns.

_____ I can double or triple a cooking recipe or carpentry measurement without having to put it all down on paper.

_____ Math and/or science were among my favorite subjects in school.

_____ I beat my friends in chess, checkers, Go, or other strategy games.

_____ I like to set up little "what if" experiments (for example, "What if I double the amount of water I give to my rose bush each week?").

_____ I've got a mind that sometimes works like a computer.

_____ I wonder a lot about how certain things work.

_____ I believe that most things have a rational explanation.

_____ I sometimes think in clear, abstract, wordless, imageless concepts.

_____ I like finding logical flaws in things that people say and do at home and work.

_____ I feel more comfortable when something has been measured, categorized, analyzed, or quantified in some way.

Intrapersonal Intelligence

This intelligence relates to inner states of being, self-reflection, metacognition (that is, thinking about thinking), and awareness of spiritual realities.

_____ I regularly spend time alone to meditate, reflect, or think about life questions.

_____ I have attended counseling sessions or personal growth seminars to learn more about myself.

_____ I have unique thoughts about things that others don't seem to understand.

_____ I consider myself to be strong willed or fiercely independent.

_____ I see myself as a loner (or others see me that way).

_____ I have a special hobby or interest that I keep pretty much to myself.

_____ I have some important goals for my life that I think about on a regular basis.

_____ I would prefer to spend a weekend alone in a cabin in the woods rather than at a fancy resort with lots of people around.

_____ I keep a personal diary or journal to record the events of my inner life.

_____ I am self-employed or have at least thought seriously about starting my own business.

Body/Kinesthetic Intelligence

This intelligence is related to physical movement and the knowing/wisdom of the body, including the brain's motor cortex, which controls bodily motion. Moving around, touching, and dramatizing are often a means for these learners to translate the understandings their bodies develop into more traditional modes, such as reading and writing.

_____ I engage in at least one sport or physical activity on a regular basis.

_____ I find it difficult to sit still for long periods of time.

_____ I like working with my hands at some concrete activity such as sewing, weaving, carving, carpentry, model-building, or a similar task.

_____ My best ideas often come to me when I'm out for a long walk, a jog, or some other kind of physical activity.

_____ I often like to spend my free time outdoors.

_____ I frequently use hand gestures or other forms of body language when conversing with someone.

_____ I need to touch things in order to learn more about them.

_____ I enjoy daredevil amusement rides or similar thrilling physical experiences.

_____ I would describe myself as well-coordinated.

_____ I need to practice a new skill by doing it rather than simply reading about it or seeing a video that describes it.

Visual/Spatial Intelligence

This intelligence relies on the sense of sight and being able to visualize an object. It includes the ability to create internal mental images. These learners are most engaged when they can explore their understandings about things by manipulating diverse media.

_____ I often see clear visual images when I close my eyes.

_____ I'm sensitive to color.

_____ I have a camera or camcorder that I use to record what I see around me.

_____ I enjoy solving jigsaw puzzles, mazes, or other visual puzzles.

_____ I have vivid dreams at night.

_____ I can generally find my way around unfamiliar territory.

_____ I like to draw or doodle.

_____ Geometry was easier for me than algebra in school.

_____ I can comfortably imagine how something might appear if it were looked down upon from directly above in a bird's-eye view.

_____ I prefer looking at reading material that is heavily illustrated.

Verbal/Linguistic Intelligence

This intelligence is related to words and language—both written and spoken. It dominates most Western educational systems.

_____ Books are important to me.

_____ I can hear words in my head before I read, speak, or write them down.

_____ I get more out of listening to the radio or a spoken-word cassette than I do from television or films.

_____ I enjoy word games like Scrabble, Anagrams, or Password.

_____ I enjoy entertaining myself or others with tongue twisters, nonsense rhymes, or puns.

_____ Other people sometimes have to stop and ask me to explain the meaning of the words I use in my writing and speaking.

_____ English, social studies, and history were easier for me in school than math and science.

_____ When I drive down a freeway, I pay more attention to the words written on billboards than to the scenery.

_____ My conversation includes frequent references to things that I've read or heard.

_____ I've written something recently that I was particularly proud of or that earned me recognition from others.

Musical/Rhythmic Intelligence

This intelligence is based on the recognition of tonal patterns, including various environmental sounds, and on a sensitivity to rhythm and beats. These rhythm and musical patterns are a means for developing understandings.

_____ I have a good singing voice.

_____ I can tell when a musical note is off-key.

_____ I frequently listen to musical selections on radio, records, tapes, and CDs.

_____ I play a musical instrument.

_____ My life would be poorer if there was no music in it.

_____ I catch myself sometimes walking down the street with a television jingle or other tune running through my mind.

_____ I can easily keep time to a piece of music with simple percussion instruments.

_____ I know the tunes to many different songs or musical pieces.

_____ If I hear a musical selection once or twice, I am usually able to sing it back fairly accurately.

_____ I often make tapping sounds or sing little melodies while working, studying, or learning something new.

Interpersonal Intelligence

This intelligence operates primarily through person-to-person relationships and communication. Social interaction and collaboration with others are used to answer questions, solve problems, and create representations of understandings.

_____ People come to me for advice and counsel.

_____ I prefer group sports like badminton, volleyball, or softball to solo sports such as swimming and tennis.

_____ When I've got a problem, I'm more likely to seek out another person for help than attempt to work it out on my own.

_____ I have at least three close friends.

_____ I prefer social pastimes like Monopoly or Bridge to individual recreation such as video games and solitaire.

_____ I enjoy the challenge of teaching another person or groups of people what I know how to do.

Appendix 4

Calculation of the Full Cost of Quality Care

To supplement the worksheets in *Reaching the Full Cost of Care in Early Childhood Programs*, the Worthy Wage Campaign developed these guidelines. They are useful to alert you to what it really costs to provide quality, rather than limiting your budgeting to the money you think you have available. These worksheets can lead to strategic planning as well as parent and public education. See appendix 5 for a invoice to parents that is based on these worksheets.

One of the biggest obstacles to raising teacher and provider salaries is the inability of most parents to pay the full cost of high-quality child care. When wages are primarily dependent on parent fees in the current system, they necessarily remain low. Most programs are reluctant to raise fees, especially if parents are already paying as much as they can. Calculating the subsidy provided by teachers is not meant to scare parents. Rather, it is a way for business leaders, policy makers, and parents to learn how expensive quality care actually is—or would be—if teachers and providers were paid a living wage.

Minnesota Method

There are two ways to calculate the subsidy. We call the first the Minnesota Method because the Minnesota Worthy Wage Coalition used it to prepare an invoice for the 1992 Worthy Wage Day. The Minnesota Method is very simple: you subtract what parents are currently paying from the estimated cost per child for a year for high-quality care. This number is then multiplied by the number of children using child care statewide (or countywide, citywide) to reach the subsidy—the amount not covered by parent fees and is instead "donated" by staff through low wages.

To calculate the subsidy using the Minnesota Method, you need the following numbers:

- the cost of high-quality care per year per child (estimated by some to be $8,000.00)
- the average cost of child care in your city, county, or state
- the number of children using child care in your city, county, or state

Once you have these numbers, the equation looks like this:

> the cost of high quality care
> − the average fee for child care
> = amount each child is subsidized
> x the number of children in child care
> = amount the system is subsidized

EXAMPLE

$8,000
−4,000
$4,000
x 5,000
$20 million

This method is not very precise because it is based on a very general estimate about the full cost of care and thus the amount of salary enhancement required. It is generally agreed that in most communities current salary levels need to be doubled to attract and retain high-quality professionals. If you would like to use this method but are unsure of what high-quality care really costs, complete the full cost of care invoice prepared by NAEYC. This will tell you how much a high-quality program in your area costs a year per child. If you need a copy of the invoice or instructions on how to fill it out, call NAEYC (1-800-424-2460) and ask for the "Red Book."

Michigan Method

The second method is called the Michigan Method because it was developed by Steve Sternberg, Director of Children's Centers at the University of Michigan. This method is adapted from a computer program developed by Mr. Sternberg that calculates parent fees based on variables like ratios, reimbursement rates, and teacher salaries. It is a more precise system than the Minnesota Method because the subsidy is calculated from specific salary figures rather than an estimate of the full cost of quality.

The process begins with a search for the total number of *paid* hours of teachers and family child care providers in your city, county, or state. This number is then multiplied by the current and average wage per hour. This gives you the total amount spent on wages in the current child care system. From there you can manipulate the subsidy figure based on what you think teachers should be earning. In some cases, you may want to double the current average wage. Others may adopt a $10 per hour minimum. Still others may want to compare the cost of care if salaries equaled those of elementary or even kindergarten teachers in their county or state.

Step One

The difficult number to find is the first number, or the total number of *paid* teacher hours. The first step is to find the total number of child hours in care. Contact your state or county resource and referral agency (or licensing agency) to find out how many children are served in licensed, center-based, and family child care programs. (You may want to calculate center-based and family child care separately because of different ratio requirements.) Also ask them the percentage of children in the various age groups, such as infant/toddler, preschool, and so on. Then estimate the average number of hours each child spends in care.

My local R&R tells me there are 100 centers in my community, serving approximately 2,500 children. There are 50 percent under two years old, and 50 percent are over two.

Since the ratio of teachers to children under two years old is 1:6, and the ratio for children over two is 1:12, the average ratio is 1:9. If all 2,500 children attend care for approximately 7 hours per day (and this may be even higher), and there are 260 working days in each year, then the equation looks like this:

> 2,500 children X 7 hours per day X 260 days per year =
> 4,550,000 *total child hours per year*

Using the ratio of 1 teacher/provider for every 9 children, divide 4,550,000 by 9 and the answer is 505,555.55 *total teacher hours per year*.

Add 15 percent to account for planning, meetings, in-service, sick pay, vacation pay, and substitutes, which totals 581,388 *total paid teacher hours per year*.

Step Two

For the second number, you need the current average wage per hour. If there is recent data available for your community, you're in luck. If you're not sure, call the Child Care Employee Project (510-653-9889) for current salary information.

Once you have an average teacher/provider wage, your equation continues:

> 581,388 total paid teacher hours X $5.00 average wage per hour =
> $2,906,940 spent per year on teacher and provider salaries

Step Three

If you want the current wages to double, your equation would look like this:

> 581,388 total paid teacher hours X $10.00 average wage per hour =
> $5,813,880 spent per year on teacher and provider salaries

Step Four

Then subtract the amount currently being spent to find the current subsidy:

> $5,813,880 (cost of wages at $10.00 per hour) – $2,906,940 (current cost of wages) =
> $2,906,398 (the amount of subsidy provided by the work force)

Submit this number on the "invoice" to community leaders to let them know how much teachers and providers are currently subsidizing the child care system through their low wages.

If you want to go a step further...

- Calculate how much each child (that is, each parent) is being subsidized by dividing the subsidy by the total number of children. In this case, the equation continues:

$2,906,398 subsidy ÷ 2,500 children =
$1,162.56 subsidy per child per year

This figure represents how much it would cost each family to raise the current wage to $10.00 per hour.

- Compare the current average wage to that of a kindergarten teacher.

To find out how much kindergarten teachers are earning, ask the State Department of Education or a reference librarian. When you divide a teacher's salary to find out the average wage per hour, divide by 1,500 hours per year (because of summer break) and not the standard work year of 2,080. (A kindergarten teacher earning $25,000 per year has an average hourly wage of $16.66.)

Final Notes

- Whichever method you use to determine the subsidy teachers and providers supply to the system, be sure to keep careful records of all your calculations. If someone asks how you arrived at your estimate, you should be prepared to answer.
- If you are planning to use the subsidy number primarily to raise awareness, the Minnesota Method may be easier. However, if your state or local officials are seriously considering a salary enhancement project, the Michigan Method may be more useful.

After computing the full cost of care for your program (see appendix 4), consider educating parents in your center with this mock invoice, perhaps on Worthy Wage Day, each year.

Full Cost of Child Care

Dear Parents,

If we were paying our staff a livable wage (about _____ per hour), here is what your monthly cost would be. We can no longer ask our staff to subsidize the cost of care. How can we work together to solve this problem?

Sincerely,

_____
Center Name

_____
Child's Name

_____
Month

_____
Service Provided

Full cost of care if teachers earned a living wage:
$_____

Current amount you pay for care:
$_____

Amount your child's teacher subsidizes your fee:
$_____

Total subsidy by your child's teacher for class:
$_____

Teacher and Director Evaluation Materials

These pages include examples of evaluation tools that can be used both as self-assessments and to assess a director or staff member's job performance. Several of these evaluation forms have been printed in an earlier form in issues of *Child Care Information Exchange*.

Possible Teacher Behaviors

Which is most typical for you?

1. When children are engaged in self-directed play I am

   ○ doing assessment checklists

   ○ doing housekeeping chores

   ○ taking children aside to teach them skills

   ○ keeping an eye on children who tend to get into trouble

   ○ joining in so I can help them focus on skills

   ○ closely observing and analyzing the flow of individual and group play

   ○ interacting by describing what I see them doing

   ○ gathering documentation with notes, quotes, work samples, sketches, photos

2. My approach to parent communications is

   ○ reminding them of our policies

   ○ posting a daily schedule, curriculum plans, and written daily report on activities

   ○ making sure children have a theme project to take home each day

   ○ writing in the monthly newsletter

   ○ holding conferences once or twice a year

   ○ conducting home visits once or twice a year

   ○ having general conversations at the beginning or end of the day

   ○ regularly telling stories of specific conversations, ideas, and activities of a child

   ○ sending home a periodic checklist, progress report, or "happy gram"

   ○ regularly sending home anecdotal notes

○ making individual photo book stories of a child's thinking, skills, or activities

○ creating visual documentation displays that analyze the significance of the ongoing activities within the classroom

3. To fulfill school requirements for curriculum plans, assessments, and documentation, I usually

   ○ fill out all the required forms (sometimes without much meaning for me)

   ○ post my schedule and weekly lesson plans

   ○ have a box of miscellaneous notes, work samples, forms, and checklists

   ○ have well-organized files for each child and program component requirements

   ○ write regular anecdotal observation notes and collect photos and work samples in a portfolio for each child

   ○ involve children in choosing work samples for their portfolios

   ○ collaborate with my co-workers in regular analysis of children's development and emergent curriculum

   ○ make books and visual displays of children's evolving ideas as well as curriculum projects

   ○ see myself as an engaged collector and broadcaster of the unfolding stories in the life of our program

   ○ analyze and translate the stories of our classroom into required documentation

4. My approach to keeping children aware of their learning is

   ○ using praise and stickers as a reward for good behavior and learning new skills

   ○ telling children what they need to be learning

   ○ letting the children know I will be having conferences with their parents

   ○ involving children in portfolio development and parent conferences

   ○ telling the children stories about what I see them doing and thinking

   ○ writing down and reading stories of what I see the children doing and thinking

   ○ making audio cassettes or videotapes of their activities and playing them back

   ○ sketching and taking photos with descriptive details and quotes to show them in book or documentation display formats

5. My approach to developing myself as a professional is

○ attending trainings required by my agency or school

○ trying to sample a wide variety of seminars and workshops

○ setting priorities and focusing on particular goals

○ looking for useful ideas and resources outside the ECE profession

○ continually cultivating an ability to describe what I understand about such things as the natural world, art, science, and human interactions

○ regularly reading stories by observers of children

○ spending time enhancing my writing skills through such things as keeping a journal and writing letters, stories, or articles

6. Overall my primary role with children is like a

○ census taker

○ paper pusher

○ court reporter

○ bird-watcher

○ storyteller

○ news broadcaster

○ archivist

○ curator

○ archaeologist

○ astronomer

○ improvisational artist

○ circus ringleader

Staff Evaluation

Employee _____

Evaluation period _____

	C (90-100%)	F (60-89%)	O (30-59%)	N (0-29%)
General Work Habits				
1. Arrives on time				
2. Reliable in attendance; gives ample notice for absences				
3. Responsible in job duties				
4. Alert in health and safety matters				
5. Follows the center's philosophy				
6. Open to new ideas				
7. Flexible with assignments and schedule				
8. Comes to work with a positive attitude				
9. Looks for ways to improve the program				
10. Remains calm in a tense situation				
11. Completes required written communications on time				
Professional Development, Attitude, and Efforts				
1. Takes job seriously and seeks to improve skills				
2. Participates in workshops, classes, groups				
3. Reads and discusses distributed handouts				
4. Is self-reflective with goals for ongoing development				
Attitude and Skills with Children				
1. Friendly, warm, and affectionate				
2. Bends low for child level interactions				
3. Uses a modulated, appropriate voice				
4. Knows and shows respect for individuals				
5. Is aware of development levels/changes				
6. Encourages independence/self-help				
7. Promotes self-esteem in communications				
8. Limits interventions in problem solving				
9. Avoids stereotyping and labeling				
10. Reinforces positive behavior				
11. Minimal use of time out				
12. Regularly records observations of children				

Staff Evaluation, page 2

	C (90-100%)	F (60-89%)	O (30-59%)	N (0-29%)
Attitude and Skills with Parents				
1. Available to parents and approachable				
2. Listens and responds well to parents				
3. Is tactful with negative information				
4. Maintains confidentiality				
5. Seeks a partnership with parents				
6. Regularly communicates with parents				
7. Conducts parent conferences on schedule				
Attitude and Skills with Class				
1. Creates an inviting learning environment				
2. Provides developmentally appropriate activities				
3. Develops plans from observations and portfolio entries				
4. Provides materials for all curriculum components				
5. Provides an appropriate role model				
6. Anticipates problems and redirects				
7. Is flexible and responsive to child interests				
8. Is prepared for day's activities				
9. Handles transitions well				
Attitude and Skills with Co-Workers				
1. Is friendly and respectful with others				
2. Strives to assume a fair share of work				
3. Offers and shares ideas and materials				
4. Communicates directly and avoids gossip				
5. Approaches criticism with learning attitude				
6. Looks for ways to be helpful				

Comments:

Master Teacher Evaluation

Teacher _____

Date _____

	C (90-100%)	F (60-89%)	O (30-59%)	N (0-29%)
Dispositions, Knowledge, and Skill with Children				
1. Values children's play and promotes it				
2. Is curious about the child's perspective				
3. Takes delight in children's development				
4. Shows respect for children's feelings				
5. Understands child guidance in developmental context				
6. Is alert to the learning process for each child				
7. Consistently communicates the worth of each child				
8. Manages the group while giving individual attention				
9. Has meaningful conversations and interactions				
10. Translates and coaches conflicts and problem solving				
11. Models anti-bias practices and cultural sensitivity				
With Planning Environment and Curriculum				
1. Plans the environment with inquiry and discovery in mind				
2. Develops curriculum around children's interests				
3. Is resourceful and timely in curriculum development				
4. Provides multiple opportunities for child representations				
5. Documents, analyzes, and plans from observations				
6. Teaches academic skills in a context, not out of context				
7. Scaffolds learning with questions, props, coaching				
8. Documents evolution of curriculum and learning (using bulletin boards, journals, portfolios, newsletters, and so on)				
9. Creates visual evidence of the life and history of the children				
10. Develops an inclusive classroom culture and community				
With Children's Families				
1. Builds relationships and consistent communications				
2. Seeks to reflect family life and values in classroom				
3. Can communicate details of child's development				
4. Has genuine empathy for parent perspectives				
5. Is self-confident and articulate when challenged				
6. Presents self as a professional ally of parents				
7. Gains confidence and respect of parents				

Master Teacher Evaluation, page 2

	C (90-100%)	F (60-89%)	O (30-59%)	N (0-29%)
With Co-Workers				
1. Seeks collaboration in developing ideas and understandings				
2. Mentors and coaches before criticizing				
3. Contributes to development of community among staff				
4. Participates in staff discussions and group process				
5. Practices conflict resolution rather than avoidance				
6. Models and promotes self-reflection				
7. Encourages leadership and self-care				
8. Consistently seeks feedback and peer support				
9. Works with conflict rather than avoids it				
With Professional Development and Advocacy				
1. Sees self as a member of a profession				
2. Is willing to take risks and make mistakes in order to learn				
3. Takes time for regular reflection and self-examination				
4. Makes progress on self-defined short- and long-term goals				
5. Has a program for self-care and renewal				
6. Is active in the wider early childhood community				
7. Can articulate the details of learning in children's play				
8. Keeps current with developments in the profession				
9. Keeps a professional portfolio of work samples				
10. Is articulate about issues of QCA and Worthy Wages				
11. Regularly reads professional literature				
12. Participates in professional activities outside the center				

Comments:

Director Evaluation by Staff

Director _____

Date _____

	C (90-100%)	F (60-89%)	O (30-59%)	N (0-29%)
Establishing a Healthy Organizational Culture				
1. Emphasizes reflection and thinking more than rules				
2. Offers clarity on expectations, norms, professional ethics				
3. Encourages vision building and innovation				
4. Responds to needs for physical resources				
5. Creates working conditions conducive to providing quality care for children				
6. Is proactive on issues of diversity				
7. Views problems as opportunities for creativity				
8. Creates collegiality and desire for collaboration				
9. Is fair and equitable in recognition and reward systems				
10. Actively involves staff in decision making				
11. Ensures that policies are clear and current				
12. Has clear systems and procedures				

Comments on specific aspects of the climate that help you thrive or improvements you want to see:

Being Available and Supportive				
1. Keeps staff informed of whereabouts when not in office				
2. Offers assistance in addressing needs of individual children				
3. Is available for help with curriculum ideas				
4. Supports staff in working with parents				
5. Offers thoughtful listening and problem solving				
6. Advocates for staff and encourages them to advocate for self				

Comments on specific aspects of the climate that help you thrive or improvements you want to see:

Director Evaluation by Staff, page 2

	C (90-100%)	F (60-89%)	O (30-59%)	N (0-29%)
Communicating and Community Building				
1. Actively seeks feedback and makes use of suggestions				
2. Creates safety and ease for people to express themselves				
3. Maintains balance in meeting individual and group needs				
4. Keeps everyone informed in timely fashion				
5. Encourages respect for differences and negotiating conflicts				
6. Creates meaningful celebrations of achievements				

Comments on specific aspects of the climate that help you thrive or improvements you want to see:

	C	F	O	N
Coaching and Mentoring				
1. Actively develops leadership in others				
2. Involves each staff member in a professional development plan				
3. Offers options and resources for learning and growing				
4. Coaches teachers in a manner consistent with what is desirable for children (that is, builds on strengths and interests, offers choices, opportunities to practice)				
5. Creates systems for reflection and peer collaboration				
6. Provides opportunities for master teachers to mentor others				

Comments on specific aspects of the climate that help you thrive or improvements you want to see:

Other evaluative comments you would like to add:

Appendix 7

Conference Attendance Planning Form

Here's an example of how you can prepare your staff to get the most out of a conference. Consider adapting it for your own use and adding a section on how this fits into the goals and focus of your individual or in-service training. Include a question on how to share and integrate what is learned into your program.

PROFESSIONAL DEVELOPMENT
CONFERENCE PLANNING FORM
developed by Deb Curtis and adopted by the
Washington Association for the Education of Young Children (WAEYC)

Making the Most of the Conference

1. Begin with a self-assessment. You can do this alone, with a friend, or with a group of co-workers. It can be an informal assessment, or you can use the CDA Competency Areas, NAEYC Accreditation Criteria, or a recent job performance evaluation or goal setting meeting.

Self-Assessment:

2. Choose one or two goals. Narrow your focus to just one or two goals that you will be able to accomplish. Choosing goals for yourself and working cooperatively with others toward a goal are two important aspects of effective training.

Focus area goals:

1)

2)

3. Select workshops. Plan a track of workshops for yourself that relate to your focus or goals. Consider choosing workshops from one of the Coordinated, In-Depth Tracks. Effective learning happens if the content is integrated and cumulative and the theoretical framework is consistent. Select workshops that offer hands-on practice and group discussion as well as content and resources. Adult learning research substantiates the need for interaction and active participation.

Workshop sessions that relate to goal:

A)

B)

C)

D)

E)

4. Attend workshops. Use the following questions to reflect on workshop content alone or with colleagues: What do I already know about this topic? What knowledge or skills do I still need to acquire? Does the framework seem consistent with my own ideas? If I feel discomfort, what is this discomfort related to? How inclusive, flexible, and respectful of diverse ethnic and cultural background is the content being presented?

Reflections on workshops:

5. Document training. You can obtain college credit, clock hours, or CDA training hours for the workshops you attend (see conference booklet for information). Determine which method will be best for you. At the very least, have the certificate of completion put in your personnel files and keep a copy for yourself.

Method of documentation:

College credit

Clock hours

CDA training hours

6. Implement new ideas. Effective training provides opportunities to practice in an actual work setting, receive feedback, and explore issues and ideas individually and with peers. Make a commitment to yourself to try out the new strategies and techniques that you have learned.

Summary of workshop ideas to implement:

Observation Form for Visiting Other Programs

Sending staff members to visit other rooms within and outside your program is a valuable professional development activity. To get the most out of this, it is useful to meet with those going to observe in order to plan how they will focus their attention for learning. From this you can develop an informal observation form to use for data collection and reflection. What you include as questions can alert the observer to the various components of the topic or focus. Here are some simple examples.

Observation Focus: **SELF-ESTEEM AND IDENTITY DEVELOPMENT**

Teacher/Program Observed: _____ Observer: _____

Date/Time _____

1. What did you see that demonstrated a child was being valued, acknowledged, or encouraged by the teacher?

2. What opportunities for self-help and independence did you see?

3. Did you see the teacher encouraging a sense of cultural or group identity for the child? If so, how?

4. How were children's lives and families reflected in the program?

5. Did you see a teacher referring one child to another for collaboration, help, or problem solving? If so, briefly describe these situations.

6. Write down specific examples you saw of how self-esteem and a child's sense of identity were promoted.

Observation Focus: **HOW ADULTS TALK WITH CHILDREN**

Teacher/Program Observed: _____ Observer: _____

Date/Time _____

Write down specific examples you saw of teachers in the room doing the following:

1. Ignoring child-initiated talk

Acknowledging child-initiated talk

2. Correcting a child

Acknowledging with interest something a child said or did

3. Using questions to test for knowledge

Using questions that indicate teacher curiosity or genuine interest

Using problem-posing questions

4. Having a conversation about mutual interests or something the teacher wanted to share about her/his life or interests

Observation Focus: **COMMUNICATION AND COLLABORATION**

Teacher/Program Observed: _____ Observer: _____

Date/Time _____

Write down specific examples you saw of the following:

1. Meaningful communication between the program staff and families

2. Teachers working together as a team, using direct or indirect communication

3. Systems in place that promote collaboration among the staff

4. Documentation of the life and history of the program

Meeting Requirements for Curriculum Planning

Most program policies and assessment tools require adoption of a curriculum model and documentation of weekly plans submitted in advance. Indeed, NAEYC Accreditation calls for a year long curriculum plan, a criterion seemingly in contradiction with their publication of the book *Emergent Curriculum* by Elizabeth Jones and John Nimmo. We've assisted programs to meet the intent of curriculum planning requirements using a more emergent approach to develop statements such as the following:

Curriculum Planning

Our approach to curriculum planning is based on several premises.

1. At the heart of children's learning is play. It is through play that they explore developmental themes and stages leading to physical, cognitive, social, and emotional development. Children are active, sensory learners and need to be provided with multiple opportunities for self-chosen exploration, investigation, social interaction, and problem solving. We are much more interested in this process than in any products they may come up with.

2. The environment is the foundation of our curriculum. This means that it is child-centered with attractive and interesting materials provided in an organized and thoughtful fashion. Materials are included to foster all the key experiences and developmental themes of early childhood. A supply of backup materials is kept in storage and used on a rotation basis or to supplement and extend a theme emerging in children's play. Some materials are introduced to the class with guidelines outlined on their use. Most are as undefined and open-ended as possible.

3. It is the children's themes, not the adult's, that we use as the basis of our planning. The teachers' plans are a thoughtful introduction of materials to stimulate the emergence of these themes. Teachers anticipate avenues the children may pursue from experience, and they preplan and prepare for this with some enrichment materials and activity options to add. Occasionally there may be a teacher-directed plan or seasonal activity, but the majority of time children spend with us is child-directed.

4. In all our work with children, we strive to present a multicultural view and to use anti-bias practices. This is reflected in our environment, materials, and interactions. We are constantly alert for developmentally appropriate opportunities to embrace diversity and divergent thought and promote activism against bias and injustice.

A webbing format is used for teacher preplanning and documentation of curriculum activities that emerge. This is posted to both guide staff and keep parents informed of our activities. Our webs code teacher-initiated and child-initiated activities to visually represent their interrelationship (see webs on the next pages).

Also included are reference articles for staff and parents. Some are given to staff as part of their orientation. Others are distributed during in-service training.

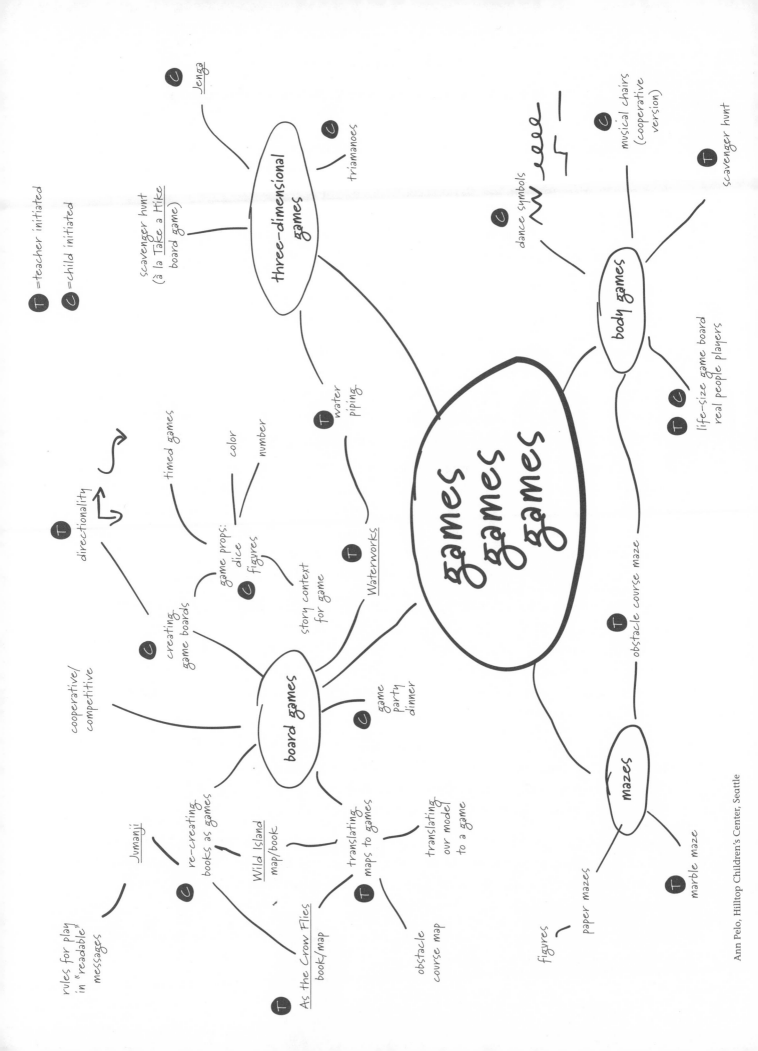

games games games

T =teacher initiated
C =child initiated

three-dimensional games
- C Jenga
- C triamanoes
- scavenger hunt (à la <u>Take a Hike</u> board game)
- T water piping

board games
- directionality T
- timed games
- game props: dice — color, number
- C figures
- story context for game
- Waterworks T
- cooperative/competitive
- creating game boards C
- game party dinner C
- re-creating books as games C
  - <u>Jumanji</u>
  - <u>Wild Island</u> map/book
  - rules for play in "readable" messages
- translating maps to games T
  - <u>As the Crow Flies</u> book/map
  - obstacle course map
- translating our model to a game

body games
- dance symbols C
- musical chairs (cooperative version) C
- scavenger hunt T
- life-size game board real people players T C
- obstacle course maze T

mazes
- figures
- paper mazes
- marble maze T

Ann Pelo, Hilltop Children's Center, Seattle

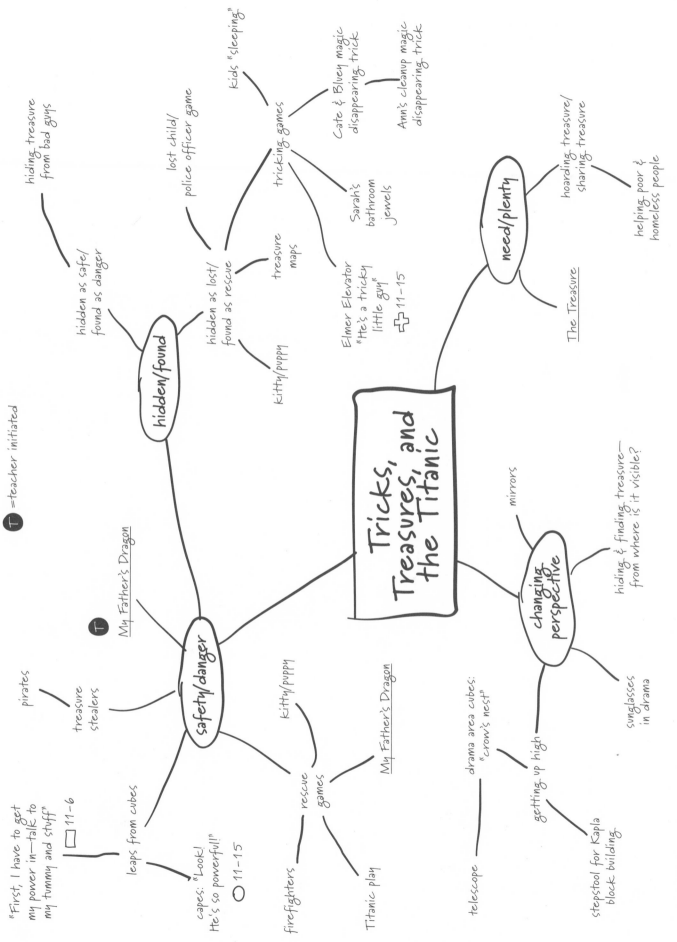

T = teacher initiated

Tricks, Treasures, and the Titanic

hidden/found
- hiding treasure from bad guys
- hidden as safe/found as danger
- lost child/police officer game
- kids "sleeping"
- tricking games
  - Cate & Bluey magic disappearing trick
  - Ann's cleanup magic disappearing trick
  - Sarah's bathroom jewels
- hidden as lost/found as rescue
  - treasure maps
  - Elmer Elevator "He's a tricky little guy" ✚ 11-15
  - kitty/puppy

need/plenty
- hoarding treasure/sharing treasure
- helping poor & homeless people
- The Treasure

safety/danger
- "First, I have to get my power in—talk to my tummy and stuff" ☐ 11-6
- pirates
- treasure stealers
- capes: "Look! He's so powerful!" ◯ 11-15
- leaps from cubes
- My Father's Dragon ⊤
- kitty/puppy
- rescue games
  - firefighters
  - Titanic play
  - My Father's Dragon

changing perspective
- mirrors
- hiding & finding treasure—from where is it visible?
- sunglasses in drama
- drama area cubes: "crow's nest"
- getting up high
- telescope
- stepstool for Kapla block building

Ann Pelo, Hilltop Children's Center, Seattle

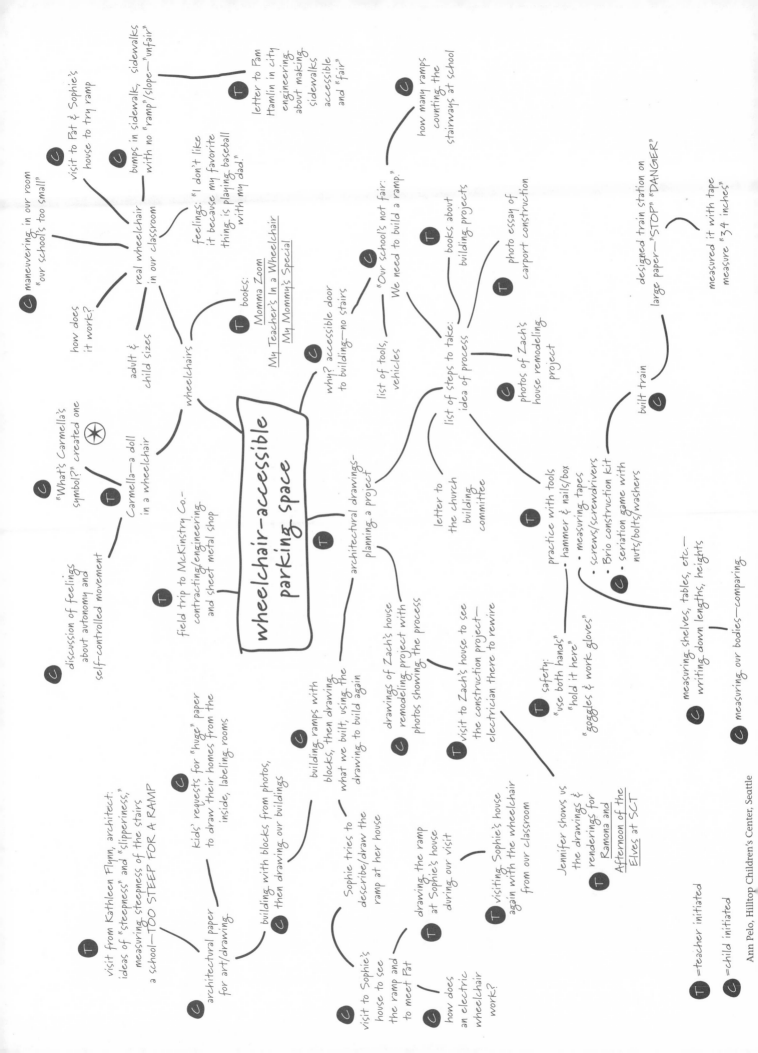

wheelchair-accessible parking space

visit to Pat & Sophie's house to try ramp

bumps in sidewalk, sidewalks with no "ramp"/slope—"unfair"

letter to Pam Hamlin in city engineering about making sidewalks accessible and "fair"

how many ramps counting the stairways at school

maneuvering in our room "our school's too small"

feelings: "I don't like it because my favorite thing is playing baseball with my dad."

real wheelchair in our classroom

how does it work?

adult & child sizes

books: Momma Zoom My Teacher's In a Wheelchair My Mommy's Special

why? accessible door to building—no stairs

"Our school's not fair: We need to build a ramp."

books about building projects

photo essay of carport construction

designed train station on large paper—"STOP" "DANGER"

measured it with tape measure "34 inches"

wheelchairs

list of tools, vehicles

list of steps to take: idea of process

photos of Zach's house remodeling project

built train

"What's Carmella's symbol?" created one ✳

Carmella—a doll in a wheelchair

discussion of feelings about autonomy and self-controlled movement

field trip to McKinstry Co.— contracting/engineering and sheet metal shop

architectural drawings— planning a project

letter to the church building committee

practice with tools
· hammer & nails/box
· measuring tapes
· screws/screwdrivers
· Brio construction kit
· seriation game with nuts/bolts/washers

measuring shelves, tables, etc.— writing down lengths, heights

measuring our bodies—comparing

visit from Kathleen Flynn, architect: ideas of "steepness" and "slipperiness," measuring steepness of the stairs a school—TOO STEEP FOR A RAMP

kids' requests for "huge" paper to draw their homes from the inside, labeling rooms

building ramps with blocks, then drawing what we built, using the drawing to build again

building with blocks from photos, then drawing our buildings

drawings of Zach's house remodeling project with photos showing the process

architectural paper for art/drawing

Sophie tries to describe/draw the ramp at her house

drawing the ramp at Sophie's house during our visit

visiting Sophie's house again with the wheelchair from our classroom

Visit to Zach's house to see the construction project— electrician there to rewire

safety: "use both hands" "hold it here" "goggles & work gloves"

Jennifer shows us the drawings & renderings for Ramona and Afternoon of the Elves at SCT

visit to Sophie's house to see the ramp and to meet Pat

how does an electric wheelchair work?

T =teacher initiated

C =child initiated

Ann Pelo, Hilltop Children's Center, Seattle

Ten Dimensions of Organizational Climate Assessment Tool

For a number of years we have adapted the work of Paula Jorde Bloom to create an assessment tool used by programs to get a "weather report" on their program (see description of this strategy in chapter 5).

The Ten Dimensions of Organizational Climate	
Dimension	**Definition**
Collegiality	Extent to which staff are friendly, supportive, and trust one another. Measures the peer cohesion and *esprit de corps* of the group.
Professional Growth	The degree of emphasis placed on personal and professional growth.
Supervisor Support	Measures the presence of facilitative leadership that provides encouragement, support, and clear expectations.
Clarity	The extent to which policies, procedures, and responsibilities are clearly defined and communicated.
Reward System	Concerns the degree of fairness and equity in the distribution of pay, fringe benefits, and opportunities for advancement.
Decision Making	Measures the degree of autonomy given to staff and the extent to which they are involved in centerwide decisions.
Goal Consensus	The degree to which the staff agree on the goals and objectives of the center.
Task Orientation	Measures the emphasis placed on good planning, efficiency, and getting the job done.
Physical Setting	The extent to which the equipment, materials, and spatial arrangement of the center help or hinder staff in carrying out their responsibilities.
Innovativeness	Measures the extent to which the center adapts to change and encourages staff to find creative ways to solve problems.

Used with permission from *A Great Place to Work: Improving Conditions for Staff in Young Children's Programs (revised edition)* by Paula Jorde Bloom (Washington, DC: NAEYC, 1977).

Sample Licenser Self-Evaluation Tool

Wherever we go, directors tell us that working with licensers and monitors is an issue for them. The experience and responsibilities of a director and a licenser usually differ greatly, and that can lead to an adversarial rather than supportive relationship. On the other hand, when licensers come to their work with an early childhood background, we have seen wonderful partnerships formed with directors and creative problem solving with an attitude of mutual support.

In our seminars with licensers we often offer this assessment tool to alert them to the knowledge they need in forming partnerships with directors. We reprint it here as a resource for you to use with your licenser and as a set of considerations should you consider becoming a licenser in your career path.

Self-Assessment and Goal Setting for Licensers

Check what is true for you

- ○ I have a clear vision of the elements of childhood I want to preserve.

- ○ I continually clarify the role I can play in advocating for child care policies and services that support this vision.

- ○ I am satisfied with my level of knowledge about early childhood education, developmentally appropriate practices, and culturally relevant programming.

- ○ I am competent in identifying the community and professional resources available for child care providers.

- ○ I am familiar with the following child care and early childhood education terms, concepts, and organizations:

❏ NAEYC	❏ Accreditation
❏ CDA	❏ Family Day Care Association
❏ NCBDI	❏ anti-bias curriculum
❏ NABE	❏ emergent curriculum
❏ DAP	❏ Reggio Emilia
❏ R & R's	❏ cultural relevancy
❏ RIE	❏ Montessori
❏ CDF	❏ High/Scope
❏ Council for Early Childhood Professional Recognition	❏ Creative Curriculum

❏ validator

❏ Zero to Three

❏ Child Care Coordinating Committee

❏ Far West Laboratory Infant and Toddler
   Training Program

❏ Schools Out Consortium

❏ Even Start

❏ National Center for the Early Childhood
   Workforce

❏ constructivism

❏ scaffolding learning

❏ portfolio assessment

❏ persona dolls

❏ *School Age Notes*

❏ *Young Children*

❏ *Child Care Information Exchange*

❏ Other _____

○ I am familiar with adult learning theory and effective methods of staff training.

○ I have effective communication skills in the following areas:

❏ active listening

❏ writing

❏ conflict mediation

❏ speaking

❏ problem solving

○ I can do objective observations and give constructive feedback.

○ I can guide providers to information and resources on small business practices.

○ I can effectively field questions and complaints from concerned parents and the
   community at large.

○ I have adequate time management skills to meet deadlines and follow through in a
   timely fashion.

○ After reviewing this assessment, use the back side of this paper to identify a learning goal
   for yourself and three action steps toward meeting it.